LEGEND

LIMIT OF STATE

LIMIT OF PREFECTURE

☐ CAPITAL

◉ CHIEF POST OF PREFECTURE

• OTHER AGG.......... S

oul

M

EM

Djouah

Djadié

Mékambo

OGOOUÉ-IVINDO

kokou ◉

indo

CONGO

OOUÉ-LOLO

toursville

• Okondja

HAUT-OGOOUÉ

a-Moutou

Ogooué

Moanda •

◉ Franceville

CONGO

The Republic of Gabon

Gabon:

Nation-Building on the Ogooué

Gabon:
Nation-Building
on the Ogooué

Brian Weinstein

THE M.I.T. PRESS

Massachusetts Institute of Technology
Cambridge, Massachusetts, and London, England

For

Ruth Imerman Weinstein
Lois Ina Weinstein
Julius Cecil Weinstein

Preface

In this study of how the Gabonese have been building a nation in Africa I started out with a general view of the nation-building process but an incomplete methodology. I believed that a methodology of dealing with information and experience would impose itself on me. This has been true, just as Gabon imposed itself on me as a place to go, as a place to study.

Gabon seemed perfect because of its size. I felt I could conceive of an entity called Gabon, or rather that I could picture in my own mind its total reality and that I could almost grasp it in my hands so that nothing would escape my view. I feared to write about anything without the assurance that I knew everything there was to know about it. Alas, size made no difference. Gabon resisted my attempts to grasp its total reality, and most of what Gabon is and has been remains a mystery to me. I have written this book even though I realized that I could never know enough about this country.

I also thought I could talk with almost everyone in Gabon to find out what they believed and what all the problems of nation-building really are. This was a fanciful idea; the Gabonese are so complex, and the problems of nation-building are so involved that it was only possible to get a glimpse of their beliefs and problems.

For six months in 1962 I traveled about Gabon and was able to go into every region and visit every major town. In 1964 I spent one month in the country and retraced some old steps. During several trips to France from 1961 to 1966 I studied and engaged in research as well. Fellowships from the Alliance Française de New-York and the Foreign Area Training Program made possible my first trip to France in 1961–1962.

I am above all grateful to the Gabonese who received me and who talked with me, and to the many Gabonese scholars whose works I consulted. No Gabonese and no one other than I is responsible for my views, however. Because my financial resources were quite limited, I am indebted to those Gabonese who graciously welcomed me into their homes or who permitted me to ride in their trucks or automobiles from one town to another. More than one Gabonese said: "And you will take your meals with me and my family"; and one truckdriver in particular who took me from one region to another said, when I offered to pay: "Forget it, brother; I might get to Amérique one of these days, and you can take me around in your truck." In Libreville my friend René Wadlow aided me a great deal, as did many other Frenchmen and Americans.

In France Professor Pierre Alexandre and others of the African section of the Ecole Pratique des Hautes Etudes and the Fondation Nationale des Sciences Politiques helped me understand change in the French-speaking countries of Africa and the French point of view. Madame Nicole Coisel and Mademoiselle Marie-Antoinette Ménier helped me explore the sometimes complex but rich French libraries and archives. In the United States I first became interested in nation-building through my study with Professor Karl Deutsch at Yale. Later, Dr. Martin Kilson and Dr. Herbert J. Spiro at Harvard challenged me with a different view of nation-building and politics.

My greatest intellectual debt is owed to Professor Rupert Emerson of Harvard University. Over the past several years he has endeavored to help me clarify a point of view and thoughts with which he did not always agree.

Colleagues and friends like James W. Fernandez, John Ballard, René and Elinor Wadlow, Henri Bücher, Roger Sillans, Hans-Otto Neuhoff, Michel François, and R. Bascou-Brescané have shared my interest in Gabon. In this group a spirit of cooperation and concern to bring to the attention of others certain aspects of Gabonese life have always prevailed.

As I did this study, I learned something important which I shall never forget, and it was the Gabonese who were my teachers: Nation-building is complex; it is as wonderfully complex as the human being himself.

BRIAN WEINSTEIN

Howard University
October 1966

Contents

CHAPTER 7

A Developing National Belief System   136

National belief system
Core beliefs
Variable beliefs

PART THREE

National Consolidation Through Human Decision-Making

CHAPTER 8

Leadership in Nation-Building   159

Problems of leadership
Pre-national leaders
National leaders
Léon Mba as the first national leader
Techniques for maintaining power

CHAPTER 9

Government Nation-Building Policies   188

Nation-building policy
Gabonese government policies 1960–1966

CHAPTER 10

The Formation of National Frontiers   210

Frontiers
Assertion of national frontiers
Frontiers with Congo
Spanish and Portuguese colonies

CONTENTS

Gabon:

Nation-Building on the Ogooué

CHAPTER 1

Introduction

Man Cannot Live Alone

Men live in groups because they fear the State of Nature. In such a state as the philosopher Thomas Hobbes described it no rules govern the actions of men: there is no government, no society, no moral system. Men's passions are unrestrained by any authority, and because man is selfish with unlimited desires, and because no one man has the power to impose his rule, there is no trust, no real peace in which men could develop themselves and a civilization. Life is unbearable.

Man knows what life would be like in the State of Nature by introspection. Man basically fears his own passions and distrusts others because he knows they are like himself. By a consideration of his own desires and fears he realizes the importance of society, which can restrain human beings.

The State of Nature is the ultimate disorder. Civilized life is impossible, and the good life is impossible. The good life is lived in such a way to prove man's superiority to others forms of life: It is a life of creativity — creation of new life and creation as an expression of man's intelligence; it is a life of progress in which man consciously seeks to improve his position in nature and to free himself from superstition, ignorance, and the forces of nature.

In the State of Nature there is no trust among human beings; they cannot be creative, and there is no progress. Nothing is sure, and nothing is safe. Nothing is sure and nothing is safe because of the absolute disorder that reigns. The sources of this disorder are capricious forces. One person attacks another person, one person steals from another person, one kills his neighbor, one person attempts to get another under his control and use him as he likes without any relation to reason or standards which the subjugated person can detect. Mysterious and fearful forces act on men too: they become ill, storms destroy their primitive shelters, and they die violently at the hands of other humans or of unknown causes. These phenomena are not understood; there is no science, no group knowledge that is passed from one generation to another. Man stands fearful and alone at war against other men and against strange forces which act on him.

Disorder and absence of a social system do not necessarily mean that the human mind itself is disorganized. Man's intelligence permits him to realize that the State of Nature must be abolished, that in order to live he must submit to rules and authorities to which his neighbors also agree to submit. Therefore social and cultural systems, groups of people, societies and communities develop and protect man from these capricious forces. In every social system there are regularized relationships which everyone is motivated to maintain. Every system has a distinctiveness that separates it from other systems. It trains, educates, and gives goals to its members. It punishes them if they do not follow the rules that enable men to be superior and that protect the group from destruction by those capricious forces called Evil.

Institutions do the work in social systems; they educate man to give him a concept of good and bad; they must deal effectively with the unknown forces that act on weak man. The forces, which were previously unknown and acted capriciously, are identified as absolute Evil, their source is traced, they are analyzed, and men are told what they can do about them. Men are told that Evil can never be completely destroyed; it is always present, but day-to-day living is possible once the group has told the individual about it and once the group can take action. Action against Evil is group action.

The group must take action against Evil because the capricious forces it represents constantly threaten group survival. The group must have power to be able to act. If the system cannot act against Evil, men will feel threatened with a return of the State of Nature. If the ways the system uses are efficacious, there is order, and the State of Nature is temporarily forgotten.

Whether or not this State of Nature actually existed at one time in history is not important. Man knows what living without a social system would be like, and this makes him act to save the system and its explanation of Evil. Original Sin, Freud's idea of the Ego, the biblical Cain, all have provided explanations of Evil to explain disorder and unknown capricious forces. They say that the sources of disorder and the failure to reach the high goals of a good life are due to man's weaknesses now or in the past. If the source of Evil is in man himself, he can act to remove it or control it. At times he may not be able to act, but he will have to be forced to do so; he will be "forced to be free" as Rousseau told us. Religion told man how to find Evil and be freed from it through group religion and in one case through submission to the Saviour who would take man's sins on himself and who would show man the way to paradise. With such religion Evil was no longer capricious, disorder could be located, and the promise of control and order was, for a time, fulfilled.

At other times Evil is found in a group or in someone who is then called a witch, a Red, a counter-revolutionary, a revisionist, a beatnik. These people are considered evil because they seem to have some demon within them which can act capriciously, because they don't abide by the rules of the system and therefore threaten it. Like the State of Nature, it is not important whether or not the capricious forces exist (we cannot know everything), but it is important to know that people feel the danger of these forces and take action.

The ways the group has of dealing with Evil may, in time, prove to be inefficacious because certain mechanisms of control no longer function or because new capricious forces present themselves. Unless the system is able to reorganize and revitalize itself, people will lose confidence in it and will seek new associations to protect themselves against a return to the State of Nature.

Rationalism, advances in science, war, association with political regimes that oppressed people so that they could not lead good lives have weakened the Church and the idea of Original Sin in Europe. Original Sin as the doctrine and the Church or religion as the system became inefficacious to explain Evil and control it. Introduction of western religions, establishment of a colonial system, and linking people with outside forces have also weakened the traditional systems of older groups which claimed man's loyalties in non-European countries. Capricious forces remain.

Man Must Live in Nations

To give man order and protect him from the threat of disorder of the State of Nature, the nation presented itself with its institutional representation, the modern state that monopolizes power. Nation-states are now regarded as the most efficacious or at least as potentially the most efficacious systems for the maintenance of order and the promotion of the noble good life for everyone. Nationalism is now regarded as the most efficacious doctrine to explain disorder and find Evil.

Nationalism can identify Evil: Sources of disorder may be some men within the new system or else some men from without and other external systems that can be fought. The nation-state has the power to explain the nature of the Evil which these enemies represent and what they must do to control, avoid, or destroy its manifestations. Also, the nation-state has the potential power to provide the rules, restrictions, goals, and a system of morality for everyone within the group.

A system like a nation that replaces another system which has become inefficacious has many of the characteristics of the doctrines and instruments it replaces. There is continuity from old systems to new systems because: All doctrines and systems have the same task to keep order and provide many of the same goals; older systems' symbols and forms never lose all their efficacity; man desires a sense of connection with his past; some methods of older systems and roles in older systems will be repeated *mutatis mutandis* as part of the cultural inheritance, because there is still some need for them. This continuity from old systems to new is a basis for the originality of a society and a culture. Each has its own past, its own threat of disorder, its own ways of identifying Evil and of controlling it to seek order.

Older systems do not disappear suddenly; they often continue to exist to fulfill different and necessary functions: religious, for example. The new systems may provide a meaningful place for old systems that might even be saved by the nation. For example, regional languages and cultures may be saved for the nation by encouraging their study and appreciation in the nation's schools. These older systems might, however, be a danger to the nation-state because they still appear efficacious in the maintenance of order for some people. Some other people no longer believe the nation-state itself is effective; perhaps it has been unjust, and they seek larger systems. In some places the nation has failed in its tasks, and the result is a downward-moving cycle of despair back to the State of Nature. It is, however, the nation-state which is the most important system today; it is the supreme loyalty group. Man looks to the supreme loyalty group as powerful enough to solve important questions and to keep order; he gives his ultimate loyalty to this group, and it influences the form and actions of smaller groups to which he belongs. Man continues to have some loyalty toward these other groups; in time of great threats to order, even to the national order, man may become uncertain about the efficacy of the nation and revert to these other levels of a system which seems to have been weakened but which still may provide limited protection. The uncertain and irregular transition to the national order is called nation-building.

Man is Building Nations

Until some larger system proves its greater efficacity, the nation-state is the end product of the sometimes irregular transition from one order-producing and order-maintaining system to another. It is a community of order which, by the intermediary of its institutions, symbols, and leaders now has the power to be efficacious in the maintenance of norms of behavior and internal peace; it is a social and cultural system whose norms for behavior are widely accepted and shared in a given territory. It is the highest level of loyalty group now — the supreme loyalty group — for which members who are not kin are expected to be willing to give their lives. Nationalism is the attempt to build, maintain, or increase the efficacity of this system in the maintenance of order and in the protection of the system and most of its members from Evil.

Nations are not fixed once and for all time. They may reach a certain level of equilibrium and stability, but they are constantly in movement as are nationalisms and nation-building. They are themselves processes. Nations are not built as a house is built; they are not constructed as a machine is constructed. A machine is over there in the corner; a person can touch it and put a little oil into it once in a while. It is something finished. Nations exist in the way a chemical reaction exists or in the way a day exists from sunup to sundown. A nation may be found on a map in the way a day is found on a calendar, but it is always changing and must be in transition if it is to be effective in its tasks. Some nations are more effective than others.

A nation is not an inert space-filling body on which forces act. It has a spirit of its own and forces of its own which produce changes. Every nation is unique with its own problems. By copying other nations closely it risks its own destruction, because it or its representatives in a government that guides the destiny of the nation may forget about the unique problems that made the nation a necessity and that continue to threaten it.

All nations have the problem of trying to inculcate norms for behavior into people who must have these beliefs to preserve the order of the system and to protect it from outside threats. People who feel the need for the nation-state may still not be willing to conform to all the rules, and people within the boundaries of the nation-state who do not feel the need for it may actively oppose those rules through antagonistic systems, which then become the supreme loyalty groups for them. Therefore the nation-state must act forcefully to promote enough consolidation and conformity to ensure its continued existence.

Acting forcefully to ensure consolidation of the nation results in the danger that a state and government might establish what is called a totalitarian regime. The result of extreme consolidation would be the subjugation of the individual to the new capricious will of his leaders. Abuses are possible, and the search for order might be used to justify oppressions and injustice. A web of groups intermediate between the state and the individual protect man, but they might threaten the nation. The ways in which each nation solves these problems add to its uniqueness. The choice of solutions means that there is a place for conscious human decision-making on the part of leaders in all countries.

Processes we call European nations have the same concerns about consolidation and order that processes we call developing nations in the Afro-Asian and Latin American *tiers monde* have. Isn't Belgium different from the United Kingdom, doesn't it have different national problems, isn't it in a sense "less" of a nation? Is it not true that the government is forced to deal with two loyalty groups below the national system which threaten the very existence of a Belgian nation in ways that recall threats to the development of a cohesive Congolese nation? Isn't Sweden different from Italy, doesn't it have different national problems? Isn't Sweden "more" of a nation? African states may even be less nations than Belgium or Italy, but they exist at an early stage of the process in that they have governments, they are independent, they have their frontiers which in most cases have been bequeathed to them by the former colonial powers, and — most important — they are attempting to build a new national order.

Nation-building is a process with world-wide implications even for those countries that call themselves old nations. Because it is an answer to deep needs felt by all men on all continents, this level of community is being built. Therefore, nation-building merits study.

Nation-Building Can Be Studied

We have become most conscious of the problems of nation-building since World War II with the independence of countries in Africa and Asia. These peoples have a conscious concern for what in other lands has been covered over with other explanations. For example, the civil-rights movement in the United States, whose goal is the cultural, economic, political, and social integration of the Negro into the American nation, is an important part of a nation-building process, but it is not usually viewed in quite this sense. Nation-building is basically as good morally in America as it is in Afro-Asian countries. Colonialism and slavery and racism are basically evil because they represent the capricious rule of one people over another. Therefore, the question of preparedness for self-government or equality is morally irrelevant.

The question that must be asked is to what extent the need for nation-building is felt on the part of the population concerned. Whatever its causes, is disorder felt by anyone? Who senses the tendency toward "anomie" and then does something about organizing a new system? This idea of anomie is a useful tool in the social sciences for the study of social change. It has been used recently because of increasing awareness in America of problems of disorder, meaninglessness, and alienation of the individual in society.[1] Anomie may refer to a condition of the social system or loyalty group to which the individual belongs. This group, for one reason or another, loses its cohesiveness; laws for governing conduct are weakened, internal relationships are no longer sure and regularized, rules are no longer regarded by everyone as legitimate. Anomie is the sociologist's name for the tendency toward disorder and the State of Nature. Complete anomie may never really exist, but tendencies in this direction do exist, and this is enough to drive some men to action.

Anomie is not felt by everyone, and all those who feel it are not able to act — if they are not numerous enough, for example. The people who do feel it and do act provide the motive force in the attempt to maintain a threatened order or in the building of a new level of order. They are the "elite" or "core nationality" leading the way in nation-building.[2] They may seek personal power and be unable to get it in other types of systems; they may have some inner dynamism; they may desire to use a new level of system to glorify their own particular loyalty group; they may desire to use a new level of system such as the nation to provide order for their own pre-national loyalty group; or they may want to escape from the old loyalty group. In the study of nation-building it is first necessary to find this core of people who want to change; they sense the need for a nation, and they act to build it. Criteria for determining whether this need is felt and who feels it must be found.

1 See the various publications of R. K. Merton, including "Anomie, Anomia and Social Interaction: Contexts of Deviant Behavior" in Marshal B. Clinard (ed.) *Anomie and Deviant Behavior: A Discussion and Critique* (New York, Free Press of Glencoe, 1964), pp. 213–242.

2 Amitai Etzioni, *Political Unification: A Comparative Study of Leaders and Forces* (New York, Holt, Rinehart and Winston, 1965).

Desire to build a new level of order is not sufficient to build a nation. People who live in the same nation must have a sense of community with other people in that nation. They must trust each other to settle disputes peacefully and in generally accepted ways. They must feel more kinship with other members of the nation than with people outside the nation, and they must be willing to fight together with other members of the nation to save it in case of external attack.

This means that communication is possible among members of a nation, that many customs are shared, that the same days are treated with reverence, that certain symbols and institutions mean the same thing to everyone, and that memories and ways of doing things are not very different. How do people from different pre-national systems develop a sense of common nationality?

To estimate the growth of a sense of common nationality and a sense of community objective, criteria such as common language, common history, common territory, common enemies, common religion, and so forth have been used. These criteria, based on European history, are ex post facto judgments. They are used to prove that a sense of common nationality and community must exist before an independent self-governing nation-state can come into being. It is true that most inhabitants of the United Kingdom speak English, are Protestants, live in a well-defined place, had common enemies in two world wars, and revere the memory of Winston Churchill. But, the Welsh did not always speak the same language as the English and the Scots still don't care much for the first Queen Elizabeth. The English, Scots, and Welsh lived under one government long before they all spoke the same language and had the same saints. The ancestors of most Americans were not in the Boston area when Paul Revere made his ride and never saw the White House burn. Yet most Americans could, like one Norwegian who escaped from occupied Norway, sailed across the Atlantic in a stolen sailboat, joined the American army, became an American citizen, got shot by a German, came back to America, got married, and lived happily ever after, speak in his heavy accent of "our ancestors, the Founding Fathers." Attempts to teach Algerian children about "nos ancêtres les Gaulois" were unsuccessful in creating a real and lasting sense of community and common nationality, but they might have been successful if the

Algerians had been treated like the Frenchmen they were supposed to be.

A sense of common nationality and community can develop, Professor Deutsch has told us, on the basis of "shared experience."[3] This shared experience, which may lead to the necessary mutual trust among members of a given society who have been brought together by the fear of disorder that they or their leaders have felt at some point in history, contributes to national unity, and living together makes shared experience more possible. Some processes and forces bring men together; they facilitate shared experience. They might mean that people work together, pay their taxes together, live together, intermarry. Some of these forces are beyond the conscious control of men; some of them can be controlled by the human will. In a study of nation-building it is also necessary to investigate the forces that create a sense of common nationality and loyalty to a particular nation-state.

A Way to Study Nation-Building in Africa

The Need for Nations and Order

To find out why people feel the need to build a new order one must know how the older pre-national systems lost their efficacity and how certain people are motivated to act in the nation-building process. One must examine the traditional or pre-national loyalty groups and their methods for keeping order in order to discover criteria which will indicate that these groups are no longer efficacious.

The most important pre-national systems in Africa are based on kinship, which is a flexible concept. Although people are kin if they consider that one is descended from the other or that both are descended from the same ancestor, whether or not this is biologically true is unimportant.[4] The organization of kinship groups into larger entities varies greatly in Africa. The Nuer are quite different from the Ashanti, and Fulani are quite different

3 Karl W. Deutsch, *Nationalism and Social Communication: An Inquiry Into the Foundations of Nationality* (New York, The Technology Press and John Wiley, 1953; second printing, Cambridge, Mass., The M.I.T. Press, 1962).

4 A. R. Radcliffe-Brown and Daryll Forde, *Systèmes familiaux et matrimoniaux en Afrique* (Paris, Presses Universitaires de France, 1953), p. 5.

from the Kissi. The problems of building a nation when one has a hierarchized, well-defined pre-national social system are different from those of building a nation when there are very egalitarian pre-national social systems which still claim the loyalty of most people who are very suspicious of any higher authority at all.

In the egalitarian social systems that are characteristic of many peoples who live in the forest clearings in equatorial Africa the important kinship groups have been the "ethnic group," the tribe, the clan, the lineage, the extended family. "Ethnic group" is something quite vague. Its members speak essentially the same language, but they may not understand everything someone else is saying; they acknowledge they had a common ancestor who lived about the time the world was created; they regard certain things or places as holy, have some of the same customs and tools; and they recognize they all have this vague ethnic identity. They may not always get along, however, and they may not see each other regularly; marriage between members of the group may not even be easy.

The tribe is a smaller system. All members claim they have a common ancestor who lived a very long time ago. They speak the same dialect of a given language although there might be some regional differences in pronunciation. The tribe represents the largest system within which one ordinarily chooses a wife or husband. The clan is part of the tribe but may cross tribal frontiers within the ethnic group. The ancestor of the clan is closer to the living than is the ancestor of the tribe, but he is not someone who has been known by the living. Male contemporaries of a given clan often consider themselves brothers.

The most important groups in these egalitarian societies are the lineage and the extended family. The lineage represents four or five generations within the clan; there is a common ancestor who is not mythical and to whom each member can easily trace his ancestry. Each member knows his relationship with the other members of the lineage and knows the standards of conduct toward them. Usually there is a living head of the lineage — an older person who represents it and arranges marriages, for example. Everyone speaks the same dialect of the same language. The extended family with grandparents, unmarried daughters, and sons with their wives and family is for many people the only important residential and spiritual unit of the whole hierarchy of systems.

The ethnic group is rarely relevant for the life of the people. Certain leaders might desire to make it politically relevant, but in this they are not always successful. Tribal unity for members of highly egalitarian societies might be important in occasional rites, in war, and in attempts to combat forces that are considered evil. Clan unity would be more important in case of war or ritual, and knowledge of clan identity would be very important for purposes of marriage. It is important that a man not marry a woman from his own clan, for this would be considered incest. For other people it is important that a man marry a woman who does belong to his clan.

A man used to know the members of his lineage and extended family best, and he saw them regularly. What he learned about his obligations to other people, to the group, and to spiritual forces was learned in these two groups, and group order was maintained. Capricious forces manifested themselves by making crops fail, by making women barren, by infecting the apparently strong with disease. Special organizations or gifted persons were designated to find the Evil that was threatening the community; once it was found, the community took action to check or destroy the Evil, which was labeled witchcraft.

Acts attributed to people who are called witches are, as far as we know, humanly impossible. Witches are supposed to be able to fly about, change into hyenas, and engage in superhuman acts that are harmful to the whole society. They are specially gifted to practice witchcraft, and probably have a magical being within them that gives them powers or that does certain tasks for them at night. After something unexplained happens, such as illness, death, or an accident, the suspected persons would have to submit to an ordeal to indicate whether or not they were witches. The people labeled witches were usually different from other people: childless women, very successful men. Once they were found by the witch-finder, actions such as banishment, purification, execution were taken. The individual was sacrificed for the re-establishment of the order of the collectivity. If there were many witches, a much larger effort would be needed to save the group; an anti-witchcraft movement or organization would be called upon.

Sorcery is not the same thing. It may be practiced by almost anyone and generally involves no special supernatural powers, although some people may be better at it than others. It may be an attempt to harm someone by the use of poisons, by drawing a figure of the person to be harmed, or by treating articles that belong to the person to be affected. The practice of sorcery is often a profession for which the sorcerer is paid. He is considered a dangerous person and might be punished for his work, but he is not considered the representative of capricious forces that threaten the whole society, like a witch.[5]

With the advent of colonial rule, the methods used to maintain order were weakened and in several areas witchcraft accusations and antiwitchcraft movements greatly increased. The white ruler, missionary, and business man attacked the ways African societies had to train and socialize the young; ways to insure conformity and methods of dealing with capricious forces were often suppressed. New areas of settlement, new ways to make money, a new type of administration, and strange economic forces released new capricious forces, such as price fluctuations for industrial crops. The new forces could not be dealt with by the old society.

The people who sense this disorder may be able to do something about it; they will need to establish a new order. If they can act, they provide the motive force in nation-building. A criterion for the disorder that makes men act to re-establish order is an increase in witchcraft.

Forces Build the Community

An examination of the consolidation of a community at a national level, once the need for such a system is felt, is the second part of a study of nation-building.

A quantitative way to examine the development of a sense of community of a given people is possible. The first stage in the process is physical contact between different people or groups of people. People who have communications with each other are "mobilized" for shared experiences and are "mobilized" into a current of communications that may eventually change a physical

---

[5] E. E. Evans-Pritchard, *Witchcraft, Oracles and Magic Among the Azande* (London, Oxford, 1937). Also Sir James George Frazier, *The Golden Bough: A Study in Magic and Religion,* abridged edition (New York, Macmillan, 1963), pp. 14–52.

relationship into an affective relationship. To measure how intensive communication is, one must use criteria such as location of markets, settlement patterns, population movements, mass media of communication, road construction, movement of vehicles, mail, and so forth.

The second stage is a change in the sentiments and attitudes of people; it is "assimilation." People find that on the basis of shared experience they communicate with increasing effectiveness with certain members of a particular system more than with others. People of one group might become assimilated by another, or several groups might be assimilated into something new. When the "communication habits" of a population become increasingly standardized, assimilation is occurring.[6]

Intensity of communication is more easily observed than is attitude change. People who ride on the same bus together and listen to the same radio have communication with each other or are subject to the same outside communications. People who live in the same village are bound to share many of the same experiences and, depending on the size of the community, are bound to have some measure of contacts with each other. Such contacts influence their opinions about each other. Opinions may be judged only by knowing about histories of conflicts between people, by extensive travel in the country. History is used to explain the present by the past; when it is oral, it is more flexible. It is useful to know the place which neighbors have in the oral histories and stories of people.

Part of the processes of mobilization and assimilation is the development of a national culture, a national history, and a national belief system, which are expressions of a growing consolidation and which contribute to the consolidation of the national system. Culture, history, and belief system will be influenced by those who provide the motive force in nation-building. Their own culture, history, and beliefs will have a special place in the national system, and the ideas they have borrowed from others will have a special place. They may even absorb aspects of the culture of another pre-national group and introduce it into the national system as their own contribution. But no one group can

6 Karl W. Deutsch, ftn. 3, pp. 91–92, 100.

build the nation without the help of others. All important groups must feel part of a growing national community with its own distinctive culture, history, and belief system. A criterion for an examination of this consolidation is shared experience.

Human Will Builds the Community

The nation-state has a government which acts for it. The institutions of the nation-state formulate the rules that govern the relations among members of the developing community and enforce them. These institutions, the articulation of collective goals of the community, and the protection of it are under the direction of the national leaders.

A single national leader and his political party have claimed the responsibility for internal order and maintenance of independence in most African countries in the first years of independence. Internal competition for power would cause so much internal disorder that national development would be impossible, the leader claims. He says that discussion will go on in the party and that decisions will still be made democratically. In some places it is believed that the party represents the people in a way better than the state; therefore, the party tells the state what to do, and the members of the legislature or administration are considered the technicians who follow the instructions of the party's leadership.

The leader may demand all the power to maintain order. With this power to maintain order a leader tries to undertake a program of education that teaches people about the nation-state and about their duties; this is civic education and is part of the process of becoming politically conscious or politically socialized. Sometimes the leader is tempted to emphasize loyalty to himself more than loyalty to the country. With his power to maintain order a leader undertakes a program of economic development for the nation-state. With his power a leader claims to be able to provide services to the people which reward them for their membership in the developing national order. And, as the single leader, he tells people what the national frontiers are and how they must be defended.

Attempts to replace the leader with someone else are called threats to order or threats to nation-building; those who make such attempts are called traitors and racists. When the national leader says he must have all the power, opposition to him is driven underground, criticism is dangerous. No one is sure who is for the leader and who is against him. People are afraid to talk. Public channels of communication are closed to the opposition; people begin to use tracts, they spread rumors, their allies in the administration and government supply them with secret information. The opposition becomes divided into old and young, religious and nonreligious, left and right. They accuse the leader of robbing the country, of not really being the national leader, of being controlled by outside forces, of being incapable of providing meaningful goals to the people and establishing a just order. It is decided that he cannot be removed by constitutional means, and violence may be used against him by the army or by someone else.

The leader who is part of the motive force must satisfy the needs that are the basis of the nation-building process. If he can do so for that core of people who make up the motive force, he may retain his power; if he cannot, he may be deposed. If he is unjust and represents a new capricious force and if an acceptable change is impossible, the nation may fail in its mission to provide a new level of system for those who need it, and the process of consolidation will not be successful. National leadership is therefore important in nation-building. A criterion for an examination of the role of human will is national leadership.

Gabon, A Developing African Nation

About half the size of France, Gabon has only one one hundredth of France's population. With its 500,000 people, Gabon's population is one of the smallest in Africa. On the equator, on the Atlantic, between Cameroun and Rio Muni to the north and Congo to the east and south, the country is in equatorial Africa where the rainfall during the eight months of the rainy season is in places almost twelve feet. Most Gabonese live in clearings of the same equatorial rain forest; it is dark. In this forest one walks along very narrow paths that extend back from the new roads which are being built. The one who walks over the path for the first time stumbles over roots of trees that must search for food in a lateral direction because the thin topsoil rests on clay. Trees fall down easily, vines hang everywhere, animals seem to move about.

During the day in the forest clearings the stranger feels as if dead in the midst of incredible life sounds: crackling, flapping, chopping, calling, sighing, moving, chirping, all under a relentless sun and a heavy, inescapable humidity. During the night one feels as if one were the only person alive surrounded by sounds: hissing, walking ten steps, scraping just outside, light tapping, distant drumming and groaning under a sky bright with stars and moon whose light cannot penetrate the thick air near the ground. One does not venture far from the fire, and a light burns through the night. And yet, wasn't that the news from the Voice of America or Radio Peking that I heard coming from that house? "What does independence mean for us?"

During the day in Libreville, the capital, Port-Gentil, the developing industrial center, or in Lambaréné, the Ogooué river port famous for Dr. Schweitzer's hospital, the sounds are different: building sounds, the latest news — "the Vietnamese government . . . ," elevators, "I have been standing in line for twenty minutes. How about some service?" clanging of metal on metal, horns, "get out of the way; what do you think this is, the Champs Elysées?" At night the sounds are from restaurants, bars, movies, lighted school dormitories: "May I have this dance?" "When do you leave for Paris?" "Yes, geology." "But give us your definition of class!"

The resources of Gabon are impressive: wood like okoumé, which is made into plywood in Port-Gentil, petroleum off shore, the second-largest manganese deposit in the world, uranium for France's bomb, iron ore that will be exploited when the railroad from the coast is built, and much more.

Under some measure of French political and economic control from 1839 to the present, Gabon became independent in 1960 with a form of government similar to that in other African countries and a developing single party based on models in other lands. The government appeared comparatively stable until February 1964, when the President was overthrown by some Gabonese military officers and then reinstalled by French troops who were flown into the country. Gabon's administration is based on the French model, with prefects appointed by the President at the head of each of the nine regions: Woleu-Ntem in the north, Nyanga and Ngounié in the southeast along the Ngounié River, Estuaire and Ogooué-Maritime along the ocean, Ogooué-Ivindo in the east on the Ivindo, a tributary of the Ogooué; Moyen-Ogooué, Ogooué-Lolo, and Haut-Ogooué along the meandering Ogooué River from central Gabon southeast to the Congolese frontier.

The country has over thirty pre-national loyalty groups, one of which, the Fang, accounts for a third of the total population. Out of these diverse groups the Gabonese are building a national order along the Ogooué.

Nation-building in Gabon, as a process that can direct the ways of men toward noble, meaningful ends, is good. As a level of system and as a process it is better than lower systems and processes because it is the one which now has the possibility of establishing and maintaining an efficacious order. Individuals may be called upon to suffer, and the true nationalist must be prepared to suffer for the nation. But history is not always good, history is not always reason; and nation-building, in some places, like nationalism has been bad because leaders and people had goals that were selfish: denial of the goodness of other nation-building processes, imposition of too rigorous an order, sacrifice of human life for stupid, ignoble reasons.

In Gabon, as elsewhere, nationalism and nation-building are the results of the needs of people: needs for belonging to a group that can bring order and protect one from Evil and needs for direction and control because every man is weak. In Gabon several people of different ethnic groups sense disorder and the inefficacy of traditional systems. They are all trying to build a new, efficacious system. The Fang people have had a particularly important role, partly because of their numbers and partly because of an attempt to consolidate their own group with a dynamism whose origins pre-date colonialism.

Building a nation has no fixed beginning and no end; no one knows when forces beyond the control and understanding of men determined that an African or European nation might exist. The observer must start at a definite point in time; this story begins with the coming of the White and the coming of the Fang.

18

PART ONE

Motive Force in Nation-Building

CHAPTER 2

The Arrival of the French and the Arrival of the Fang in Gabon

French Imperialism

During the fifteenth century the Portuguese discovered for themselves the coast of what is now called Gabon. In those days the west coast was the coast, not of Gabon, Congo, Dahomey, but just of Africa; it was undefined by frontiers which the Portuguese could see. It was a series of gulfs, rivers, islands off the coast where trading stations could be established and what appeared to be impenetrable places like the rain forests.

The Portuguese thought they were free to call anything by any name. They chose names of people, saints, kings, things of which places reminded them. These men, like all explorers, thought of going into Africa one day and made note of rivers, for one might go to the Nile. Some rivers were not rivers, and none went to the Nile. Rio Gabon, so named because someone thought an estuary just north of the equator was the mouth of a great river and because someone else thought it looked like a cape (gabão), was not a rio and does not really look like a cape. This was the first

Gabon, not an empire, not a great river, just an estuary with some people called Mpongouè who were of course named "Gabonese."

This nonriver attracted other traders and explorers from Holland, America, the United Kingdom, and France for wood, slaves, ivory, rubber, adventure, souls. Later, the roles of these men, spurred on by noble or ignoble ideals, were in large part determined by nationalism in Europe. The French were concerned with British commercial successes and wanted to build a strong, prestigious France to maintain its grandeur. One of the signs of prestige, according to them, was an empire and a large navy which needed coaling stations and trading posts to insure and justify its existence; chambers of commerce, a society of geography, and navy men like Bouët-Willaumez were interested.

For Edouard Bouët-Willaumez, the power of any nation rested on the size of its navy and on the extent of its commerce; naturally, he reasoned, colonies were necessary:

> If one examines ancient or modern history, one recognizes immediately that every nation which has desired to have commerce and a navy (the indispensable element of the power of a state) has recognized the necessity to found far away colonies to exchange its riches and to maintain a permanent force of men at sea.[1]

Although Bouët's ship, *La Malouine,* was supposed to assist in attempts to seize vessels transporting slaves, both he and the Chamber of Commerce of Bordeaux thought he could combine this mission with an investigation of commercial possibilities in the area called Gabon, where the English were reputed to have a profitable trade and where the Portuguese had obtained slaves for their base on the islands of Saint Thomas and Prince.[2] Thus attracted to the Gabon estuary, Bouët signed a treaty on 9 February 1839 with the first of the Gabonese, "King" Denis. "King" as head of his family and as an important slave merchant, not as head of some kingdom, Denis ceded forever to France territory in the estuary on which it could build anything it liked. France would give Denis merchandise in return. More important for Denis was the offensive and defensive alliance which was included

---

1 Le Comte Bouët-Willaumez, "Les Colonies françaises en 1852," *Revue des deux mondes*, 1952, p. 23; extract in Bibliothèque Nationale, Paris.

2 Henri Brunschwig, *L'Avènement de l'Afrique noire* (Paris, Armand Colin, 1963), pp. 58–59.

in the treaty, for he knew that someone was moving toward the coast in great numbers: "The above-mentioned king commits himself to an offensive and defensive alliance with France which, for its part, guarantees him its protection."[3]

An American observer who arrived three years later as a missionary from the American Board of Commissioners for Foreign Missions (A.B.C.F.M.) surmised that Denis saw in an alliance with the French a way to extend his highly localized authority: "He had hopes, too, that the partiality of the French might place him at the head of the whole of the native population of the country. He determined, therefore, to give them his hearty support and did all he could to induce others to yield to their wishes."[4] For the next ten years the French negotiated treaties with other Mpongouè dignitaries, such as King Glass, and their relatives; they got control of most of the estuary. Other American observers said that "by deception and the free use of brandy, signatures were obtained to a document under which French officials claimed and took possession of land including King Glass's town; and the Gaboon has ever since been held by them as a naval station."[5] (In spite of comments by teetotaler missionaries, it is unlikely the French had any monopoly on the use of spirits to gain certain advantages.)

In 1843 blockhouses had been constructed on the left bank of Rio Gabon to fight the slave trade and to promote commerce; the area was under the Ministry of the Navy which had most responsibility for overseas possessions until a separate Ministry of Colonies was officially set up in 1894. (A Ministry for Algeria and the Colonies existed briefly between 1858 and 1860.)

This estuary naval station cost too much money to maintain, and the French government was not always sure that its protection of merchants of all nationalities and missionaries, mainly American and French, was worth the francs and centimes spent. An old rival was, as usual, taking much of the financial benefit

3 "Traité conclue au Gabon, le 9 février 1839," in Bernard Schnapper, *La Politique et le commerce français dans le Golfe de Guinée de 1838–1871* (Paris, Mouton, 1961), p. 263.

4 J. L. Wilson, *Western Africa: Its History, Condition and Prospects* (New York, Harper, 1856), p. 295.

5 William Ireland, "Historical Sketch of the Gaboon Mission," 1863, extract from the archives of the American Board of Commissioners for Foreign Missions, Boston, pp. 29–30. See also Abbé André Raponda-Walker, "Notes d'histoire du Gabon," Mémoire de l'Institut d'Etudes Centrafricaines, No. 9, Brazzaville, 1960.

from the colonies. Britain's industries were superior to those of France, and it flooded Africa with its goods. French merchants were even reduced to selling English products. At one time two thirds of what French ships were carrying to Africa were English products![6] The financial losses were so serious after the Franco-Prussian War that the French thought seriously of trading Gabon for Gambia because they were commercially more successful in the British possession than in their own. But Gabon was destined to become more important as the French were able to restrict the activities of foreign merchants and as explorers reported on interior territories which would one day constitute the equatorial part of a vast empire. For these men and one English lady, Gabon was the opening to the interior, to the Congo, to Oubangui, to the unknown.

Paul Du Chaillu was one of the most popular of the explorers. He arrived in Gabon in 1856, when he was about twenty years old, in order to

> ascend the various rivers, hunt in the woods, and acquaint [himself] alike with the haunts and habits of the gorilla, and with the superstitions, customs, and modes of life of the black tribes, who had not hitherto been visited by white men . . . .[7]

He was, like travelers of all time, also claiming to look for a kind of ideal place for a home for someone, for a pure and fertile land:

> Another purpose I had in view was to ascertain if in the interior, among the mountainous ranges in which the rivers took their rise, there was not to be found a region of country fertile and populous, and at the same time healthy, where the missionaries, who now suffer and die on the low coast, could work in safety and to advantage.[8]

Du Chaillu is called the first explorer in the interior to have encountered the fierce people who were moving south; he claimed to know a lot about them and to admire them. They carried a shield, a large knife, and they filed their teeth, the better to eat their enemies with — or so Du Chaillu would have his reader believe. He sensed their dynamism and predicted that they would

[6] Schnapper, ftn. 3, p. 118.
[7] Paul B. Du Chaillu, *Exploration and Adventure in Equatorial Africa* (London, John Murray, 1861), p. 2.
[8] *Ibid.*

"eliminate" their neighbors or, in his words, "leave the other tribes behind" and would one day "take possession themselves of the whole line of seashore . . . ."[9]

In the 1870's the Marquis de Compiègne penetrated the forest by going up the Ogooué above what is now Lambaréné. Omyènè traders advised him not to continue, for he would certainly die at the hands of the supposedly fierce cannibals who lived up the river.[10] The Mpongouè were, however, more worried about the loss of their position as commercial middlemen than concerned about the health of this nobleman.

The explorer who did the most for the establishment of French sovereignty in equatorial Africa was Pierre Savorgnan de Brazza, a navy man, Italian by origin, who was attracted to France to participate in the building of its empire. Because of these travels and contacts with many different peoples in equatorial Africa there are still those who claim to have helped him, canoed for him, or at least to have seen him, that man with the black beard. During his three voyages in 1875, 1880, and 1883 he explored the Ogooué River by traveling from the Atlantic through the interior into what is now Congolese territory; by his signing of treaties which established French sovereignty over increasing areas, France gained control of important parts of what are today Congo-Brazzaville and Gabon. Because the French government was not at first enthusiastic about gaining control over this region, he was obliged, according to documents in colonial archives, to use his own funds and those of influential friends to make the trips possible; what is more important is that he signed treaties that were unauthorized by that same government.[11] The territory added to France's empire extended to the River Congo, just across from the place where Stanley had founded another empire.

Stanley, as a representative of King Leopold and the International Association of the Congo, obtained protectorates over areas which de Brazza claimed to be under French control, par-

9 *Ibid.*, p. 89. Du Chaillu was actually preceded by American missionaries who met Fang in the 1840's, but they wrote reports for a very limited audience while Du Chaillu's publications were written with the general public in mind. This no doubt influenced his exaggerations and inaccuracies.

10 Marquis de Compiègne, *L'Afrique équatoriale: Okanda, Bangouens, Osyeba,* third edition (Paris, Plon, 1885), p. 80.

11 Brunschwig, ftn. 2, pp. 143–163. See also Henri Brunschwig, *Brazza explorateur: L'Ogooué 1875–1879* (Paris, Mouton, 1966), pp. 11–19.

ticularly near the mouth of the great river. Portugal also advanced claims and called for an international conference to save its interests and to avoid more confusion. At the Congress of Berlin in 1885, rules of colonialism were drawn up and imperialism began in earnest.

In the same year Jules Ferry, amid cheers from the center and left benches of the French National Assembly, proclaimed his ideas of colonialism: markets, civilizing missions, and power for France.[12] France could not, according to the imperialist theory, become a second-rate power.

From then on France began to consolidate its hold over equatorial Africa by sending missions to invade and bring the whole area under French control. It was no longer a question of mere blockhouses or trading stations. European powers had agreed at Berlin to notify each other about their new claims and had decided that representatives of the colonizing country were effectively to occupy these areas in order to have them recognized by other imperial powers as possessions. In 1886 the colony of Gabon was officially established. Military missions left Gabon for northern Congo and for Oubangui-Chari; it was the military which "pacified" and ruled most of the interior of each colony well into the twentieth century.

Trading rules were tightened up to discourage commerce between Gabon and countries like Britain. American missionaries were no longer allowed to teach English and eventually gave up their mission to the French Protestants. The administration sent the Cottes Mission into Woleu-Ntem and other missions to the south to examine the effectiveness of the French presence and to investigate the possibilities of commerce and development. There were many attempts to resist white penetration, along with revolts against white rule. The last such attempt about which there is some documentation was in 1928–1929 when a Bawandji revolt was put down. Frontiers were changed to suit European needs, and they were changed in the north and changed in the south.

Until 1910 France's equatorial possessions across from Leopold's Congo were called Congo Français; its capital was in Libreville. In 1910 the federation of Afrique Equatoriale Française (A.E.F.)

12 Henri Brunschwig, *Mythes et réalités de l'impérialisme colonial français 1871–1914* (Paris, Armand Colin, 1960), pp. 73–77.

was organized and separated into three colonies: Gabon, Moyen-Congo, and Oubangui-Chari-Chad. (In 1920 Chad was made into a separate colony.) The capital had been transferred three years before to Brazzaville, just across the river from Léopoldville.[13] The French were concerned about Belgian expansionist desires and wanted to have a strong, clearly French area across from the Belgian territory which was no longer the personal property of the king. A federation capital on the Congo also meant that the French on a large river that was used at least since the sixteenth century as an important commercial route would have comparatively good communication with interior regions. The best of the few schools of the federation, the railroad Congo-Océan, and the largest city were built on the site, which bore the name of the French nationalist.

Gabon lost its strategic importance. It was no longer the stepping-off place to equatorial Africa and was considered a rather insignificant colony in a federation which was itself regarded with disdain. No longer just the estuary, Gabon became a country between Cameroun and French Congo, between the Fang and the Batéké, from the Atlantic to the place where the Djouah, a tributary of the calm Ivindo River, turns southward. After World War I Gabon was governed mainly by the immense Service Colonial, whose officers took their training in Paris at the Ecole Coloniale, the school on rue de l'Observatoire just across Luxembourg Gardens from the Senate. They shared power with representatives of the trading companies, which were granted huge areas of Gabon to exploit because the French government was not interested nor had the money to develop African resources.

Until the abolition of forced labor and the *indigénat* system which permitted an administrator to jail and fine certain categories of noncitizens without trial, the administrators and businessmen had immense power over the lives of the Gabonese in their jurisdiction. One man far from Libreville had executive, judicial, and legislative powers with little or no check on him before World War II. Atrocities reportedly committed all over A.E.F. by some administrators and the companies brought Savorgnan de Brazza back in order to make a report on the situa-

13 See Jean Suret-Canale, *Afrique noire: l'ère coloniale* 1900–1945 (Paris, Editions Sociales, 1964), p. 119.

tion. He died during the return trip, and no report was ever published. The concessionary companies in forgotten Gabon still had almost complete control over their territories although they were supposedly subject to investigation and control by the administration.

René Maran was the first to write briefly about the sufferings of the African in this federation in the preface to his book *Batouala*.[14] After his own trip into this part of the world André Gide was candid in his views of the big companies and the absence of concern on the part of the French government: "What have these big companies . . . done for the country? Nothing. The concessions were given with the hope that the companies would develop the country. They have exploited it, which is not the same thing as development; they have bled and squeezed it like an orange whose skin is sooner or later discarded."[15] Other Frenchmen in the administration and in colonial activities recognized the failings of the federation, and vain attempts were frequently made to reform and to develop it. "In Equatorial Africa we expected everything to come from private initiative, and . . . we were wrong."[16]

Seemingly isolated from the rest of the world, with a reputation as a hell on earth for the Africans and the Europeans who worked there, Gabon was also used as a dumping place for political prisoners. The Malinke warrior Samory spent his last days on an island in the Ogooué near the town of Ndjolé; in 1900 Ago-li Agbo, king of Abomey, was deported to Gabon, and Allal el Fasi from Morocco was also here. Because laborers were badly needed since the population seemed to be dying out or fleeing the forced-labor practices of government and company, Indo-Chinese were sent to work and to marry Fang women. According to the plan of one governor, they would supposedly produce a hardy race of laborers. The Asians died as they worked to fill in the swamp land on the southeastern edge of Libreville where small bungalows now house civil servants.

14 René Maran, *Batouala* (Paris, Albin Michel, 1921).

15 André Gide, *Voyage au Congo* (Paris, Gallimard, 1927), p. 78. For a map of the territory controlled by these companies and a full (if Marxist) discussion, see Suret-Canale, ftn. 13, pp. 29–41 and 57.

16 Arch. Nat. Col. A.E.F. 649, dossier 14, M. Chailly, Directeur général de l'Union Coloniale, "Plan dressé en vue d'améliorer la situation économique de l'Afrique Equatoriale Française," 14 December 1919.

Changes came during and after World War II. The Free French government of General de Gaulle was given support, Gabonese served in the French army in Europe, and Félix Eboué, the first black Governor-General of A.E.F., called for some African participation in ruling. During the Fourth French Republic from 1946 to 1958, Gabon had the status of an overseas territory along with the other sub-Saharan possessions of France (plus Madagascar), and was part of the Union Française, the new name given to the French Empire. In spite of the failure to make all the reforms that were necessary, increasing African participation in the affairs of state was a result. With the return of General de Gaulle in 1958 Gabon voted yes to the constitution of the Fifth Republic, gained internal autonomy, and became a member of the Community until this French Commonwealth of Nations disappeared in 1960 with the political independence of its members, 121 years after Bouët-Willaumez of the French navy signed his first treaty with the first Gabonese.

The First Gabonese and the Latter-Day Gabonese

The Mpongouè, like King Denis, considered themselves as the elite of Gabon.[17] When they had arrived, nobody knows — someone has suggested 1300 with a question mark — and from whence they arrived nobody really knows — someone has suggested the east.[18] As the tribe which had the most contact with the White and which monopolized trade with the interior, its language became widespread; it was adopted by other tribes who lived in the area.

The Galoa and the Oroungou who live near the Mpongouè probably came from the southeast,[19] the Nkomi and Enenga came from elsewhere, and the Adyumba were once part of the Mpongouè. These five tribes became what is known as the Omyènè ethnic group or (unfortunately and incorrectly) as the Omyènè "race." They now speak the same language and begin

---

[17] Evidence of prehistoric habitation of the Libreville area has been found, but very little is now known about the people there. B. Farine, "Sites préhistoriques gabonais" (Libreville, Ministère de l'information, 1963).

[18] André Hauser, "Notes sur les Omyènè du Bas Gabon," *Bulletin de l'Institut Français d'Afrique Noir*, série B, July-October 1954, pp. 406–408.

[19] *Ibid.*

conversations or call to someone by "I am saying — eh." which in their language is miè nè — whence their name.

Gabon has the following ethnic groups (defined mainly on the basis of language) and the following tribes (defined mainly on the basis of dialect).[20]

Groups	Tribes
Omyènè	Mpongouè, Adyumba, Enenga, Galoa, Orungou, Nkomi
Séké	Séké, Benga
Eshira	Eshira, Ngowe, Bavarma, Bavoungou, Bapounou, Baloumbou, Babuissi, Massango
Okandé	Bapindji, Mitsogo, Pové, Bassimba, Okandé, Baveya
Bakèlè	
Fang	Fang, Ntoumou, Mvaè, Okak
Bakota	Bakota, Mahongoué, Shaké Dambomo, Shamaye, Mindassa, Bavoumbou, Mbahouin
Mbédé	Ambamba, Bambama, Mindoumou, Bakanigui, Bandjabi, Batsangui, Bawandji, Badouma
	Plus the Bakwélé and Batéké tribes, which belong to Congolese groups.

Most of these people, who are considered Bantu, probably came in waves from the northeast or east in an order that depended on who was fleeing from whom or what. The Eshira and Mbédé groups probably came from the south.[21]

All these groups are then ethnic groups. The Mahongoué say

20 Part of this basic outline is found in Marcel Soret, "Introduction" to Abbé Raponda-Walker, "Notes d'histoire du Gabon" (Brazzaville, Institut d'Etudes Centrafricaines, 1960), p. 6. The spelling is mine and corresponds to how people refer to themselves or to government-preferred spellings. The plural form of tribal names is generally used here.

21 In addition to a linguistic classification of the Gabonese there is a new tendency to classify them according to the place in which they live, with subclassifications for linguistic differences. The people have been divided into geographical groups like south, central, north, and so forth. Conceptions of tribe and language are still more relevant. See Hubert Deschamps, *Traditions orales et archives au Gabon* (Paris, Berger-Levrault, 1962), p. 18.

they belong to the Mahongoué tribe or "race" ("race" was used quite indiscriminately by French administrators for tribe or ethnic group, while the word "tribe" was used for "clan"; this confusion and incorrect use of terms has been inherited by many Gabonese), not to the Bakota tribe; they claim, however, that they are related to the Bakota and to everyone whom the ethnographer has placed in the Bakota group. They say: "Il n'y a pas d'interprète entre nous." Some members of the various tribes of the Omyènè group say they belong to the Omyènè "race"; others say they belong to the Galoa "race."

The Fang of Gabon are really part of a larger ethnic group historically called "Pahouin" in French, "Pamué" in Spanish, and "Pangwe" in German. This group is divided into the Fang of Gabon and Rio Muni, and the Bulu and Betsi of Cameroun. They all consider themselves part of the larger group even though there are no chiefs or institutions at this level and even though the term Pahouin is considered very derogatory. All the members of the Pahouin group speak essentially the same language and consider that they are descended from the same ancestor; they are separated geographically, by dialect, and by their descent from different children of that same ancestor. The total ethnic group, Fang, Bulu, and Betsi, number over 800,000 of whom about 150,000 Fang live in Gabon, about 150,000 Fang in Rio Muni, and over 500,000 Bulu and Betsi in Cameroun.[22]

In Gabon the Fang account for about 30 per cent of the population; the Eshira group with almost 100,000 accounts for over 20 per cent because of the Bapounou, a very large tribe. The Mbédé group accounts for about 15 per cent of the total because of the numerous Bandjabi; the Bakota group has between 10 and 15 per cent of the population, the Omyènè, about 5 per cent, and the rest of the groups between 10 and 15 per cent of the total. The Mbédé, Okandé, and Eshira who live south of the Ogooué sometimes call themselves Mérié people.

Those who call themselves Fang, whom I call members of the Fang "group," live from the Atlantic coast at Libreville along the Ogooué River to the region of Ogooué-Ivindo and north into Woleu-Ntem, Rio Muni, and the southernmost part of Cameroun.

---

[22] P. Alexandre and J. Binet, Le groupe dit Pahouin (Fang-Boulou-Beti) (Paris, Presses Universitaires de France, 1958), pp. 8–13.

Some Betsi may live in the eastern part of Ogooué-Ivindo, but most live in Cameroun. Differences in dialect separate the Fang of Gabon into tribes such as Ntoumou, Okak, Mvaè, and "Fang." These are parallel to the tribes in the Omyènè group but most Fang of Gabon consider themselves to be Fang; they might specify their dialect group as Ntoumou, but they say *Fang* Ntoumou, and increasingly just *Fang*. The tendency is to forget these particular subcategories. In practice almost all Fang in Gabon call themselves Fang.

Geographical distribution of the various ethnic groups and their neighbors was determined by who got there first. The Fang were the last to arrive.

Fang on the Move: The News and the Fear

People on the coast knew about the reportedly fierce men from the northeast long before they arrived. Thomas Bowdich on a ship that was buying wood in the estuary in 1817 talked to an English-speaking African who told him about some people called "Paam-way" who lived near the Wole River, "the largest river in the world, which" Bowdich was told, "ran further than anyone except, God knows, further than Indee."[23] The news of the Fang spread as new tribes came into the forest country by the rivers and as a trading network with the White developed; the Fang were at the distant end of the interior trade routes. They passed the ivory or the rubber to others who passed it on until it reached the Mpongouè, who sold it to the Whites.

The Fang disliked all these middlemen and did not like to be subject to the capricious wills of other traders. They had heard stories about the white traders with different ways and reportedly strange powers; could they have been sent for a special mission, could they be the "elder brothers" of the Fang? According to one legend of Fang origin about which President Léon Mba has written, God gives this advice to his black children just as he is about to die: "After my death you will go down to Nki the west. Down there you will find men white as the foam of the sea, as white as

---

23 Thomas E. Bowdich, *Mission from Cape Coast Castle to Ashantee* (London, John Murray, 1819), p. 428.

ghosts. They are very rich, they are your elder brothers."[24] Professor Pierre Alexandre writes that this is a transformation of an earlier legend in which the coastal Africans are portrayed as the elder brothers.[25]

If the trading stations were removed and all the Whites took their goods to Senegal, a Frenchman speculated that it might take the Fang twenty years (no more) to reach Dakar.[26] In 1846 the Whites sent word to some interior Fang that it might be worth their while to trade directly with the White.[27] As the Fang tried to do so, they fought wars with everyone, particularly the Galoa and Enenga near the coast and the Shaké, Bakota, Badouma, and Okandé further in the interior. There were "annual wars" between the Bakota and the Fang as the Bakota were first favored as traders by the Whites:

> Six Bakota of Djambala, including an old chief, had come to Ndjolé about the 15th of this month and took two canoes. The 21st, having finished their business, they peacefully went back up the river; when they passed before the pahouin village of Nsegke, that of Chief Emane-Tole, some miles above Ndjolé, they were attacked by the inhabitants of this village who killed three men including the chief, seized the canoes and merchandise therein.[28]

The Badouma often shared the fate of the Bakota when they worked for the Whites; as used by de Brazza they served as carriers of mail along the Ogooué or the Ivindo and as such were called upon, it was said, to serve as meals for the Fang: "Received serious news," one administrator wrote, "I have just learned that three Badouma (Special Couriers) going to Lastoursville were stopped, killed, and eaten by the Pahouins of Zabouré."[29]

They moved down the Ogooué. The people near the mouth of

---

24 Most people in Gabon believe that even if God is alive, he plays very little role in what goes on. See Léon Mba, "Essai de droit coutumier pahouin," n.d., p. 51.

25 See Pierre Alexandre, "Proto-histoire du groupe Beti-Bulu-Fang: Essai de synthèse provisoire," *Cahiers d'études afraicaines*, 20, 1965, pp. 503–560.

26 R. P. Martrou, "Le Nomadisme des Fangs," III, *Revue de géographie*, 1909, p. 521.

27 Schnapper, ftn. 3, p. 58.

28 Arch. Nat. Col. Gabon IV, dossier 10, letter from administrateur principal de N'Djolé, Franceville et Dépendances à M. le Commissaire Général, N'Djolé, 29 July 1896.

29 "Livre de Correspondance," *Station de Booué*, Letter from Booué, 9 November 1889.

the river had naturally heard about the Fang. It was only a question of time now; all they could do was wait. The "enemy," whom an American missionary called Fañwe, arrived on 20 September 1875:

> On Monday the 20th there was loud shouting on the opposite side of the river, and news of Fañwe having killed one Akèlè and wounded another. This was the beginning of what eventually proved to be a revolution in the tribal conditions of that part of the Ogowe . . . . The tribe had emerged on the right or northwest bank of the river and had come into conflict with the Bakèlè . . . who were now beginning to flee to the left bank . . . . Ten years later, the entire river was practically in possession of the Fañwe.[30]

Those in the way of the Fang either fled or eventually disappeared; those considered inferior were not tolerated — men were often killed and reportedly eaten while women were taken into the group; and those considered superior were copied. Once the Fang surrounded a tribe, it was said to disappear. Père Trilles observed their absorptive capacities:

> No foreign tribe can live in the middle of them; it is purely and simply "eaten" . . . . The influence of foreign tribes cannot act on them because they are literally "absorbed," as "Fan" as their conquerors . . . .[31]

Reported anthropophagy has always been overestimated by Europeans who have long had an odd fascination with the idea of cannibalism. European traders, explorers and missionaries like Trilles never really saw acts of cannibalism but depended mainly on what other Africans told them. These accounts were designed to frighten the Europeans and prevent them from trading directly with the peoples of the interior. Africans also used the word "eat" in an ambiguous way: Killing someone meant often "eating" his soul. Confusions of language led some Europeans to exaggerate and even embellish stories about the Fang. The idea that Africans were cannibals also served to justify colonialism by insisting they did not have the rights of human beings. Cannibals, according to the historian of the French Revolution, Georges Lefebvre, were

---

[30] Robert Hamill Nassau, *My Ogowe* (New York, Neale, 1914), pp. 101–102.
[31] H. Trilles, *Le Totémisme chez les Fans* (Münster, Bibliothèque-Anthropos, 1912), p. 123.

not covered by the Declaration of the Rights of Man and Citizen: "For cannibals, for example, the rights of man can have no real application; and if it be argued that even cannibals are human beings, still they are scarcely human in our sense."[32] If some Whites claimed that Africans did not have the rights of human beings because they were supposed to be cannibals and thus "scarcely human," then the Whites could easily justify civilizing missions and control.

Non-Fang conquered in war could also be accepted into the tribe as Fang, and those who could not be conquered risked a different type of absorption by finding that the more numerous Fang had simply adopted their customs. Evidence indicates that the Fang did not move rapidly to the coast but took about a century to move the 200 kilometers from the place in Woleu-Ntem where they were known to live to the coast, according to Professor Sautter, French geographer at the University of Paris. This slowness of movement and apparent patience were a help in keeping enough unity to absorb neighbors. Relations with new neighbors were therefore not always violent.

A late-nineteenth-century traveler indicated that when the Fang could not conquer a village by battle, they would send a single man to the village chief to request hospitality and a bit of land. The man would work hard and make friends with the villagers; one day he would "timidly" ask if he might send for his wife. Time passed. Another Fang would arrive with his family and very courteously ask permission to settle. Gradually, the traveler from France thought, so many Fang came that the original inhabitants began to complain. They were then told in less courteous terms to leave if the place didn't suit them. They stayed to be ruled by the more energetic Fang and were absorbed by them or they left.[33]

The French were able to use the Fang invasion threats to gain the compliance of other tribes. Near the turn of the century everyone in the northern part of the country feared the Fang; when they had a choice of the European or the Fang, many people chose the French, or so the French said.

32 Georges Lefebvre, *The Coming of the French Revolution* (New York, Random House, Vintage Series, 1947), p. 183.

33 J. de Montaignac, "L'Ogooué: ses populations et son avenir commercial," *Revue des Deux Mondes*, 1884, p. 192.

For example, after Robert Nassau, missionary and Princeton graduate, had noted the Fang arrival on his section of the Ogooué, they advanced to the coast and Fernan Vaz area where the Nkomi, another tribe of the Omyènè group, were living. They are a small tribe and are still somewhat isolated from the rest of the Omyènè. As the invaders came into their country, the Nkomi appealed to the French for protection. The French agreed to protect them on condition that they recognize French sovereignty. The Nkomi signed a treaty immediately. The French then demanded that the Fang liberate Nkomi whom they had captured and that they submit themselves to the authority at Libreville; the Fang complied, but only after a few battles.

Their southerly movement was thus stopped, as it was in other places, by a general submission of the country. The Fang became less feared: "The effect produced by this operation," said the man who directed it, "is great on the N'Comi who had not believed it was possible to push back the Pahouins. We should take advantage of this by collecting the taxes for 1899 immediately."[34]

The French continued to crush resistance to their rule in Gabon and to explore the country. The Fang largely submitted to their authority, although the Woleu-Ntem did not effectively become a part of Gabon until after World War I. Other tribes, such as the Bapounou, were unaffected by the Fang invasion but felt the French variety.

The Whites said they found the Fang an attractive and useful people. This was the same as in Cameroun where the Germans had used Bulu and Betsi dynamism to advantage, thus encouraging the latter's spirit of dominance over other tribes. The Betsi who lived around Yaoundé

> were considered . . . as the best natives of southern Cameroun. . . . They were also the most intelligent of all, the most open, the most eager before the White whose language they passionately desired to learn. They were sought from everywhere for their vivacity of spirit, their robustness, their passion for work. . . . Thus, their preponderance over all the other tribes of southern Cameroun was assured.[35]

[34] Arch. Nat. Col. Gabon IV, dossier 10, Report from H. A. Tondere, Commandant de la Région à M. le Commissaire Général, Région de l'Ogooué, 24 July 1899.

[35] G. Perrault, "Les Fangs du pays Yaoundé," *Les Cahiers d'Outre-Mer*, 1948,

The Spanish used the Fang in the territorial guard of Fernando Poo and Rio Muni.

The French view of the Fang is in a way one of the curiosities of their imperialism; it is also sentimental. The Fang was regarded as superior, not because he submitted to French material superiority but because he did not. The French were impressed by stories of how this group conquered others and thought they might benefit:

> It is necessary to note that these populations for which the Pahouins substitute themselves after having eaten them are uninteresting; they are cowards, vicious, profoundly corrupted. . . . We have no interest in protecting them against the invaders concerning whom we may permit ourselves some hopes.[36]

They also thought they saw long-lost brothers in the Fang and claimed they saw Fang who looked like Frenchmen. This was written for European readers who might be more willing to contribute money to missionaries if they thought there was an isolated band of Christians or Whites surrounded, as it were, by "pagan" and "dark" Africa.

In a little pamphlet published in 1905, for example, one Louis Franc (a pseudonym, probably) insisted that a very long time ago a section of the Germanic people left for Africa; they were Franks who, observed in North Africa after they had crossed the Ocean, were called Feran or Fan as they moved south. He then discussed the ways in which the Fang make weapons and how they look; his conclusion was that they showed a real kinship with the Germanic folk and must be the lost tribe.[37] Père Trilles who as a missionary had studied the Fang for many years wrote that he had seen black, red, and white Fang, all of whom were ferocious, but often friendly and hospitable; he calculated that they numbered from four to five million. "The Black Peril is perhaps not so far away as some people think. It is," the priest concludes, "the secret of tomorrow."[38] The Europeans wanted to see these Fang, who

---

pp. 326–27. See also, Dr. Karl Ritter, Veröffentlichungen des Reichskolonialamts No. 4 (Jena, Fischer, 1912), p. 23.

36 V. Largeau, *Encyclopédie pahouine* (Paris, Leroix, 1901), pp. 31–32.

37 Louis Franc, *De l'Origine des Pahouins: essai de résolution de ce problème ethnologique* (Paris, Maloine, 1905).

38 R. P. Trilles, *Chez les Fang ou quinze années de séjour au Congo français* (Lille, Desclée de Brouwer 1919), pp. 14, 25, 73.

they were, these so-called "savages"! A Belgian came to "recruit" these people for an exposition in his country; a German requested that he be allowed to recruit some for a project of exploration.

The white imperialists needed labor and needed help in governing; they said they were disgusted by the "Gabonese" or coastal tribes who had in effect been decivilized by them:

> The Gabonese have become so lazy that if the Pahouins (who are the future because they are energetic workers) did not bring in bananas and sticks of manioc, the former would have nothing to eat.[39]

It was Savorgnan de Brazza who suggested that Fang might be used as auxiliaries to the French in part to pacify them and in part because they were capable and attractive:

> These new recruits have come without too much repugnance to be integrated into the ranks of our first auxiliaries: Badoumas, Kandé, Bapingis, Bakotas, Bangoués. . . . Little by little these Pahouins will come to double and triple the number of our auxiliaries; their natural aptitudes, their physical force, their extreme sobriety make them perfect to back us up in these new regions.[40]

The missionaries thought they could use the Fang as well. Bishop Bessieux, the first priest to arrive in Gabon in 1844, thought that the "lazy people" on the coast might be replaced in Christian hopes by the "vigorous people" in the interior.[41] Not only were the Fang attractive to the missionaries as vigorous types, they seemed to Catholics to avoid the Protestant English and Americans and to be easier to evangelize because they all spoke the same language.[42] The missionaries and the explorer-administrators did not act together on all things, but they all tended to encourage, educate, and favor the Fang at first.

The military sent Fang to mission schools at Libreville to be

[39] Arch. Nat. Col. Gabon-Congo I, dossier III, 21b, Letters from the Capitaine de fregate Masson, commandant du Gabon, au Ministre de la Marine et Colonies, Libreville, 18 September 1882.

[40] "Exposé présenté par M. P. Savorgnan de Brazza, Lt. de Vaisseau dans la séance générale extraordinaire," 21 January 1886 (Paris, Société de Géographie, 1886), p. 22.

[41] Letter of Bessieux cited in *Revue Coloniale* (Paris), Tome XII, August 1847, p. 446.

[42] *Bulletin Général de la Congrégation du Saint-Esprit et du St. Cœur de Marie* (Paris), Tome VII, 1863, pp. 455–456 and Tome XII, 1882, p. 572.

educated so that they could be used by explorers and administrators. De Brazza wanted the Fang to become the expert canoers that the Badouma were; he signed treaties with the Bakota, the Okandé and the Bapindji to take in young Fang whom they would teach their methods of canoeing.[43] Fang were sent on missions of exploration such as the Fourneau mission into Congo. Monsignor André Raponda-Walker, the well-known Gabonese historian and scholar, reports that in his youth, well before the turn of the century, there was a building in Libreville called "Pahouin House" where the French recruiter of Fang lived; it was he who brought them to Libreville to engage in hard labor, such as construction and road work.[44] When there was a corps of sharpshooters ("tirailleurs gabonais"), the Fang played an important part in it. The commander indicated that out of 187 Africans there were 55 Fang, of whom one was a corporal; the widely used Senegalese were, of course, more numerous (79); of these four were corporals and four were sergeants. There were also 47 Omyènè.[45] In 1891 the corps was suppressed because the French were disappointed by the Fang who did not always cooperate, as hoped; in addition, since many of the battles were against the Fang themselves it was better to have a corps 100 per cent Senegalese, the commander wrote. The French later wanted to use Fang as soldiers in World War I. Instructions concerning recruitment were explicit: the government wanted Sara and Banda from Chad and Oubangui-Chari, and they wanted Fang from Gabon.[46] Of the 2,065 Gabonese recruited for the World War I most were not, however, Fang.[47]

In school at Libreville the Fang were by far outnumbered by the Omyènè in whose territory the schools were, after all, located. The first Roman Catholic schools were set up in 1844 (two years

43 Arch. Nat. Col. Gabon IV, dossier 10, "Rapport Général sur la Haut-Ogooué-Alima-Congo," Capitaine Pradier, Commandant Supérieur des Etablissements Français du Golfe de Guinée, 17 March 1886. The Fang has long had the reputation of not liking the water.

44 A. Raponda-Walker, personal communication.

45 Arch. Nat. Col. Gabon XVI, dossier 12 (3), "Rapport du Capitaine Laumonnier, sur le recrutement des indigènes qui composent le dit Corps," Libreville, 25 September 1888.

46 Arch. Nat. Col. A.E.F. 661, dossier 1, telegram, Ministère des Colonies, 6 January 1916.

47 *Ibid.*, letter from Lt. Governor to Governor-General, 13 May 1919.

39

after those of the Protestants), and by 1898 Gabon was reported to have twenty schools with 1,118 students, while Congo had only seventeen with 465 students and Oubangui-Chari had a bare ten with 640 students.[48] In 1856 the church had even set up a secondary school in which by 1900 there were enrolled 38 Mpongouè plus 12 other Omyènè, 10 Fang, and 57 Senegalese, Congolese, southern Gabonese, and children from the Portuguese islands of Saint Thomas and Prince. Graduates of the school were supposed to continue their studies and become priests, but they got jobs with local businesses and in the administration. The administration suppressed the school, for it had decided that what Africans needed was a simple vocational or technical education with a heavy emphasis on French and agriculture so that they would become teachers and very low-level clerks.[49] It was almost a century later that another secondary school was established in Gabon although in the meanwhile the Ecole Renard had been set up in Brazzaville.

The Fang did not become the "younger brothers" and did not assist the French the way in which they were expected. For example, there was an early resistance to going to school in Libreville. It may have been that, while the Fang wanted to trade with the White and learn his ways, he feared going to school far from home because that would have meant being cut off from his family and being mixed in with the disliked coastal tribes. There are Fang who say they never got a chance to attend school in Libreville because their families feared they would surely die in that place. One administrator wrote: "I have tried to engage some Pahouins to go to Libreville, and I have not been able to conquer their hesitations...."[50] Schools were not set up in the Woleu-Ntem until 1929, but once the Fang saw what the benefits of education would be, they overcrowded these small schools.

With the exception of a few important Fang in European enterprises and the administration, like Léon Mba, Edouard Ekoghe,

---

[48] Gouvernement Général de l'A.E.F., "Histoire et organisation générale de l'enseignement en A.E.F." (Paris, 1931), pp. 7–9. By 1901 the Protestants along the Ogooué had 311 children in their schools. (Americans had founded a mission at Lambaréné in 1876.) Register of Letters, Mission at Ngomo, Letter 14 February 1902.

[49] A. Walker, "Une Mise au point," No. 3, *Réalités Gabonaises*, October 1959, p. 3. See also Gouvernement Général, ftn. 48, pp. 10–13.

[50] "Livre de Correspondance," Station de Booué, 16 July 1890, pp. 150–151.

Jean-Hilaire Aubame and François Mèyè, a graduate of the Ecole Renard, it was the Omyènè who, in spite of early explorers' scorn and administrators' disdain, flocked to whatever schools were available. The grandson of King Denis was the first high-school graduate, and a great-grandson, Prince Félix Adandé, worked for some years in the (Belgian) Congo for a large private company. The Omyènè were sent into various parts of A.E.F. and into West Africa as well, particularly to the Ivory Coast and to Guinea. (The present bishop of Guinea is a descendant of Gabonese who accompanied Dr. Ballay, a colleague of de Brazza, when he left Gabon.) Men like Laurent Anchouey and some administrators originally from the Antilles published a highly sophisticated newspaper in Dakar, called *l'Echo Gabonais*, in 1922. So-called "committees for *l'Echo Gabonais*" were established and were transformed into, or linked with, an Omyènè-run section of the League of the Rights of Man. A "Pan-African Association" was directed by these men as well. Later, the Omyènè attempted to found a political party, the Parti Démocratique Africain, and in 1945 an Mpongouè organization affiliated itself with the French trade union, C.F.T.C. The first priest, the first pastor, and the first African president of the Territorial Assembly were all Omyènè.[51]

In a year like 1930 six Omyènè and no Fang were appointed accountants; ten were appointed interpreters along with two Fang. Four Omyènè were appointed as clerks at the telegraph bureau, compared with two Fang. In the same year five Omyènè were admitted as primary-school teachers with no Fang, while fifteen Omyènè and only five Fang were granted *certificats d'études* for primary-school studies.[52]

When opportunities for education in France became more accessible to Africans, the Omyènè were the first to send their children to Paris. The first college graduate was an Omyènè of Libreville. Until 1964 the only member of the President's cabinet to have completed a full secondary-education program was an

[51] I am grateful to Dr. John Ballard for having directed my attention to the early Gabonese newspapers in the Bibliothèque Nationale in Paris. An account of Omyènè activities is found in John Ballard, "The Development of Political Parties in French Equatorial Africa," unpublished dissertation, Fletcher School of Law and Diplomacy, December 1963.

[52] Gouvernement Général de l'Afrique Equatoriale Française, *Journal Officiel*, 1 February 1930, pp. 124, 130; also year 1946, pp. 125, 184, 268, 648, 945, 1335, 1502, 1503.

Omyènè Eurafrican. This has now changed. Eurafricans were mostly born of Omyènè mothers, and only when they were recognized by the European father could they become French citizens. The Eurafricans had organized themselves into a cooperative organization called the *Amicale des Métis* and had set up a school called the *Internat* which was generally regarded as superior to other schools.

The Omyènè and the Eurafricans generally had more money than other people. One reason was that they lived in the zones where exploitation of wood had begun and were allowed to cut it down and sell it under a system called the *coupe familiale.*

Today, the Fang predominate numerically in all areas of Gabonese life, with the Omyènè and the Bapounou coming in second. At the lowest and the highest echelons the Fang predominate in leadership positions; for example, the first Gabonese bishop is a Fang from the estuary, and the president of the now independent Protestant church is also a Fang. The first Fang to be ordained were from the estuary, but increasingly they have come from Woleu-Ntem. Out of twenty-eight priests in 1964, five were Omyènè while eleven were Fang. Eight of these eleven were ordained in the last fifteen years and seven of them were from Woleu-Ntem.[53]

In the diocese of Libreville the Fang and the Omyènè now account for most of the teaching positions in Roman Catholic schools: Out of 383 teachers in 1962–63 no less than 261 were Fang, with 53 Omyènè. In the government school system there were, in 1960–1961, 697 teachers at the primary-school level, of whom about half were Fang.[54] In the highest civil-service posts the Fang also predominate; they are the prefects, sub-prefects, assistant sub-prefects: 23 out of 54 prefects and sub-prefects named to posts then filled by Gabonese in 1962 were Fang, and so were at least 24 out of 47 in 1964. The army, the gendarmerie, and the police are about 50 per cent Fang; the Omyènè and the Bapounou are also well represented. The first President is a Fang, as is the

53 "Annuaire de l'archidiocèse de Libreville et du diocèse de Mouila," Gabon, 1964, pp. 24–25.

54 Ministère de l'Education Nationale, "Liste nominative du personnel de l'enseignement officiel en service dans la République Gabonaise pendant l'année scolaire 1960–1961."

former head of the former opposition. In the National Assembly in 1962 the Fang had 24 out of 67 seats, or a little more than one third; in 1966, 18 out of 47 seats (the total was reduced), or slightly more than one third, were held by Fang.

Youth and women's organizations are mainly run by both Fang and Omyènè, as are trade unions. Important companies in the private sector are controlled by Europeans, but an Africanization of skilled and unskilled jobs has been taking place. Laurent Biffot, a noted Gabonese sociologist, found in a study of one forestry enterprise that of 46 Fang, who constituted only 15.2 per cent of his sample, 17 were illiterate laborers in the lowest job category while 20 occupied the top jobs of mechanic and "bureaucrat." Among the Omyènè, who were only 2.3 per cent of the total work force, there were no laborers, and eight out of twelve employees interviewed occupied the top posts of mechanic and "bureaucrat."[55]

The Fang believe they have an important role to play in Gabonese nation-building. In the foreword to his essay on Fang customs, Léon Mba cites with pride one European who wrote that the Fang would be the "race [sic] of the future of Gabon."[56] At the same time the Omyènè and the Eurafricans are resentful and consider what their place will be as the old elite which has contributed immensely to Gabonese history but which, for lack of numbers, finds it is playing a decreasing role.

The French said they would use the Fang as "partners" in colonization, but there is no such thing. They could not have their "noble savage" and an orderly administration. They did not appear at first to realize that the coastal peoples whom they despised for their apparent alcoholism, debauchery, and degradation had been made so by the coming of the White. It was the coastal people who, once they lost their control over commerce, took greatest advantage of the limited opportunities for education, jobs, and new ways. Their present importance in Gabonese national life is due to this acceptance of education and employment in the colonial system prior to that by others. The turning of the Fang toward Gabon, their predominance, their dynamism cannot be at-

---

[55] Laurent Biffot, *Facteurs d'intégration et de désintégration du travailleur gabonais à son entreprise* (Paris, ORSTOM, 1960–1961), p. 58.

[56] Léon Mba, ftn. 24, p. 5.

tributed to the supposedly preferential treatment they received at the hands of the White. They have felt a need for a new social and cultural system, and they have acted along with other Africans to build a new order.

CHAPTER 3

Anomie and the Motive Force of the Fang

Fang Pre-National Order

When the Fang first came into Gabon, perhaps in the eighteenth century, they were, as warriors, feared for their numbers, their special urge to dominate and to absorb others on their path to the sea. Their villages which moved, split, and fused were small fortresses with houses attached to one another.

Since the White has known the Fang, the latter had no well-organized, clearly defined hierarchy of authority. The Fang themselves indicate no ancient kings that were important in the land from which they came. This land may have been the savanna of northern Cameroun, or it may have been closer to the Nile. No one really knows, not even the eldest of the Fang.

Egalitarianism does not mean there were no leaders, for they did have men who were "pre-eminent": These were the elders charged with certain ritual observances for the lineage or clan and were considered temporary clan chiefs; they were judges empowered to settle disputes and restore order; they were military leaders who organized many, but not all, of the tribesmen to fight their enemies.[1]

1 Henri-Marcel Bôt ba Njock, "Prééminences sociales et systèmes politico-re-

These leaders could not expect to have much power nor to maintain it very long, for a leader would be suspected of witchcraft if he were too powerful and rich. He would be suspected because it was believed that there was a given quantity of riches and power in the world; a man who had more than others must have taken some of theirs by witchcraft powers. A witch could get the power of others by a type of cannibalism, it was believed.

A spiritual form of cannibalism is important in the Fang conception of the world. The man considered a witch does not consume human flesh; he has a force within him that supposedly consumes the soul of someone else who becomes ill, loses his possessions, or dies. The force is called *evus* by the Fang and *ignemba* by the Omyènè.

Evus, a way to explain the unknown, is considered a "magical being" that lives in the body of a person. It helps man gain riches and power because it can leave his body to perform cannibalistic acts that will appropriate the riches and power of others. This "supernatural agent" leaves no traces. *Evus* is not absolutely evil, for the man who possesses it can decide how to use it. For example, there are three types of men in Fang society: *mimia* does not have the benefit of the magical being; he is poor but honest, a harmless fellow; *engolengola* possesses *evus* but is not considered a witch; he is "reasonably" rich and powerful, but no one seems to suffer by his presence; *nnem,* however, is a real witch; he is very rich and very powerful and is considered to have an *evus* that has stolen much from others.[2]

Evus is one of the potentially evil forces that surround mankind, the Fang believe. In a dangerous world, it is believed, the individual can act in some small ways to face life and protect his family. The Fang had rituals, societies, and medicines to insure that some member of the family might have *evus* to be used moderately or to act against enemies who themselves had *evus*.

---

ligieux dans la société traditionnelle Bulu et Fang," *Journal de la Société des Africanistes,* Tome xxx, Fasc. II, 1960, pp. 150–171.

2 Dr. James W. Fernandez has written extensively about *evus*. See particularly his "Redistributive Acculturation and Ritual Reintegration in Fang Culture," unpublished thesis, Northwestern University, June 1963, pp. 80, 150–151. And James W. Fernandez, "Christian Acculturation and Fang Witchcraft," *Cahiers d'Etudes Africaines,* No. 6, 1961, p. 247.

46

They had ways to protect themselves from the mysterious forces of disorder that were considered evil.

The first of these methods was *bieri,* an ancestor cult that centered about a basket containing parts of the ancestors' skulls. Young men were initiated into the cult, and kinship groups were strengthened by the ceremonies and by membership in it.[3] Ties with the ancestors and the tribal past were strengthened; the ancestors who could act on earth to punish evildoers were expected to help the members of the cult in wise decision-making and to protect them from evil capricious forces like *evus. Bieri* was used in time of misfortune because the ancestors were considered an efficacious force in the reestablishment of the familiar order.[4]

The Fang had other ways to protect themselves against the capricious force of witchcraft. Special societies were organized when crisis was widespread: famine, universal sterility — any series of mysterious and harmful forces that threatened the group. The *ngil* society would, by a complicated ritual, find the evil as represented by witches, and the Fang would be purified of evil forces among them.[5]

Witch-hunting was rare. Like any other society, the Fang had methods to insure social control and to socialize the young or integrate them into society by making sure they upheld the cultural standards which made the society distinctive and maintained order. These had little to do with witchcraft or protection from it although the person who knew the rules, the person who was normal in the strict sense of the word, was in less danger of being called a witch than the one who was a bit strange or a little abnormal. To insure normality and a social control there were age groups, initiation societies, and in each *corps de garde* of the village or section of village young men learned what they had to do to be Fang and to be faithful to the ancestors. If people broke the rules, they met efficacious punishments.

Marriage was, of course, central to the Fang order. It served as an alliance between two families, and in a world in which evil

3 Georges Balandier, *Sociologie actuelle de l'Afrique noire* (Paris, Presses Universitaires de France, 1955), pp. 141–142.

4 Fernandez, "Redistributive Acculturation," ftn. 2, pp. 158–161.

5 For the Omyènè a society called *mwiri* had the same function.

was regarded a constant threat, marriage alliances built up larger zones of security and order. More close relatives meant more places where one would be helped in time of need and more places where one could go in safety. The bridewealth, as a transfer of goods from the family of the groom to that of the bride, was a material sign of the legitimacy of the union and also a material sign of the new alliance.[6]

Whatever the Fang concept of the world, they had come to terms with it as well as with their environment in the forest clearings. Ways to preserve his order existed and were adapted to the unknown forces that threatened it. Until the coming of the White these ways were efficacious.

The Fang were warriors, but the French imposed their own kind of peace. Peace was necessary so that the colonialists could rule according to their ideas of order. In peace the Fang became what Balandier, professor at the Sorbonne, has called "available conquerors" (*des conquérants en disponibilité*).[7] They continued to try to block trade routes, and one administrator complained that the Fang had surrounded his post: "It is indispensable to make the Fang know that their prohibitive lines which now encircle the region . . . must be open for all."[8] Attempts on the part of the Fang to resist control and to disrupt trade routes and administration plans were met with strong reactions on the part of the French who in the 1920's and 1930's were responsible for great changes in the old Fang order.

Weakening of the Pre-National Order

Movement toward the coast had proceeded in a voluntary way. The White, however, introduced a new kind of migration. When he occupied the interior regions of the country, he began to move villages, to recruit for commercial activities and military expeditions. Such recruitment, which resulted in population movements, often really meant forced labor and the kidnapping of young men.

---

6 Balandier, ftn. 3, p. 124.

7 Georges Balandier, "Le Fan du Gabon: des conquérants en disponibilité," *Tropiques*, No. 316, December 1949, pp. 23–26.

8 "Livre de correspondance," Letter to Lt. Governor from Commandant de la Circonscription de l'Ivindo, Mvahdi, 2 March 1911.

In the 1920's the White began in a more systematic way than in the past to exploit the wood, particularly okoumé which is valuable and which Gabon has in abundance. He set up camps where the wood was located and most easily transportable. This meant forestry exploitation would begin south of the Woleu-Ntem near the coast in the area along the Ogooué from Lambaréné to Port-Gentil and south from Lambaréné along the Ngounié River. In 1921, 939 out of 2,167 workers recruited came from Woleu-Ntem.[9] It has been estimated that as many as 75 per cent of these young men recruited for work on the coast never returned to their homes.[10] In the ten years from 1921 to 1930 a third to a half of the young men of Woleu-Ntem were working in forestry enterprises far from their homes.[11]

The population further decreased and the confusion increased with the epidemics caused by diseases brought by the White. In the early 1920's, for example, there were epidemics of influenza and smallpox which killed 4,000 out of a total population of 17,000 in the area of Mitzic.[12] In the mid 1920's a famine killed one third of the remaining population in some areas, because there were not enough young men to clear the fields for cultivation and because women were compelled to prepare what food they had for the administration. Isolated villages which were unknown to the colonial administration had no famine.[13]

In the 1920's and 1930's the administration needed workers for the construction of the Congo-Océan Railroad which was being built in the Congo from the port of Pointe Noire to the capital of A.E.F., Brazzaville. Little has been written about what the Fang and other Gabonese, to say nothing of the Congolese, must have suffered at this time; reports by missionaries in Fang areas give some idea of it: "The whole sector is in disorder; six militiamen have gone there to recruit. All available men are in the brush sharing bed and board with the antelopes while others with ropes

9 Colonie du Gabon, "Rapport Politique — 1921," cited by Gilles Sautter in "Les Paysans noirs du Gabon septentrional," *Cahiers d'Outre-Mer*, 14, April-June 1951, p. 131.

10 Personal communication from Gilles Sautter to Balandier, cited in Balandier, ftn. 3, pp. 165–166.

11 Personal communication from Gilles Sautter. I am grateful to Professor Sautter for having permitted me to read his unpublished manuscript on Gabon.

12 Sautter, ftn. 9, pp. 133–134.

13 Gilles Sautter, personal communication.

around their necks are taken toward the Congo after having spent several nights in prison, of course."[14] This recruitment was called the Terror; to escape it some men fled to Spanish Guinea: "At the time of my arrival not a soul was in the village; everyone under the reign of the Terror has fled into the bush or into Spanish Guinea."[15]

One of the serious effects of continued recruitment, voluntary movement, and breaking up of villages was the disorganization of the clans. A 1943 census of the district of Libreville indicates that fifty-four clans were represented in a total Fang population of 3,500 but that only eight of these fifty-four could muster more than 150 members in the district.[16] The Fang were concerned about clan organization because it was a far more important level of system to the individual Fang than the tribe. Male and female contemporaries in a clan were considered brothers and sisters, and marriage partners had to be found outside the clan. When members of the same clan lived in different administrative circumscriptions set up by the French, they were subject to different non-clan authorities such as cantonal chiefs, who were often appointed by the French on the basis of their loyalty to the colonial administration.

Separation also meant that customs might change. The Fang on the coast changed in ways different from those of their relatives in Woleu-Ntem. They learned the languages spoken there, such as Omyènè, the language of the Libreville Mpongouè; they became Christians, they changed their way of dressing; they forgot some of the old customs. The people of Woleu-Ntem began to regard those who had migrated to the coast as traitors to the past; they had been, it was thought, corrupted. At the same time, the meaning and purpose of bridewealth deteriorated. The transfer of goods and perhaps services from one family and from one clan to another was not supposed to be a get-rich scheme for the father of the bride. As a result of the introduction of a money economy and the general disorganization of Fang society, fathers of the bride began to "sell" their daughters to the highest bidder. Daughters and wives were treated like gold bullion, and only older

14 "Tournées," Catholic mission of Oyem, entry 28 May to 5 June 1938.
15 *Ibid.,* entry 15 to 21 June 1938.
16 Cited by Balandier, ftn. 3, pp. 85–86.

men could afford to get married. Marriages became very unstable as families might try to disrupt a recent marriage if they thought someone else would pay more, and secondly, adultery increased because many young men could not marry and because missionaries had suppressed traditional effective means of dealing with it. Missionaires, administrators, and businessmen weakened the older order.

In the 1930's the French introduced the cultivation of coffee and cocoa into the Woleu-Ntem.[17] Because a market was guaranteed, most of the voluntary movement out of the region stopped as people were encouraged to remain and cultivate industrial crops. This policy helped stabilize the population, but a challenge to the egalitarian order was created when a new way for people to enrich themselves was open and when the cocoa and coffee were tied to world-market prices. Rich people would be suspected of witchcraft, and world prices were capricious forces over which the cocoa producer of Gabon could have no control: one year he might make much money, and the next year he might starve.

The missionaries attacked the role of ancestors in Fang life. The *bieri,* which symbolized the concern which ancestors had for the living, were considered uncivilized and un-Christian. They had to go. With the support of the administration, missionaries often raided villages and seized these baskets and destroyed them. Furthermore, certain ceremonies were forbidden, often without very much knowledge about them;[18] among these were the techniques used to find witches and to destroy them, *ngil,* and the anti-witchcraft societies. The old methods of dealing with disorder, of insuring conformity to the group's rules were weakened, and new capricious forces were introduced. The Fang found that his society was tending toward anomie and disorganization. Customs were rejected by the young who tried to free themselves from the authority of elders and ancestors. Elders have everywhere lived to see a revolt of the young against their authority and principles. As one young Fang wrote: "With these principles disappear a certain number of privileges which the old men of the family, clan, and

17 The Germans had experimented with cocoa and coffee in Cameroun and in Woleu-Ntem when it was under their control, but the French started the cultivation on a large scale.

18 A sign posted on a church door in Lambaréné simply says: "Bad dances are forbidden."

tribe possessed." The elders fear damnation by ancestors "for not having kept the customs they left."[19] Witchcraft accusations as labels given to the capricious forces which man feels threaten him increased as uncertainty, confusion, and a sense of frustration increased.

The number of people who had *evus* and used it capriciously is believed to have increased, and new types of antiwitchcraft movements emerged. An administrator noted in 1908 that very few Fang were said by their neighbors to have this "magical being," but an anthropologist who worked for two years in the Woleu-Ntem reports that Fang now say about one out of every two people has it.[20] In the 1940's a missionary noted an increase in witchcraft accusations in Gabon as elsewhere in Africa.[21] Most people don't like to talk about this, but an increase in antiwitchcraft movements of various kinds has been an observable indication of an increase in witchcraft itself. One antiwitchcraft movement has been *Mademoiselle*.

Mademoiselle was particularly important in the 1950's and apparently started in the Congo from where it spread into several regions of Gabon. In 1957 missionaries in Fang areas reported that trees or wooden stakes had been planted by a representative of this movement to protect people against witchcraft: "N. has planted two trees; all the men attended the ceremony: no Mass, they refused the sacraments and penitence. The chapel has fallen. . . ."[22] The people who had sought protection in the church saw no need for it when *Mademoiselle* came. Representatives were requested to visit villages. Those who called for the representatives of this movement were the poor and the young who wanted these witchfinders to rid them of the witches who had made them weak and less successful in all things, including the production of coffee and cocoa.[23] The witchfinders also condemned *bieri* and other traditional practices, for this movement was an indication of a desire to modernize Fang society as well as to purify and protect it.

19 Jules Mbah, "Coutumes gabonaises et civilisation française," Mémoire, Institut des Hautes Etudes d'Outre-Mer, 1958–1959, pp. 32–33.

20 Fernandez, "Christian Acculturation," ftn. 2, p. 249.

21 Henri Lavignotte, *L'Evur — Croyance des Pahouins du Gabon"* (Paris, Société des Missions Evangéliques, 1947), p. 72.

22 "Tournées," ref. 14, entry 13 to 23 June 1957.

23 Fernandez, "Christian Acculturation," ftn. 2, pp. 251–252.

Although *Mademoiselle* is no longer as widespread as it was, it still exists. In Oyem, the administrative capital of Woleu-Ntem, I interviewed one of the representatives of the movement who still works in this Fang area; he gave me the following explanation of it and how the spirit came to him in 1957:

Mademoiselle is a spirit, not a religion; I am a Catholic. It is a spirit sent by God and is the beginning of the liberation of man from the habit of eating other men. Traditionally, people have killed by witchcraft and have eaten their victims who were usually members of the same family. They might call in a special witch for a rite of black magic or they might do it themselves. Two days after the rite the man becomes sick and two days later he dies from poisoning; he is buried and later his body is taken away to be eaten by those who killed him and by their friends. They also make drugs from parts of the body. *Evus* is the killing force.

God saw all this and he wanted to do something about it. One day a very pretty girl was killed by a jealous suitor; she was only 18 years old and was killed by *evus*. In heaven she asked God for the power to destroy *evus* once and for all. God said, "You are dead and cannot return to earth; but I shall send your spirit. You will enter into men who have never eaten human flesh. These people will do your work for you." "First," God continued, "go to see Lucifer who wishes to render a service to be cleansed of his sins, and Lucifer's spirit will also enter into the body of the agent on earth."

They entered the body of B., a merchant of Ouesso, Moyen-Congo, in order that he rid the country of filth and destroy the bones of those killed. B. was sick for eight days and eight nights; he did not eat and was seized with the spirit during this time. He then commanded all the people to give him their skulls and fetishes or he would kill them.

B. traveled and arrived at Makokou, Gabon; the spirit told him that he had reached the edge of his territory and must leave the work here to others. N. was named by *Mademoiselle* to continue the work and was mad for days; during this time he sang and shouted: "Lucifer, *Mademoiselle*." B. tested him to find out if he had the spirit: "Point out someone with *evus,* someone who has eaten his brother." N. showed him, and he was accepted into the profession. They worked together for six days; then, B. returned.

N. worked the Makokou area against the filth. In Oyem a young man with a mortally sick mother summoned N. to find the *evus*. Even before N. came to Oyem I was seized with the spirit.

53

On Monday my mother was dying; I was worried about how I was going to take care of my wives and children without my mother. On Tuesday morning I went mad [*j'étais fou*] my mother was dead; I beat up my wives and my children. At nine o'clock relatives of my mother came. I was able to tell that her sister was carrying human flesh in her basket. I kicked her out of the house; we looked in her basket: There it was, human flesh. I was also able to determine the existence of skulls in another person's house.

Then N. came to Oyem. I went to him on 12 September 1957; he saw that *Mademoiselle* was at work within me. During one year we worked together in Woleu-Ntem and gained co-workers. The group has 58 members today — women and men. I am the chief; we kill those who are witches.

We plant trees which cover the filth, the skulls, the fetishes and protect the village against sorcery. The missionaries opposed us and destroyed the trees. Father M. uprooted one and then he fainted; he did not breathe for five minutes. I am a Catholic; we help the Church. I don't understand why they don't like us.

Bwiti and *evus* are the same thing. Bwitists ate men but I got rid of the bones and now all they can do is dance. *Ngil* also used bones.

Makokou and Oyem are well worked by *Mademoiselle*; there is little witchcraft now. In other places we have not had much luck. I was put in prison eight times in Bitam. I wrote to the President to get permission to work in Libreville, but he has not answered me. One chief helped me and so did one deputy. The other deputies were against us.

When I look for witches, I put white paint on my face and drink a little wine; afterwards I feel very tired, but I have succeeded in killing many witches.

The trees this man and N. planted are all over certain regions of Gabon, particularly where the Fang live and where the Bakota live. It is important to note that N. was not a Fang; he was a Bakota, yet he had power over them. He could kill them, he said. A man with special spiritual powers has authority even over those who do not belong to his tribe. In one Fang village a "tree" is still there; it is really a post. People said that N. promised that a little snake would leave the post if there were witchcraft and would kill the witch. Some people said that now there is no more witchcraft; others said that after N. left things became worse than before. "He took all our things." By this they mean that he destroyed the protective devices and the *bieri*. *Mademoiselle* was a failure. It was attacked by the French and by many Gabonese who saw it as a danger. It failed because it could not deal with all the forces of disorder.

The White was not ignorant of the problems facing the Africans, and he did not remain completely inactive. The missionary who had helped to destroy the old methods of protection from evil had an ideal in evangelization; he knew that the African had ways to protect himself and he knew that the Africans had a religion, but he judged it as inferior. The ideal of some missionaries was to free the African from the evil spirits that surrounded him. Missionaries proclaimed that Christianity would protect the Fang from the *evus* of others and would protect him better than all those things the White called "fetishes," and "pagan" anti-witchcraft rites.

The administration tried to analyze the changes that were taking place and to determine what to do about them. In 1918 a commission to study changes in Fang society was organized; their concern was mainly what was happening with marriage customs. They knew very well that there was a decline in the efficacy of the old means of social control. The commission attempted to restrict the bridewealth, but without success.[24] In 1946 another commission, the *Commission de la population*, made a study of the reasons for an apparent decrease in Gabon's population. Their remedy was absurd. The members of the commission proposed a Fang reservation where traditional customs could be re-established, but the reservation was not to cover areas from which forestry companies were recruiting.[25]

The Fang themselves knew their society was becoming disorganized: Why were there fewer births, why more witchcraft, why more *evus*, why rule by the Whites? Concern with what appeared to be a decrease in the population led many to write articles for the A.E.F. cultural review, *Liaison*, and to write essays for contests sponsored by churches or the administration. A Fang administrator wrote that "in 1906 census data . . . indicate 1,638,000 inhabitants in Gabon. But by 1954 the number was reduced to 420,000." Was part of the reason, he speculated, that

[24] Balandier, ref. 3, pp. 187–190.
[25] *Ibid.*, pp. 197–198.

"the Christians" had taken away traditional means of protection so that now "disease ravages the country?"[26] Men passed through Woleu-Ntem and claimed to be able to restore fertility to barren women; there were large meetings once near Minvoul at which 5,000 women were reported present.[27]

Did attempts to solve these problems mean a return to the past, a reassertion of old ways in the face of new threats and changes? Did they mean adoption of completely new ways and completely new institutions? Or did they mean new leaders at new levels of system? If so, would one leader be acceptable to all Fang who sensed differences among themselves and who always feared stronger men as possible witches?

All Fang were swept up in the various attempts to reorganize. The various movements and institutions suggested or tried were neither completely traditionalist nor were they completely new and cut off from the past. They all had elements of an antiwitch-craft movement like *Mademoiselle* and claimed to have the power to keep order. There were attempts to reassert traditional values and reorganize the tribe independently of any state; there were attempts to use state institutions to help the tribe. Lastly, there has been the beginning of a use of state institutions to develop the nation for its own sake as the only level of system and community that can maintain order and give meaning to man's life.

Attempts to Restore Order

Order Through the Old

Those who looked back at past or imaginary orders demanded a reassertion of the "true" Fang customs. In 1936 Léon Mba, who had been a cantonal chief and judge in Libreville, wrote an essay on customary Fang law in response to this demand.[28] Mba, who had been required to settle many conflicts involving marriage, divorce, and inheritance, wrote about the one true Fang custom which could be used to govern relations among these people. The

26 Edouard Ekogha Mengue, "Un gros problème: populations gabonaises en voie d'anéantissement," unpublished manuscript, Libreville, 12 July 1962.

27 Jean-Marie Mbeng, "Ella-Akou, prophète ou charlatan?" *Liaison*, No. 44, 1954, pp. 25–26.

28 Léon Mba, "Essai de droit coutumier pahouin," n.d., pp. 5–51.

greatest danger to order, people believed, was in the weakening of marriage customs.

Ten years later, in 1947, Fang leaders met in Mitzic in the Woleu-Ntem at the administration-sponsored Fang Congress; their purpose was partly to discuss a renewal of Fang customs. The meetings were held in the Fang language, and documents were drawn up in the Fang language, the use of which had been discouraged or forbidden by the French administration since World War I. The delegates to the conference, who were mainly chiefs, called for the election of a Grand Chief, a suppression of "false" religions which some people were adopting, purification of Fang customs, and a decrease in the bridewealth. At the same time they suggested the construction of new roads.[29] Attempts to get people to follow the customs of the fathers would be useless if the kinship groups were in disarray. Therefore the Fang tried first to reorganize the clans, then to establish a unified tribe, and then to unify the whole Fang-Bulu-Betsi or "Pahouin" group at a level which had not in anyone's memory ever existed. This movement was called *alar ayong.*

The Fang who participated in *alar ayong,* or regroupment of the clans, had several expectations about the benefits they could get from it: preservation of Fang values, particularly those concerning marriage; solidarity and friendship; reassertion of a moral system; and progress. One Fang wrote that it was a "moral and sociological effort" to combat divisions among people who now are enemies.[30] Missionaries reported that each clan chose a motto in which the word "progress" was often mentioned; the Fang wrote: "Tribal regroupment has no ritual character; it rests on principles of modern evolution; it assists in the evolution of the African world." It was thus partially, according to the writer, concerned with sending children to school, improving hygiene, but to do these things unity would be necessary: "The tribe, thus united, becomes solid, elaborates what is mutual, creates a new society." This was something which attracted many Fang; people were "excited to find themselves in the *alar ayong.* Everyone was *poussé par un espoir.*"[31]

29 Gouvernement Général de l'Afrique Equatoriale Française, "Congress Pahouin de Mitzic 26–28 Février 1947: Vœux" (Brazzaville, n.d.).

30 Simon Mbeng, "Elar-Ayong chez les Fangs du Gabon," *Liaison,* September 1951, p. 16.

31 *Ibid.*

The goals of the movement did not remain what they had been, and they differed among the supporters. It had started in the early 1930's among the Bulu in Cameroun. Later a sympathetic administrator who realized the Fang were trying to unify clans and purify their customs permitted them to set up chiefs for each clan in his district. This encouraged its supporters, and it spread into the Spanish colony, Guinea, and into Gabon in the early 1940's. Concerned about any possible misunderstanding of its goals on the part of missionaries or the administration, Fang leaders tried to reassure the French. In 1942, for example, a trusted Protestant missionary was shown a large loose-leaf book and was told he could look through it for one night while he stayed in a village in Woleu-Ntem. It was, the missionary told me, a "book of the tribe"; it was proof that all Fang had a common ancestor and that they all belonged to certain clans. This was the story of Afrikara, the father of the Fang, Bulu, and Betsi.

The missionary thought he was permitted to view the book to see that *alar ayong* was merely a traditionalist movement which had no anti-French goals. Money was given to the various Christian churches by leaders of *alar ayong* to show they were not anti-Christian. Administrators were permitted to attend some meetings at which the tricolor, the cross of Lorraine, and the Christian cross were prominently displayed. Still, the administration continued to be very concerned about this movement.

This was the period after World War II, and France was losing possessions in the Middle East and in the Far East. The Brazzaville Conference at the end of the war called for some changes in the empire, but independence had been ruled out. Cameroun was a trusteeship territory whose right to independence was affirmed by the United Nations Charter. Fearful of possible political implications, the administration was always concerned about ethnic conflict. Gabon had no history of the conflict Guinea and Congo had known and would know, but some thought that organization of one tribe might encourage others to do the same. To find out the real goals and implications of *alar ayong*, the administration assigned the task to Edouard Trezenem, an experienced administrator with a long service in the colonies.

Trezenem wrote two secret reports for the governor of Gabon in 1948 in which he analyzed with care and with what appears to be considerable documentation the origins and nature of this Fang movement, how it was organized, how it spread, to what extent it was an attempt at tribal unity, and whether or not French interests could be affected.[32] It was difficult for Trezenem to trace the exact manner in which *alar ayong* ideas had spread down from the Cameroun, but he had some information: People had come down from Cameroun, and Fang had gone north from Gabon and Spanish Guinea to visit relatives; also an official history of the Fang was brought into Gabon. Once the idea had caught on in Woleu-Ntem, it spread, the administrator thought, to the Ogooué-Ivindo and Moyen-Ogooué regions rather than to the coast, where the Fang were not on good terms with their relatives in Cameroun or in Woleu-Ntem: "Regroupment was introduced into Ogooué-Ivindo through the district of Mitzic. Emissaries from Woleu-Ntem arrived, without being controlled, by the path from Angouna. . . ." Because the Fang had their own paths off the main routes and their own system of communication, they were more likely to avoid control by the administration, Trezenem reasoned. Local organization was established and certain ceremonies to which Trezenem got himself invited were held.

One of the ceremonies the Frenchman said he was permitted to witness had something to do with protection of the members from evil. He wrote, probably incorrectly, that two men were sacrificed to *evus* in order that *evus* would protect the people rather than harm them; ceremonies about which he heard reminded him of what he knew of the older antiwitchcraft *ngil* society. He noted that officers were elected, and the names chosen for them were copied from those of the French administration and army. For example, there was a president of each clan who was elected by a grand congress of all adult male members of that clan; below him there was a vice-president, and then governors general who were to act as judges to resolve conflicts between members of the clan. If they could not solve the conflict by means of discussion, the dispute would be submitted to the president who would settle

[32] The information here presented comes, unless otherwise noted, from the two reports Trezenem wrote: "Rapport à Monsieur le Gouverneur des Colonies, Chef du Territoire du Gabon, sur le Regroupement des Fan," Booué, 30 March 1948; and "Second Rapport à Monsieur le Gouverneur des Colonies . . . ," Booué, 25 September 1948. I have also talked with a former colonial functionary (Trezenem himself died several years ago) and with Fang who confirm much of Trezenem's information.

it arbitrarily. *Chefs de département* were supposed to organize grand meetings of the clan (*esulan*) which would take place regularly; *chefs de subdivision* were supposed to make sure that all villages were clean.

Villages that were to be organized by clan were to have men called colonels, one of whom would serve as a frontier guard to check on people who came through the village and one who would supervise a special clan dance called *enienge*. Among the other officers the commissioners were the most important. Aided by a force of police, their function was to maintain order; it was their duty to make sure that correct customs were followed in the villages and that the reputation of the clan was maintained. Clans had to maintain their reputations for hospitality, for example. A last officer, the customs man, was supposed to ensure that all men took their meals together. For an egalitarian society like that of the Fang the organization being set up by *alar ayong* was extraordinary; it was influenced by the men who had achieved a certain status in the colonial order; this meant that they had *evus*.

Two of the presidents whom Trezenem mentions were a cantonal chief and a former *tirailleur* for the French; among the vice-presidents were an interpretor for the French, a *tirailleur*, and a village chief. A merchant was the governor-general, a farmer and a teacher were lieutenant governors. Another observer reports that out of thirty-two high-ranking officers in the various clans he studied five were chiefs, and the rest were cocoa or coffee planters, merchants, or employees of the colonial administration.[33] This was a movement led by men who were part of the order the White had installed but who knew customs of the old order. A president had to be, in the words of one Fang informant, wise, clever, possessed with an *evus* that would be used for the good of the collectivity, and a man who knew how to handle discussions.

Mass meetings of the clan and dances were used to teach the "catechism" of the clan and tribe so that everyone knew his ancestors and so that people knew the rules of marriage. (The bridewealth was fixed at 2,500 francs plus two sheep.)

The clans were organized in a hierarchical way; some of them were combined, and one large organization which would include

33 Balandier, ftn. 3, pp. 216–217.

all Fang-Bulu-Betsi was attempted. Most decisions on these matters were made in the Cameroun, Trezenem thought: "The Esakura had been called an important *ayong* but they became a part of the Yeminsem. The Fang scholars of Cameroun had decided thus." These Camerounese apparently called for meetings of all clans in Cameroun in 1948. Another French administrator has written that there was a grand esulan, or meeting, which formed the *Union Tribale Bantoue* which in July 1948 transformed itself into the *Union Tribale Ntem-Kribi*.[34] Clans of the three tribes were represented in this organization whose goal was unification of all Fang into one group. Trezenem confirmed that such a meeting was held and indicated that statutes were drawn up and, most important, the term Fang was to have been adopted for everyone: "The new fact which this meeting brings out besides the transformation of the *Union Tribale Bantoue* into the *Union Tribale Ntem-Kribi* and the publication of statutes is the recognition by these . . . tribes . . . of their membership in the same 'Fang stock.' " He believed the *Union Tribale Ntem-Kribi* was linked with the radical *Rassemblement Démocratique Africain* which had been formed in 1946 in West Africa.

Trezenem believed *alar ayong* was a threat to French sovereignty in Gabon and in Cameroun. He found out that dues were collected and sent to Cameroun, "certainly not with the purpose of helping the French administration"; the money was to be used, he had heard, to purchase weapons to be used "to chase away the French." He was also concerned that an administrative structure parallel to that of the colonial power had been set up which would eventually be able to challenge the colonial structure. Administration-appointed chiefs were already without power: "It is certain that once their regroupment is entirely finished, once the presidents of the *ayong* are all elected so that they will form a kind of government presided over by an elected official, then the Fang will present us with their organization as an entity capable of governing itself. It would be organized democratically and would arrive at the stage foreseen by article 75 of the Charter of the United Nations (we should not forget that the chiefs of the movement are Camerounese who are under trusteeship), which gives

[34] M. Rolland, "Le Mouvement Fang au Moyen Congo," unpublished report at Centre des Hautes Etudes d'Administration Musulmane, 1955, p. 4.

them the right to demand their independence. The recent example of the Gold Coast ought to inspire us." In the Gold Coast, whose precedent worried the administrator, a boycott at the beginning of 1948 against high prices and a demonstration of former soldiers led to violent manifestations against the British. And it is true that Camerounese were well-informed about events in other parts of the world. A group of Camerounese reportedly approached American Presbyterian missionaries after World War II to ask them to request the American government to take over the trustee territory of Cameroun "so that they too could become independent as had been done in the case of the Philippines."[35]

The Americans were suspected by Trezenem of having encouraged *alar ayong* first by having taught the Bulu about their common ancestry with the Fang and second by having published a little newspaper, *Mefoe,* at their mission in order, he thought, to pass on information about clan meetings and to translate the Charter of the United Nations into the African languages. American missionaries who worked in the southern part of Gabon and who had no connections with the Presbyterians in Cameroun were closely watched, and searches for hidden arms were occasionally carried out during this period.

Some Fang, particularly those of Libreville, distrusted the Camerounese and suspected they wanted to use Fang-Bulu-Betsi (or "Pahouin") unity for their own political goals in Cameroun. The Bulu, for their part, had always considered the Gabonese Fang to be inferior and to have lost the pure customs of the people. There was opposition from within the African group and from the administration, which acted to suppress the movement. Large meetings were prohibited, collections of funds were forbidden or confiscated, movements of population were strictly controlled, and local leaders, like Léon Mba and Jean-Hilaire Aubame, were watched.

Alar ayong failed for most people, and some of its leaders turned to Gabonese politics. But it is still being tried by a few clans, such at the Yemveng clan of Woleu-Ntem and Ogooué-Ivindo: "In northern Gabon this regroupment is far along. There are frequent meetings, tribal laws are examined, people are enlightened. We

35 L. K. Anderson, The United Presbyterian Church in U.S.A., personal communication.

arrange cooperative efforts for purchases: For example, at Minvoul the president of the Yemveng [clan] purchased an automobile through contributions of all the Yemveng of Woleu-Ntem."[36]

Order Through the New

At the same time that movements to restore something from the past were important, some people looked to new systems through religion and the state, in the running of which they were allowed but a very small part. The two religious movements were *Bwiti* and the Great Revival.

Something called *Bwiti* had originally been practiced among the Mitsogo and Bapindji people in the southern part of the country. Slaves who had been brought to the coast danced the *Bwiti,* so that the non-initiated, including Fang who had been sent to the south as traders for French-owned companies, saw it.[37] The Fang changed *Bwiti* to fit their own needs, and it is now a syncretistic religion which combines some aspects of traditional Fang religion with Roman Catholicism. It is considered a way to come to terms with the older religion and the power of newer European religions.

Members of the church believe they are protected from witchcraft and that they have values to live by; ancestors are regarded as once again efficacious forces on earth which will strike down anyone in the religion who might practice witchcraft. A non-Fang Gabonese claimed *Bwiti* gave great power to its adherents. He claimed when he wrote about the alleged *Bwiti* bible that it would be the beginning of the assertion of the black race: "Three Magi Kings came to the cradle of the white Christ: a yellow man, a white man, a black man. The Yellow has spoken and is silent, the White is speaking now, the Black has not yet said anything. Is he mute? I should like these pages to be the first words of his response."[38]

A syncretist religion, *Bwiti* was considered by missionaries as a threat to the integrity of the western religion from which it had drawn many of its elements. Even the clothes of the members

36 Mvë Ondo, "Quelques coutumes et sciences d'hier," unpublished essay, 1962.
37 In villages near Lambaréné, where Fang live near Mitsogo, they dance the Mitsogo *Bwiti* together.
38 Prince Birinda, *La Bible secrète des Noirs selon le Bouity* (Paris, Omnium Littéraire, 1952), p. 125.

clearly recall the robes of priests. The missionaries noted its appearance in Woleu-Ntem in 1945 and wrote what they did about it: *"Bwiti* is spreading more and more in this region — of Asucbere; it has won over Nkein, then Aderayo and finally Elelem. . . . I have had their hut at Aderayo destroyed, also that of Nkein, but once I leave they build it again and even more beautifully than before."[39]

The administration sent troops to raid and destroy the chapels because people reported that *Bwiti* adherents were engaging in ritual murder and cannibalism. Chapels were sought out deep in the forest and burned to the ground. In recent years the administration, French and Gabonese, has more or less permitted the practice of the religion, although some of the Fang leaders in Woleu-Ntem and all missionaries preach against it. People in Libreville related that at one time the Bwitists marched to the Roman Catholic church to take part in a Mass or to conduct their own service there; they reportedly claimed that it was their church just as much as it was that of the Roman Catholics. As a way for the Fang to reorganize, *Bwiti* has been a failure because of pressures from the Whites and Blacks who were nonadherents and because it was not really efficacious; only about 8 per cent of the Fang belong today.[40]

To seek a new order and to protect themselves against witchcraft the Fang turned to a Christian religious movement introduced by a European. This was the Great Revival which started about 1935, after it had already become an important movement in Europe and America.

Pastor Vernaud who, like many French-speaking Protestant missionaries, is Swiss, began his work in Gabon in 1930. During a vacation in Europe in 1934 he was, according to his own testimony, "possessed with the Holy Ghost."[41] In 1935 he returned to Gabon and preached the Revival, about possession by the Holy Spirit; his prayers were answered and the Revival took place among the Fang and among the non-Fang south of the Ogooué as well. It spread fantastically, particularly in Woleu-Ntem; people

39 "Tournées," ftn. 14, entry 13 to 23 April 1945.
40 Fernandez, "Redistributive Acculturation," ftn. 2, p. 181.
41 Pastor Vernaud was kind enough to tell me the history of the Revival during an interview in Paris; the details of it are also found in a brochure written by him, "Le Plein Evangile au Gabon" (Peseux, Editions Evangéliques, 1957).

rushed to the Protestant and Roman Catholic churches; people said they had a thirst: "I had thirst, thirst for prayer, thirst for — God." At Lastoursville in the South there had been no mission because an early missionary had been mistreated by the Badouma. These same Badouma in 1936 begged the Roman Catholics to set up a church and to send a priest. The missionary who went to them, Father Hee, reported that prayers were said everywhere, chapels were built before he asked for them to be built, people brought him their "fetishes": "We don't need them." Along the river the priest collected 2,141 people who said they wanted to become Christians. "In one grandiose ceremony we baptised 504 people together."[42]

Although Hee did not appear to understand the Revival, Protestant pastors knew very well what was going on, for there had been revivals in Europe and there was a church, the Pentecostal Church, which preached possession by the Holy Ghost. A pastor who was in Woleu-Ntem at the time told me the following: Easter 1936 in one mission of Woleu-Ntem there were 5,000 Fang who had come for the service; most stood outside the church as there was not enough room. A loudspeaker was set up. During the morning service the pastor saw about eighty people faint or go into a trance, and everyone visibly trembled: *"L'Esprit va venir."*

The Fang brought this pastor all their *bieri* which had not been taken from them previously; they were not asked to do so but said that they needed them no longer. They were saved, protected, they were possessed by the Holy Ghost. Possession by the Holy Ghost was regarded as protection against witchcraft and was regarded as a source of power. People asked the pastor: "Can a Black receive the power of the Holy Ghost as well as a White?" During another Sunday service he requested an African pastor to preach and he, the missionary, sat in the rear of the church near the door. The door was open, the sun beat down outside; suddenly, the pastor reported, a crab crawled into the church. The European pastor saw it and placed it outside. Later, a woman was seized with the Spirit and went into a trance; she rose from her place, stumbled out of the church, fell to the ground. Relatives followed to help her; when they lifted her up they saw the crab on which she had

---

42 R. P. Hee, "Les Adouma du Gabon" in *Les Missions Catholiques* No. 3.299 and No. 3.300, n.d.

apparently fallen. They shouted, people ran from the church: *"Evus, evus, evus!!* She has been saved!" They believed, the pastor says, that once she was possessed with the Holy Ghost, *evus* was expelled from her body and took the form of a crab. They believed that they would be protected from witchcraft by the Holy Spirit. After that, people came to the church regularly. They confessed that they had in the past stolen things, that they had cheated, and they sought absolution through and protection of the spirit. More recently the pastor of one Pentecostal church reported that a Fang who had just joined the church claimed that in so doing he had been relieved of an *evus* that was causing a pain in his chest.

In the course of my sojourn in Gabon I sought out people who had been affected by the Revival, particularly the Africans who said they had received the Spirit. (There were Europeans who had received it as well.) In a Fang village I talked with an African who took part in the Revival; he said that it was the custom during that time to pray during the day, any day. "We had the thirst." He was a student in a small trade school and one morning everyone wanted to pray, "We had the thirst." They all prayed, and suddenly everyone was seized by the Holy Ghost, including the white teacher who knelt with his students: "Hallelujah." They sang "Hallelujah" and they prayed together, "We had the thirst."

"I felt freed, I was freed. We felt light and we flew. Hallelujah. I was reborn. I confessed my sins; I had been evil and sinful, but no more. We prayed. We had the thirst."

People were also cured miraculously. Even those who did not belong to the movement say they saw miraculous cures; this is one of the things that disturbed the Protestant Church. Church officials did not want what was going on to continue; it was a mass movement that was getting out of any kind of control in a colony, and supernatural things like miracles were happening. The administration was also concerned, for they saw a relationship between this movement and kimbanguism in the Congo — a movement which was anticolonialist as well as religious. At the end of 1936 Church headquarters in Paris sent two of its high officials to preach against the Revival; they told the eager people crowded into Protestant churches that it was all a fake, that they were confused, that there was no miracle, that the Holy Ghost could not seize them and could not protect them. That was the end.

The pastor who started it all has continued his work, however, and has formed a Pentecostal Church in Gabon; it is most active among the Fang, although it is very small. The headquarters is at Medouneu in Woleu-Ntem; there are branch churches elsewhere: one among the Omyènè south of Lambaréné, one in Libreville with a Fang pastor, one at Booué among the Fang, also with a Fang pastor, and one near Makokou. The latter has an Omyènè pastor.

Neither syncretistic religion nor a Christian Pentecostal movement, as combinations of the old and the new or as rejection of the old for something new, was successful, although each of these attempts still has its adherents. Those who were part of these movements but who are so no longer say they feel a certain sadness that they failed.

After the end of World War II Africans were permitted to take part in politics with the reforms following the establishment of the Fourth Republic in France and the *Union Française*. In 1947 Gabon elected a deputy to the French National Assembly. He was a Fang, much of whose support came from the Woleu-Ntem area. As the most important and most powerful Gabonese, he sponsored a program of regroupment of villages. The plan called for a decrease from 4,111 to 770 villages in four regions; the population of each village would be between 500 and 1,000. Under this program every village would have a primary school, an infirmary, a meeting place, and a sports area.[43]

Such a program would permit many Fang to regroup by clan; second, such a program would permit more children to go to school; finally, it would mean that long trips to hospitals in towns would no longer be necessary. The Fang adopted the idea of regroupment, and it has been far more successful in the Woleu-Ntem than elsewhere. The Fang gave credit to their Fang deputy who worked through state and colonial institutions to help them reorganize.

The Fang have accepted change that will contribute to a new order. They, more than any other Gabonese, adopted the coffee

[43] Jean-Hilaire Aubame, "Renaissance Gabonaise: programme de regroupement des villages" (Brazzaville, Ministère de la France d'Outre-Mer, 1947). Aubame was given the support of the administration. Sociologists Georges Balandier, J.-Cl. Pauvert, and André Hauser did considerable research into the idea of regroupment. See, for example, Georges Balandier and J.-Cl. Pauvert, "Les Villages Gabonais," Mémoire (Brazzaville, Institut des Recherches Congolaises, 1952).

and cocoa culture; to market the crops they were often forced to build their own roads by hand. Many Fang remember that as children they assisted in the cutting away of enough of the equatorial rain forest to permit men and women with heavy baskets of beans on their backs and heads to walk several miles to the place where the products were being purchased.

During a recent school-building campaign undertaken by the Peace Corps it was decided to put a school in one village at a considerable distance from the road. The villagers insisted it be located on the road where everyone could see their school. When they were told they would have to clear the thickly wooded area themselves and without any help from the various machines which were to be used to clear the designated area, they cleared it themselves, and the school was constructed where they wanted it.

The Fang have turned to the political and economic institutions first set up by the French (they had already used French terminology in the *alar ayong* movement). They have done so because these institutions were sources of power; they saw certain benefits such as ways to help in the reorganization of the clans with this power or as a way to establish a new kind of order. This they have done because they seek progress and believe that new ways can improve their lives through material benefits and through knowledge about how to control what appear to be capricious forces. The other peoples of Gabon have felt the threat of disorder too and they fear witchcraft; but the Omyènè are too small a group to be able to lead, and there is some resentment against them for their elite and separatist attitudes. The southerners have often retreated in the face of disorder, such as one tribe whose birth rate has decreased sharply and whose leaders say: "We are lost; we don't want children, for our values do not fit the world; we are becoming cut off from our ancestors."

The Fang have taken leadership in all areas of Gabonese life. First the Fang who were closest to the coast and later the Woleu-Ntem Fang began to participate in the new organizations and institutions that are part of modern nation-building. Whether or not their motives are reorganization of a narrow tribe or organization of a new nation, the results are that they provide the dynamism and the motive force for nation-building in Gabon. They do so in four ways:

1. They have the spirit of warriors. They are aggressive and impose themselves on other Africans or absorb them into their own tribe. They are not exclusionist like others and accept non-Fang as kin.

2. They fear the possibility of losing all their customs and of forgetting all traditional ways. This has encouraged concern with the customs of the Fang and this in turn has caused the Fang to look at his social organization and attempt to restore it through an *alar ayong* movement.

3. They sense the weakening of the tribal order and the threat of capricious forces and have tried to do something about it. They have sought order in different systems.

4. The Fang sensed the possible role of the state in helping them re-establish the old order and also establish a new order more efficacious than the old. A new order means modernity and equality with other people — Blacks and Whites.

Not all Fang have accepted Gabon as the solution for their problems. They fear that the true Fang custom will, in the end, be lost by association with other tribes even when the Fang appear to be dominant. Slow development of a new community at the national level is the greatest threat to the pure Fang custom, but the Fang have taken the lead in the formation of that culture and will leave their imprint on the form which national consolidation will take.

PART TWO

*National Consolidation Through
Shared Experience*

CHAPTER 4

Measurement of Shared Experience

Problems of Communication

The road to Okondja extends for about one hundred miles over the Plateau Batéké. Twice a week Jean, a Congolese, leaves Franceville to drive a Mercedes truck owned by a European merchant over the plateau; he carries goods and news along this road of sand. At the height of the dry season in July and August it may take two or even three days to reach Okondja because the truck sinks into the sand, must be unloaded, pushed, reloaded. And there are rivers to cross on ferries that sometimes get stuck in the middle of the fast-flowing rivers of the Republic of Gabon.

While Jean waits for his men to unload the truck, he talks to villagers who come to watch or to help by spreading leaves on this curious road. Leaves make the trip a little easier. The truck is finally loaded and moving; a boy runs up to give a message to the driver to pass on to the next village, and a woman who must be eighty climbs on the truck to go as far as Akieni.

In the village of Akieni the truck stops because some passengers want to get off and because the villagers have fruit for sale. The driver inspects the fruit and some eggs displayed on a wooden bench: "Your prices are too high," he says. "In Franceville, the prefecture of this region, pineapples sell for fifteen francs, and didn't you know that the standard price for eggs is just ten francs all over Gabon?" As they continue to discuss the prices, the village chief comes up to one passenger. He sees the wristwatch and asks the time: "11:15, Monsieur." The old man is pleased. "That's what my wristwatch says too; my wristwatch must be right, it's right."

The road to Okondja is a dead end. Maps indicate that roads have been started from other towns to Okondja but they always end in dotted lines, indicating they are far from completion. At the end of one of these lines is Lastoursville. There are two deputies to the legislative assembly, the National Assembly, from this district. One lives among the Badouma people and says he is Badouma; the Badouma claim that both deputies are Badouma. The second deputy says he is Bawandji, but the Badouma retort that he grew up among them after his Bawandji parents died and that makes him Badouma, whether he likes it or not.

Gabon is sparsely settled (the density of population is about 1.5 per square kilometer) with a population whose social structures are all now of a decentralized egalitarian character. In times of peace, loyalties have been limited to a relatively restrained family circle, and in times of organized violence comparatively few people have been involved. The country has a very poor system of communication; there is no railroad, many roads of sand or clay are impassable during the rainy season, and three of the nine administrative regions into which the country is divided have had practically no direct land communication with the capital, Libreville. There are many roads to places like Okondja, and there is no one to decide whether a man is Bawandji or Badouma.

The regions of the country were originally based on ethnic or tribal differences and were called by such names as Region of the Badouma and Region of the Oroungou. In Lastoursville the Bawandji objected to the name "Region of the Badouma," and it has been changed to Ogooué-Lolo because the two most important rivers are the Ogooué and the Lolo. Other regions and administrative circumscriptions bear the names of rivers — mainly some combination of the River Ogooué, such as Moyen-Ogooué and Haut-Ogooué. The regions or prefectures are then divided

74

into a total of 28 districts and 103 cantons. The districts get their names from their capitals, but the cantons are often called after small rivers which determine their frontiers.

Officials at the levels of region and district are civil servants and agents of the central government; the only exception to this is the rural council or *collectivité rurale* in each district, whose members are elected from the cantons. It is in charge of some road and bridge construction in the district. Cantons that name their own chiefs by election or by following some rules of heredity have an ethnic identity, although several tribes may be living in the same canton. Formerly the cantons were divided into *terres* on which the population was ethnically quite homogeneous. Six towns in the country have their own elected mayors, whereas all other towns are under the government-appointed sub-prefects. Communication within a region between the offices of the prefecture, the sub-prefecture, and the canton has depended mainly on the administration's Land Rovers, and communication with Libreville has depended on the telegraph and airplane.

The colonial administration had several projects to build a railroad through Gabon, but nothing was ever done except making surveys. Between 1908 and World War I France took steps to improve communications in Equatorial Africa and to occupy it more completely than it had done. In 1910 and 1911 the Perriquet Mission traced a railroad from Libreville east into the Congo to Ouesso. The war cut short these plans.[1] When the Congo-Océan railroad was still in the planning stage, Port-Gentil was considered a terminus on the Atlantic, Gabonese civil servants claimed, but the decision to build it from Brazzaville to Pointe-Noire was made, according to the Governor-General, to weaken the Belgian railroad: "There is no doubt that the best solution for the general interest of A.E.F. is the route Brazzaville–Pointe-Noire . . . which will, at the expense of the Belgian railroad, absorb most rapidly and most surely the transit traffic coming from the Upper Congo."[2] To exploit the manganese in southeastern Gabon a railroad was proposed, but as early as 1954 Gabonese students in Paris objected to the administration's idea

1 Comité de l'Afrique Française, *Chemin de fer du nord et mission hydrologique* (*Rapport de la Mission Periquet*), Paris, 1913.
2 Letter from Governor-General Victor Augagneur, published in *L'Echo Gabonais*, No. 10, July 1923.

that a railroad from the site of the deposit through the Congo to the port of Pointe-Noire would be most efficient. They proposed that the railroad be built through Gabon and that a port be constructed at Owendo, for Gabon did not then and still does not have a real deep-water port with facilities permitting ships to dock: "To say that the Franceville–Pointe-Noire solution would be the most economical is to oppress Gabon, to prevent its well-being, to brake its economic development. . . . In unity the youth of Gabon demands a railroad from Franceville to Owendo."[3] A cable-car line was eventually built to the Congolese frontier from where a railroad extends via the Congo-Océan Railroad line to the port of Pointe-Noire. This railroad which takes passengers as well as manganese ore facilitates movement from one region of Gabon into the Congo. A Gabonese railroad will be built, however, from Owendo on the estuary near Libreville east to a great iron-ore deposit near the Congolese frontier.

Although there are almost 3,000 miles of roads, they are in such poor condition during much of the year that communication and commerce between regions and with Libreville has been very difficult. Even though there is supposed to be one passenger vehicle for every 127 inhabitants, compared with one vehicle for every 180 in the four states of the former federation, only 6 per cent of all vehicles are used for interior road transportation, compared with 25 per cent in Chad.[4] To travel from the Haut-Ogooué and Ogooué-Lolo regions to Libreville it is necessary to pass through the Congo, and this has meant that the two regions have been more closely tied with the Congo than with the rest of Gabon. The same is true of Woleu-Ntem which at least until recently had far better communications with Cameroun and Spanish Guinea than with the rest of Gabon. Until 1950 a fourth region along the Congolese border, Ogooué-Ivindo, was also more closely tied to Congo than to Gabon. Traders and goods came from Brazzaville, and men went to work in the Federation capital rather than in the rest of Gabon. Since a road was built into the region, it is more closely linked with Gabon. Merchants come into the region from Libreville, and it is possible to get to Libreville to work.

---

[3] *Jeunesse Gabonaise*, Paris, Nos. 3–4, February-March 1954.
[4] Service national de la statistique, "Le Parc automobile du Gabon au 1er janvier 1962," supplément *Bulletin mensuel de statistique de la République Gabonaise*, August 1963, p. 2, 6.

Roadbuilding in Gabon has always been linked to the needs of the forestry companies. The first road in the interior was built to facilitate the hauling of logs around a rapids in a river. The forestry men are now moving further inland, into what they call the second zone of exploitation, and roads being built with the aid of a twelve-million-dollar loan from the World Bank will facilitate the exploitation of okoumé and other woods as well as provide links with the Haut-Ogooué and Ogooué-Lolo regions. In 1959 only 750 million francs were spent to build and maintain roads; in 1963, 1,290 million francs were spent.[5] In 1964 a road was cut through the Cristal Mountains from Medouneu in Woleu-Ntem to Libreville; although the road could only be used by jeeps and Land Rovers, it is being steadily improved. Improvement from 1962 to 1964 meant that a Fang entrepreneur in Woleu-Ntem could begin to transport coffee beans purchased in Ogooué-Ivindo back to Woleu-Ntem and then sell them in Rio Muni. There is an internal airline company with many landing strips in the country.

Although there are two radio transmitters, one in Libreville and one in Haut-Ogooué, many people in the north prefer to listen to Radio Cameroun and many in the south listen to Radio Brazzaville. A television station has programs for two hours each day; its audience is limited to Libreville and is composed mainly of expatriates and high government officials. There are no national newspapers. One weekly sheet called *Gabon d'Aujourd'hui* has a circulation of about 400, and its subscribers are almost exclusively civil servants and foreigners. A daily bulletin published by a press agency is distributed mainly in the capital. New publications have been started, such as the mimeographed *Femmes Gabonaises* for women, and *L'Educateur* for teachers, but the distribution of these magazines is faulty. There is telephone communication between Paris and Libreville but until recently none between Franceville and Libreville. There is also since 1964 telex communication between Libreville and Paris and between Libreville and Douala, Cameroun.

Mountain ranges, rivers blocked in places by rapids, and the great forest have contributed to the difficulties of building an

---

[5] Service de statistique, "Rapport annuel sur la situation économique, financière et sociale de la République Gabonaise, fin 1963" (Libreville, July 1964), p. 71.

adequate communications system that would bring Gabonese into closer contact with the central government and into contact with other Gabonese. Problems in communications have also been a factor in maintaining egalitarian social structures and in creating problems of ethnic or tribal identity.

Problems of Identity

Every tribe in Gabon had a similar type of government when the White arrived. There was no centralized authority. An empire in the south — more in what is today Congo than in Gabon — had already begun to disintegrate before de Brazza signed a treaty with Makoko, king of the Batéké. In normal times authority was very limited.

The French found that the chiefs they appointed or with whom they were allied had very little authority: "In certain administrative divisions, auxiliaries known as village or land chiefs exercise their authority over a small area only; when they are accepted, their authority extends over a small group composed of a few families, rarely counting as many as one hundred people."[6] Today a chief in any one of Gabon's 4,500 villages has, on the average, only about eighty-four people under his supposed authority.[7]

Without a rigid hierarchy and with steady movement toward the coast by several tribes, problems of loyalty and identity increased. As tribes moved, the populations of some villages were left behind or struck out on their own, some were tired and found good stopping places, and no one could make them follow the others unless they were attacked; even when they were attacked by members of a foreign tribe, they might be helped by other members of that same tribe. For example, an administrator noted in 1896 that the Bakota who survived an attack by chief Emane-Tole's village were able to escape and return to Bakota country with the aid of Fang in another village.[8]

If it were mixed in with another people, a tribe might become

---

[6] Circulaire, No. 5a, le Lieutenant-Gouverneur du Gabon à M. le Chef de la Circonscription des Adoumas à Lastoursville, 10 April 1916.

[7] Cited in Ministère d'Etat chargé de l'Economie Nationale, "Situation économique, financière et sociale de la République Gabonaise, fin 1962" (Libreville, May 1963), p. 147.

[8] Arch. Nat. Col. Gabon IV, dossier 10, Letter from Ndjolé, 29 July 1896.

part of another tribe. If it were isolated, it might consider its customs purer than those of relatives who lived in close contact with other tribes. Because its customs were considered purer, it would be proud, but isolation might also bring the disdain of others who regarded themselves as closer to what were eventually considered more civilized ways of living. And if it were isolated, it might become a separate tribe like the Adyumba who, originally a clan of the Mpongoùè, fled to an isolated spot on a lake after a war and over the years became what is now considered a separate tribe.[9]

The White was more concerned about population movement than he was about tribal identity. One source of the confusion and movement was that ship hulks, used as trading stations where ivory and rubber were traded for cloth, moved along the rivers: "The hulks change their position every two or three months. That is how nomadism, the antithesis of civilization, is perpetuated in the rivers. We must try to force the natives to settle permanently around commercial centers."[10] To stop the movement the villages were grouped around military and trading posts.

Village regroupment as a way to stabilize the movement of a very small population and to provide services which would be impossible to organize if villages were tiny and dispersed has been continued after a system for regroupment was proposed by the Gabonese deputy to the French National Assembly, Jean-Hilaire Aubame.

The administrator was less concerned about tribal identity and often seemed to believe people did not have names before the White arrived. The Mpongoùè were called Gabonais for many years because they lived along the Rio Gabon; the Nkomi were called the Sette Cama after the place in which they lived. Clan names were confused with tribal names, and until the present day the word "race" has been used indiscriminately and incorrectly. In his records an administrator also grouped tribes together under one name; sometimes he would forget about smaller tribes. Gabonese administrators do the same thing. For example, a census

---

9 Abbé Raponda-Walker, "Notes d'histoire du Gabon," Brazzaville (Institut d'Etudes Centrafricaines, 1960) pp. 60–61.

10 Arch. Nat. Col. Gabon IV, dossier 10, Letter from Capitaine Masson to the Ministre de la Marine et des Colonies, 7 July 1883.

in 1954 listed the inhabitants of the district of Mbigou as "Band-jabi, Batsangui, Massango, Bavoumbou, and Bakèlè." In the 1956 census the inhabitants of this district were listed as "Bandjabi, Boumouéllé (part of Bandjabi), Massango, Bavoumbou, Bakèlè, Toumbidi (part of Bakèlè)." In 1961 estimates of the population size made by local administrators divided the population only into Bandjabi and Massango. The 1954 Batsangui were supposed to account for 20 per cent of the population, but by 1956 they had disappeared and the Boumouéllé were supposed to account for 20 per cent of the population. In the most recent village census conducted by the central government no Boumouéllé and only about two and one half per cent Batsangui are indicated.[11] Further to confuse the question, a former French administrator wrote that the Boumouéllé were really part of the Bapounou tribe, which does not even live in the district.[12]

The many people one meets in the district who call themselves Boumouéllé are no longer counted as Boumouéllé or as Batsangui, although the ethnographer Marcel Soret claims that the Boumouéllé are a clan of the Batsangui tribe, "a clan that has lived slightly isolated."[13] That they are really Batsangui is of no consequence, because the administration now considers them Bandjabi and has counted them as such. A sub-prefect who was taking a village census at the time of my visit to Mbigou hesitated when I asked him about the Boumouéllé; he was not absolutely sure who they were but had decided to count them as Bandjabi.

In some regions confusion of tribal identity has nothing to do with the administration. Some people claim that neighbors are their kin because they want to increase their numerical importance, and relative size of tribes is considered to be very important. Other people change their tribal and ethnic identity to escape the opprobrium of belonging to an outcast group or to gain the prestige enjoyed by one tribe. For example, the Eshira who live along the Ngounié River south of the town of Lambaréné accuse the Galoa who live in Lambaréné of being "social climbers."

11 Data from "Estimations démographiques," Bureau d'Agriculture, Mbigou, n.d.
12 Jacques Hubert, "Esquisse de la coutume Bapounou et généralités sur la dégradation des coutumes au Gabon," mémoire, Centre des Hautes Etudes de l'Administration Musulmane, Paris, n.d., p. 15.
13 M. Soret, personal communication.

The Galoa say they are part of the prestigious Omyènè group, the first Gabonese, but the Eshira maintain they are really Eshira. Consideration of the true identity of this people has prompted leaders in both camps to defend publicly their points of view on this matter. An Eshira priest wrote a pamphlet in which he proved to the satisfaction of the Eshira that the Galoa were really relatives in disguise. But a Galoa pastor wrote an answer to this allegation. He explained that in 1920 the Galoa at Port-Gentil got into a fight with the (other) Omyènè. As a result of the ill feelings that developed because of this fight the (other) Omyènè disowned the Galoa and called them the worst name he says they could think of — Eshira.[14]

There are dozens of examples of tribal change and confusion, but it is necessary to systematize this information with what is known about communications in order to estimate the extent to which people have increasing, shared experiences that contribute to national consolidation. Investigation of shared experience by a person with limited resources means that he must find one or two manageable criteria as a basis on which trends in physical contact or mobilization and attitude change or assimilation might be estimated.

Tools for Measurement[15]

Once arrived in Gabon I discovered that a census that was still in progress would have to be my main source of statistical information. The *Service de Coopération* of the French Institut national de la statistique et des études économiques began a census of Gabon in 1960. French and Gabonese statisticians and their employees, who visited every village in the country, used one census form for each household. Every member of a given household was therefore accounted for: Name, age, occupation, place of birth, and relationship with other members of the household were noted. Tribe or ethnic group was indicated for all persons fourteen years

---

14 Pasteur Ogoula-M'Beye, "Galoa ou Edongo d'antan?," translated from the Omyènè by Paul-Vincent Pounah, Port-Gentil, 1957. A pamphlet written by Abbé Hilaire Ngouba, called "Les Galoas sont des Gisaras," is cited.

15 Parts of this section have appeared in shorter form: Brian Weinstein, "Social Communication Methodology in the Study of Nation-Building," *Cahiers d'Etudes Africaines*, No. 16, 1964, pp. 571–588.

old and over. Dossiers were then grouped by administrative unit: village, canton, district, region.

The canton was the smallest unit with which I could work because it could be located on a map more easily than villages and because global ethnic data were available at the level of the canton.[16] On the basis of the canton it was possible to make an ethnic map. The zone map at the end of this volume shows where the major tribes live. Arrows show, in an incomplete way, approximate directions of population movement calculated on the basis of where people said they were born compared with where they then lived. Within a given canton I could examine patterns of intermarriage and settlement when two different tribes lived in contiguous villages or in the same village. These quantifiable data served as a basis for a study of mobilization for communication and shared experience.

In order to validate conclusions based on the quantitative census data I lived in a few selected villages for periods of three days to a week. I found that one way to investigate attitudes and assimilation was by oral histories and conceptions of kinship.

Historians collect oral histories as an aid in the writing of general history, and they are naturally interested in accounts which are accurate or which lead to a discovery of the truth.[17] For me, as a political scientist, the "truth" was irrelevant. If a certain people crossed such and such a river and had not really fought such and such a tribe one hundred years ago, as they said, this was not important. I was interested in history as ideology: How were present relationships between tribes justified and explained in the history, what was the place held by neighboring tribes in a given history, how were history and conceptions of kinship influenced by present settlement patterns? I thought that these criteria, settlement patterns, and oral histories supplemented by interview data could serve as a basis for an estimation of trends in assimilation and mobilization and could show the relationship between nonquantifiable attitudes and quantifiable social communications.

16 I am grateful to the *Service de Cooperation* and particularly to M. Michel François for permission to consult their unpublished data.

17 Professor Hubert Deschamps had visited the country in 1961 to collect oral histories as part of a large project to write the history of Gabon. He published his preliminary findings in *Traditions orales et archives au Gabon* (Paris, Berger-Levrault, 1962).

Mobilization

Gabon may be crudely divided into three general zones of mobilization: places where people are relatively nonmobilized, where they are partially mobilized, and where they are mobilized for intensive contact with people of different tribes or ethnic groups. I have called these zones Heartland, Contact, and Nationalizing zones, respectively.

The Heartland Zone is a group of contiguous cantons in which one tribe clearly predominates with at least 80 per cent of the total population. Internal communication is fairly good and is better than means that link the area with other parts of the country. Contact Zones are on the edges of Heartland Zones; from about 50 to 80 per cent of the people belong to one tribe. Such zones are cantons in which people of different tribes live in adjoining villages or even in the same village, or else they are centers of attraction such as administrative posts and markets to which people from different Heartlands travel regularly. They are most likely along roads and rivers that provide a link between Heartland Zones. There may be more mechanical means of communication in a Contact Zone than in a Heartland, and one tribe is clearly more important than the others.

Nationalizing Zones are groups of contiguous cantons and large centers of attraction in which no tribe accounts for 50 per cent of the total population, and no one tribe dominates the others. The internal means of communication are best here: They are public, mechanical, and regular. It is usually the one place where most decisions affecting the whole country are made.

A Heartland

The largest Heartland in Gabon is that of the Fang. Its center corresponds with the administrative region of Woleu-Ntem. The region is relatively isolated from the rest of Gabon but has regular contact with Cameroun and Rio Muni both by land and water. The road to Libreville has been in poor condition, but improvements have been made since 1962. While there is regular air and telegraphic communication between Libreville and the administrative centers of Woleu-Ntem, such as Oyem, where the prefect has his office, and Bitam near the Camerounese and Rio Muni frontiers, there is no frequent and regular land transportation.

Fair roads extend into Cameroun and Rio Muni where close relatives of the Fang, the Bulu, live. Merchandise is imported along these routes, while coffee and cocoa exports leave Woleu-Ntem through Cameroun and increasingly through Rio Muni. Fang have long taken advantage of the road to Cameroun to attend Camerounese technical schools and to go to Camerounese hospitals (particularly a missionary-run hospital not far from the frontier). They also go into frontier towns of Rio Muni for the purchase of cloth, canned food, beverages, and other goods which are much less expensive than in Gabon or Cameroun because tariffs are low. From Bitam it is much easier to get transportation to Rio Muni than to any place in either Gabon or Cameroun. Taxis dash back and forth and charge a mere eighty cents per passenger. (A one-way trip to Libreville costs over twenty dollars.) Spanish merchants in the town of Ebebeyin speak French, and Fang members of the *guardia territorial* are friendly, particularly when the Spanish commandant is not around. About twice each day taxis or cars that can carry about twenty people leave for Cameroun.

The concentration of the Fang along the Rio Muni and Camerounese frontiers and their isolation from the rest of Gabon constitute a recent phenomenon. The French geographer Gilles Sautter believes that when the Fang population decreased after World War I because of famine, recruitment, and disease, they regrouped themselves and also were regrouped by the administration in such a way that practically no one lives in the eastern and southern parts of the region. They regrouped along the Camerounese and Rio Muni frontiers where the density of population is between four and six persons per square kilometer, and in some places even as high or higher than ten. As a result, Professor Sautter indicates there is an economic region that does not correspond with political frontiers and that links the Fang of Woleu-Ntem with part of Rio Muni and part of Cameroun.[18] That such a concentration of people and comparative isolation have not always been so is further indicated by A. Cottes, who headed a mission which delimited the northern border of Gabon with the Cameroun. He explored the interior of Rio Muni and noted that

18 Gilles Sautter, personal communication.

the Fang who had formerly organized caravans to the coast in order to trade with the White had changed their routes. Once the Germans established trading stations in southern Cameroun and northern Gabon and paid better prices than anyone else, the direction of the caravans changed and the intensity of communications with southern Cameroun increased.[19] Once the railroad is built, the Fang might again move closer to the Ogooué and the rest of Gabon. The region south of Woleu-Ntem in which the railroad is to be located is relatively uninhabited.

Within Woleu-Ntem there is a regular service of autocars that link the administrative centers and fourteen of the sixteen cantons of the region. From 1962 to 1964 the service has improved. In 1962 two little Renault buses left Oyem every day for each canton except that of Medouneu to the far west and Lalara to the south toward Libreville. In 1964 two to four buses left every morning for points north and east, and it was possible to travel between Oyem and Bitam at almost any time of day. The region has about 500 miles of roads, which is more than any other Gabonese region although Ngounié has almost as many because of forestry exploitation.

Another means of internal communication was a regional newspaper published by a Fang teacher. In 1962 it contained mainly Fang stories and essays on "the true Fang customs." In spite of the great preponderance of Fang in the region, it was printed in French and was issued in seventy-five copies. It is no longer published.

About 55,000 out of a total adult population of 56,500, or 98 per cent, in this region are Fang.[20] In the canton of Woleu which is around Oyem there are 5,531 Africans of whom 5,473 are Fang. The non-Fang live in well-defined quarters of the town of Oyem; most of these people are Bulu merchants from southern Cameroun or Bakota who have moved from a neighboring region to work as servants or to attend a Roman Catholic secondary school.

While these "foreigners" move into the Woleu-Ntem, the present Fang residents appear to be fairly stationary. The census

19 A. Cottes, "La Guinée espagnole," *Annales de Géographie* (Paris, 1909), p. 447.
20 Unless otherwise noted, all census figures refer to people 14 and older.

indicates that 83 per cent of the males were born in the place where the census taker found them. However, only 29 per cent of the females were born in the place where they were counted.[21] This does not mean that many Fang have not moved outside the Woleu-Ntem, for many have; it merely means that Fang males, who still live in the region, have an interest in continuing to live in the village where they were born and that they find wives outside their village, in other cantons, or in Rio Muni and in Cameroun. There are indications, however, that people do travel within the region. For example, primary-school students change schools more frequently in Woleu-Ntem than elsewhere. A sample of students in Bitam changed 1.59 times on the average and a sample in Oyem changed 1.38 times, compared with 0.89 in Libreville and 0.77 in Ndendé where the Bapounou live.[22]

Contiguous with Woleu-Ntem are eight cantons that constitute an extension of the Heartland. Movement into these particular cantons was determined partly by the existence of means of communication. For example, the administrative region of Ogooué-Ivindo has four cantons adjacent to the Woleu-Ntem. Two of these have a Fang population that exceeds 80 per cent of the total, whereas in the third and fourth they represent no more than 5 per cent of the total population. The two cantons with high Fang percentages are linked to the Woleu-Ntem by a river and a road. In the canton of Laké, for example, many Fang indicate they were born in Woleu-Ntem. In one of the 17 villages of this canton, Sougalam-Fekelée, 54 out of 251 people were born either in Woleu-Ntem or in the neighboring Fang-dominated canton of Ntang-Louli, and most of these 54 were women.

In the sixteen cantons of Woleu-Ntem plus the eight cantons in adjacent regions which constitute the Heartland there are 70,000 Fang out of a total Fang population in Gabon of 106,000. On the basis of settlement patterns, 66 per cent of the Fang are therefore nonmobilized. Their contacts are almost exclusively with other Fang. Table I indicates that more than half the Gabonese have no contact with people of tribes different from their own.

21 Service de Statistique, "Recensement et enquête démographiques 1960–1961: Résultats provisoires ensemble du Gabon" (Paris, 1963), p. 24.

22 Jacques Proust, "Essai d'analyse des mouvements d'effectifs dans l'enseignement du premier degré au Gabon," *Tiers-Monde*, 1964, p. 135.

Table I

Heartland Populations

Tribe	Population in Heartland	Total population in Gabon	Per cent in Heartland
Bandjabi	26,500	36,200	73
Bakwélé	1,700	2,500	68
Fang	70,000	105,600	66
Ambamba	6,800	10,570	64
Mitsogo	5,500	8,840	62
Bapounou	22,300	37,400	60
Batéké	5,000	8,540	58
Massango	7,200	13,600	53
Eshira	7,000	13,370	52
Bavoungou	1,500	3,400	44
Bakota	5,700	14,200	40
Bawandji	900	3,380	27
Totals	160,100	257,600	62

Not all the tribes of Gabon have Heartlands, because their cantons have been settled by other tribes or because they are too dispersed. The Omyènè no longer have a Heartland because of the movement of all Gabonese toward the coast, and the Bawandji, with only 27 per cent of their total population in the Heartland, are being surrounded by the Bandjabi in Ogooué-Lolo. Census data indicate that most Bandjabi in the area were born in neighboring cantons while the Bawandji were born in the place where they were counted. The invading Bandjabi are admired in the region for their comparative dynamism, just as the Fang were admired by the Whites. As one man wrote some years ago: "Already several Bandjabi villages have begun to settle down; fortunately, that creates a little life around here as the few Bawandji villages are lifeless."

The Bakèlè are widely dispersed. They live in 8 of the 9 regions and in 61 out of 103 cantons, although there are only 5,066 adult Bakèlè in the whole country. The 1,812 Bakèlè in the region of Ngounié live in 21 of the 22 cantons without any significant concentration. Bakèlè in Ngounié say the French used them as hunters and they were therefore assigned to various administrative posts; there was also a famine which reportedly dispersed them.

Of those Gabonese who do have Heartlands, 62 per cent live in them. In 1962 the total population (14 and older) was approximately 285,000.[23] If the total population of Gabon is taken into account, 56 per cent live in Heartlands and are nonmobilized. They have no, or practically no, communication with members of different tribes or ethnic groups.

Table I also indicates that only the Bandjabi and the Bakwélé have a higher percentage of their total population in the Heartland than the Fang — 73 and 68 per cent, respectively, compared with 66 per cent — but as the map indicates, the 26,500 people in the Bandjabi Heartland are separated administratively into two regions, Ngounié and Ogooué-Lolo, while the Fang have a Heartland population of 70,000 of whom 55,000 live in one administrative region and completely dominate it. All tribes except the Fang must share a regional administration with other Heartlands; they are all paid the same prices for their coffee or cocoa; they use many of the same facilities; they belong to the same sections of the single political party; in the elections of 1964 they had to form joint electoral lists; and their representatives often serve together on elected bodies like the *collectivités rurales*. In other words, it is more difficult for them to remain completely without any contact with different tribes than it is for the Fang.

A Contact Zone

The Bandjabi moving into the Bawandji area around Lastoursville were apparently drawn to the administrative post of Lastoursville and traveled along the road that links their own Heartland with this center of attraction. But the Bandjabi are not the only people who are moving or who have moved toward Lastoursville; the Bakota have moved down from their Heartland in Ogooué-Ivindo as well.

In one canton between Lastoursville and Makokou, the administrative capital of the Ogooué-Ivindo Region, the Bakota account for one third of the total population of 3,000. They cleared a

---

[23] All the calculations, unless otherwise noted, are my own; they are based on what were unpublished census data. The data used here are absolute numbers, whereas the published data are extrapolations based on a sample. The validity of this discussion, which depends on proportions and comparisons rather than absolute numbers, should not be affected by any difference between the two.

path from Makokou when workers were needed in the gold mines near Lastoursville. Out of 56 villages in the canton, 35 have mixed populations. In these mixed villages there is sometimes considerable intermarriage. Doumé, for example, really consists of 3 villages that have been regrouped by the government. The dossiers indicate that there are 129 marriages of which 59, or 46 per cent, are between partners of different tribes.

There used to be more Bakota in this canton of Ogooué-Amont-Lassio. Gold is no longer mined by the company that used to be there, and the Bakota have been moving back to their Heartland. In one village, Behamba in the Bakota Heartland in Ogooué-Ivindo, there were only 32 inhabitants in 1954 and 93 in 1956. Census data indicate that the newcomers were born near Lastoursville.[24] The fact that the newcomers were born in a Contact Zone did not prevent them from moving to a Heartland. Once the center of attraction disappeared they had no more interest in remaining and became "demobilized." This instability is characteristic of Contact Zones, just as considerable movement of population is characteristic of Gabon.[25] De Brazza observed a temporary Contact Zone along the Ogooué. He noted that, at a place called Lopé, "once a year in the month of February and perhaps more often the Inenga [Enenga], the Galais [Galoa], and the Okandé get together. Once the market is over, everything becomes deserted and it is even impossible to find a village."[26] A more important Contact Zone is around Makokou where the Fang, the Bakota, the Bakwélé, and others meet.

The town of Makokou exists by day only. It is located on a main road and two rivers which are used by people to travel to this "post." They come to deal with the administration, to go to the market on Saturday, to buy sugar or cloth at one of the European-owned or state-owned shops, to go to school or to church. People travel by canoe or by the trucks used by the administration to

[24] Data from partial village censuses, 1954–1959, Makokou.

[25] The census experts found that for every hundred residents in a given place twelve, on the average, were absent at the time of the census and seven of those present were visitors. Service de Statistique, ftn. 21, p. 26.

[26] Archives de la Marine, Paris, Série BB4, Volume 1448, "Rapport de P. Savorgnan de Brazza sur son expédition dans l'Afrique Equatoriale août 1875 à novembre 1878," 30 August 1879. Professor Henri Brunschwig, who discovered this document, kindly permitted me to read it in photocopy form prior to its publication in his book *Brazza explorateur: L'Ogooué 1875–1879* (Paris, Mouton, 1966), pp. 93–194.

collect coffee beans for the small factory where they are sorted and bagged for export. The only regular transportation by land is provided by privately owned Renault buses, each of which holds twenty people. Once or twice a week it is possible to take one of these buses or possibly a truck to Libreville.

At night Makokou disappears. Everyone except the European merchants and civil servants goes home to the surrounding villages. The Bakwélé live up the Ivindo River, which extends northeast from Makokou toward the Congolese frontier; the Bakota and Shaké live along roads to the east and south and along the Liboumba River which extends east; the Fang live to the west and northwest along the road to Libreville and near the Mvoung River, which comes into the region from Woleu-Ntem.

Two of the four cantons around Makokou are mainly Bakota and Shaké who account for 5,000 out of a total population of 5,800. One of the cantons is Fang; they number 4,400 out of 4,900. The fourth canton is Bakwélé with 1,700 out of 2,300 of the population of the canton.[27] All these people have tended to move toward Makokou or have been regrouped in villages closer to Makokou where they meet at the market or where some of them work during the day.

Census data indicate that some few people are even moving into areas of tribes different from their own. For example, Fang and Bakota are sent to Bakwélé villages, and Bakota catechists are sent to Shaké villages. Some Bakwélé have moved into Fang and Bakota areas.

There are examples of intermarriage, but they appear to follow certain patterns. For example, in a village of 100 people there may be five or six married couples, but the men are Fang and the women are Bakwélé and Bakota. There are fewer examples of Fang women married to Bakota or Bakwélé men. Data show that of 170 Fang-Bakota marriages in Ogooué-Ivindo only 34 are between a Bakota man and a Fang woman; 136 are between a Fang man and a Bakota woman.[28]

The people of Makokou listen to Radio Gabon and Radio Brazzaville. The prefect receives the Gabonese newspaper about

[27] The total population of the region is 25,876, of which there are 8,595 Bakota 14 years and older, 7,251 Fang, 2,278 Bakwélé, and 1,581 Shaké.

[28] Service de Statistique, "Recensement et enquête démographiques 1960–1961: Résultats définitifs ensemble du Gabon" (Paris, 1965), p. 79.

two weeks after it is printed. Many men have worked in Brazzaville before the road to Libreville was completed.

At the other end of Gabon in the region of Ngounié there is a Contact Zone along the river Ngounié from Mouila, the administrative capital, to Lambaréné. People move toward the river and road, and once they arrive they begin to move north. It is also a region which along with Moyen-Ogooué has many forestry camps whose workers represent most of the Gabonese tribes.

The Bapounou, whose Heartland is in Nyanga and in southern Ngounié, come into contact with the Eshira, Mitsogo, and Baveya at Mouila and Sindara. The Baveya used to have a *terre* within a canton and thus had a certain degree of autonomy and identity. Since the *terres* have been abolished, Baveya have become insignificant numerically and have a Mitsogo chief of canton. They are now caught between the Mitsogo Heartland to the east and the Eshira Heartland to the west, and because they live near the centers of attraction of Sindara and Fougamou, they are being inundated. What once were Baveya villages have become very mixed. The village of Madaguia, with sixty-nine inhabitants, is regarded as a Baveya village. It has been settled by Eshira who have crossed the Ngounié River from another canton into what used to be the Baveya *terre*. Twenty-one marriages are recorded for the village: Twelve are between Baveya men and Baveya women, two are between Eshira men and Eshira women, five are Baveya-Eshira, one is Eshira-Baveya, and one is Bavili-Eshira (the Bavili who are related to the Baveya live mainly in Congo).

When people move into a new village, they ask permission of the chief to settle there. The chief may lend some land which has already been cleared, or he may not. Because Gabon is underpopulated, there is no scarcity of land, but there may be a scarcity of land that has already been cleared. Even if a chief does not give the newcomers land, they may not be dissuaded from settling in a place because it is likely that they will keep their old plantations in the place they have just left.

It is in the Bapounou Heartland below Mouila and in the Nyanga Region that 63 per cent of the Bapounou live; most of the goods they purchase have come through Congo. Dolisie on the Congo-Océan Railroad has long served as a center for commerce with Gabon and as a center of attraction along with the port of

Pointe-Noire for workers. This is changing as attempts are made to ship the rice grown in the region to the north instead of south to Congo as Lambaréné becomes an increasingly important inland port for the distribution of imported goods.

It has been reported that in 1961 imports into Gabon from outside Africa but via Congo exceeded importations by way of Libreville and Port-Gentil by $10,000,000, but this was due to the construction of the COMILOG mining camp in Haut-Ogooué which required importation of much material and machinery.[29] In 1962 goods worth about $38,000,000 passed through Port-Gentil and Libreville compared with slightly over $7,000,000 which came through Congo for Gabon. About 10 per cent as a rate of importations from Congo and about 5 per cent of the total Gabonese importations from Cameroun were the 1963 estimates.[30]

Trucks continue to move between Congo and regions of Ngounié, Nyanga, Haut-Ogooué, and Ogooué-Lolo particularly to supply the needs of European merchants, many of whom came into Gabon from Congo or even from Angola. That the traffic is one-way in nature is indicated by the tonnage of goods carried: The average tonnage of goods per truck that enters Gabon from Congo is 6.5, while the average tonnage of goods per truck which returns from Gabon to Congo is only 1.3.[31]

Transportation facilities have increased greatly within Ngounié due to the actions of a European who established regular and frequent bus and trucking service from Mouila. Large buses holding about forty passengers leave five days a week for Lambaréné, and a bus leaves Lambaréné five days a week for Mouila. Twice a week it is possible to go into Congo and into Nyanga; there is one bus a week to the eastern administrative posts of Mbigou and Mimongo. A truck follows each bus in order to carry whatever the passengers want to transport. Another White has a bus but his schedule is more irregular.

Although communications have improved, comparatively few people live near one another in Contact Zones. Table II indicates this.

29 *Marchés Tropicaux,* 14 April 1962.
30 Ministère d'Etat chargé de l'Economie Nationale, *Situation Economique, Financière et Sociale de la République Gabonaise — Fin 1962* (Libreville, May 1963), p. 107. There is, of course, no way to calculate the smuggling.
31 *Ibid.,* pp. 77–78.

Table II

Contact-Zone Populations

Tribe	Population in contact	Total population in Gabon	Per cent in contact
Bawandji	2,300	3,380	68
Bakota	6,500	14,200	46
Batéké	3,400	8,540	40
Massango	3,900	13,600	29
Bavoungou	950	3,400	28
Bakwélé	680	2,500	27
Ambamba	1,900	10,570	18
Mitsogo	1,600	8,840	18
Bandjabi	4,800	36,200	13
Fang	13,000	105,600	12
Eshira	1,400	13,370	11
Bapounou	3,600	37,400	9
Totals	44,030	257,600	17

Seventeen per cent of those who do have Heartlands live in Contact Zones. If the total population is taken into account, 21 per cent of the Gabonese are partially mobilized.

A Nationalizing Zone

The single Nationalizing Zone of Gabon is in the shape of a triangle formed by eighteen cantons roughly between and including the three cities of Libreville, Lambaréné, and Port-Gentil. There is a regular system of land and water communication in this area. Libreville and Lambaréné are connected by the best national road in the country, part of which was paved in 1964 and on which regular transportation is assured by small buses and trucks. Lambaréné is then linked with Port-Gentil and the Atlantic Ocean by a navigable section of the Ogooué River. Ships and boats move regularly between Libreville and Port-Gentil and between Port-Gentil and Lambaréné. Merchandise is brought to Lambaréné from Port-Gentil and Libreville. The weekly newspaper *Gabon d'Aujourd'hui* is more likely to be found in this triangle than elsewhere, and the Gabonese national broadcasting company is heard more frequently than other stations.

The area delimited by Libreville, Lambaréné, and Port-Gentil has been called an island because of its long isolation from the rest of Gabon. Since 1958, however, a road has extended south parallel with the Ngounié River from Lambaréné to link the Nationalizing Zone with the southwestern part of the country. Regular transportation assures communication between Lambaréné and this area.

Sundays a truck leaves Tchibanga, in the far southwest near the Congolese frontier, to collect manioc and vegetables for workers in Port-Gentil. The truck, which also has taken passengers, is driven to Lambaréné where the vegetables are transferred to a boat that leaves on Monday afternoons for Port-Gentil, down the Ogooué River. This boat also takes passengers.

In the Nationalizing Zone there are about 84,400 people 14 years and older; the Fang, the largest single group,[32] account for only 22,600 or 27 per cent of the total. Few of these people were born in this zone: for the age group 15 to 59 only 25 per cent of the men and only 20 per cent of the women were born in the place where they were counted.[33]

No tribe occupies a single solid zone, and most cantons are not like the contact areas contiguous with a Heartland Zone. Villages are interspersed ethnically, and within each village several tribes are represented. In canton Lac Nord there are 1,800 people: 500 Fang, 400 Bapounou, 190 Omyènè, 140 Eshira, 50 Bakèlè, and 520 others from almost every tribe in the country. The twenty-eight villages are all mixed, and intermarriage is frequent. In the village of Guelimoni, for example, there are twenty-five married couples of which fourteen are unmixed and eleven are mixed. Contrary to the "patterns" in Contact Zones there are examples of people from any given tribe in this canton marrying people from any other given tribe.[34]

Libreville, with a population of about 50,000, is divided into five "groups" each with four or five quarters which have chiefs.[35] Some "groups" used to be predominantly Omyènè, but now members of other tribes, particularly the Fang, have moved into every

---

[32] In spite of poor communications with Woleu-Ntem many Fang have, of course, moved to Libreville and the rest of the Nationalizing Zone. With the decrease in cocoa prices more Fang are now moving to Libreville.

[33] Service de Statistique, ftn. 28, p. 24.

[34] This is, however, not so true of the Omyènè and the Eurafricans who marry within their own groups.

[35] See Guy Lasserre, *Libreville: la ville et sa région* (Paris, Armand Colin, 1958).

part of the city. Two quarters, that of Nombakèlè and Akébé have a highly mixed population. Nombakèlè (the word means Bakèlè hill) used to be inhabited by the Bakèlè who had fled the Fang, but now all new arrivals in Libreville live here. Along labyrinthine paths are countless tiny houses which shelter the new arrivals until they are lucky enough to get a job which will permit them to move elsewere. This is also where the non-Gabonese Hausas, Congolese, Dahomeans, and others have lived. Akébé, also highly mixed (including some Europeans), has houses for low-ranking civil servants and teachers.[36] The Omyènè dominate the groups of Louis and Glass; Lalala, abandoned by the Mpongouè, is now almost completely Fang; smaller quarters like Petit Paris are inhabited by Bandjabi and Massango workers from Ngounié or by the other tribes of Gabon.[37] Many residents of Libreville have plantations of bananas or manioc a few miles from the city or in some cases within the city limits.

Port-Gentil and Lambaréné are also divided into various quarters; in Lambaréné the Omyènè used to predominate on the island where the town is really located, but there are now so many other tribes and nationalities that the Galoa (Omyènè) have been somewhat submerged. The Fang, however, tend to live on the right bank of the Ogooué, and the Bapounou live with other southerners on the left bank.

In Libreville the Fang account for 34.2 per cent of the total African population and 40.5 per cent of the total Gabonese population.[38] Other large groups in Libreville are the Omyènè with 15.1 per cent of the Gabonese population and the Bapounou with 10.9 per cent. Naturally, the major educational, religious, and some of the major economic institutions are in the Nationalizing Zone. Port-Gentil has a number of industrial installations including an important plywood factory and will soon have an oil refinery. Libreville has all the offices of the central government, and

36 Europeans with money tend to live along the ocean near the central part of town, but Libreville is not a segregated city, whereas Brazzaville, Abidjan, Kinshasa, Nairobi, and many other African capitals have been.

37 See Abbé A. Raponda-Walker, "Toponymie de l'estuaire du Gabon et de ses environs," Vol. 2, *Bulletin de l'Institut de Recherches Scientifiques au Congo*, 1962, pp. 96–98.

38 There were Congolese and Dahomeans in the capital during the census. Service de Statistique, ftn. 21: Résultats pour Libreville (Paris, 1962), p. 26.

Lambaréné has the best communication links with the rest of the country.

Most intensive intertribal contact is possible in the Nationalizing Zone although there is still a tendency toward tribal regroupment. One of the two major Roman Catholic churches is predominantly Omyènè, while the other is predominantly Fang; one of the largest primary schools located in an area where there are both Fang and Omyènè has gradually become exclusively Fang. If an area or an institution of one kind or another has a tribal rather than a national label attached to it, the most likely labels are Fang or Omyènè. (If the Bapounou continue to migrate to Libreville, there may develop "Bapounou" schools, and so forth.) Each of the groups of Libreville has its own market; there are tiny shops that sell canned goods, cigarettes, and other European articles, but there is one central shopping area. Outside Libreville but still in the Nationalizing Zone there are individual villages where, for example, the Omyènè account for all the population and almost consider themselves bulwarks against their neighbors.

Table III indicates percentages of the various tribes in the Nationalizing Zone.

Table III

Nationalizing-Zone Populations

Tribe	Population in National	(Of which in Libreville)	Total population in Gabon	Per cent in National
Eshira	4,970	370	13,370	37
Bapounou	11,500	1,800	37,400	31
Bavoungou	950	—	3,400	28
Fang	22,600	6,600	105,600	22
Mitsogo	1,740	137	8,840	20
Ambamba	1,870	1,250	10,570	18
Massango	2,500	493	13,600	18
Bakota	2,000	900	14,200	14
Bandjabi	4,900	1,200	36,200	14
Bawandji	180	—	3,380	5
Bakwélé	120	—	2,500	5
Batéké	140	—	8,540	2
Totals	53,470	12,750	257,600	21

Of those tribes that have Heartlands, 21 per cent live in the Nationalizing Zone, and 23 per cent of all Gabonese live where intensive contact with people of tribes different from their own is probable. These people are "mobilized."

According to this table, the Batéké, the Bawandji, and the Bakota are poorly represented in the zone. Yet they are the tribes with the highest percentages in the Contact Zones. This means that although they move around considerably, their contacts with the rest of the Gabonese are rather superficial. They are only partially mobilized, and they do not share many experiences with other peoples. They do not necessarily move from Contact to Nationalizing Zones.

There is no inevitable and logical migration in states from Heartlands via Contact Zones to Nationalizing Zones; people may move directly from their Heartland Zone to the Nationalizing Zone. Partial mobilization does not necessarily indicate that people are on the way to full mobilization.

Table III shows that four out of five tribes with the highest percentages of their total population in the Nationalizing Zone (the Eshira, Bavoungou, Bapounou, and Mitsogo) come from the same region, the Ngounié, which is linked with the Nationalizing Zone by the Ngounié River and the major route extending from Lambaréné to the south.[39] The people of isolated Haut-Ogooué and neighboring Ogooué-Lolo are but poorly represented in this zone: The Batéké have a bare 2 per cent, the Bawandji 6 per cent of their total population, and the Ambamba 18 per cent.

These percentages correspond with certain political realities. The three most important recent political leaders in the country have been Jean-Hilaire Aubame, a Fang of Libreville, Léon Mba, also a Fang of Libreville, and Paul Gondjout, an Omyènè from Port-Gentil who was the secretary general of the major political party and was, for a time, president of the National Assembly. The ministers who founded the B.D.G. (Bloc Démocratique Gabonais) party and who were in every cabinet from 1957 to 1966 were an Omyènè of Libreville, a Bapounou from Ngounié, and an Eshira from Ngounié. The Omyènè, Bapounou, and Eshira are not, after the Fang, the largest ethnic groups in the country (the Bapounou may be second to the Fang, but my data indicate that the Bandjabi outnumber them slightly), but the largest percentages of their

39 This does not of course count the Omyènè, almost 100 per cent of whom live in the Nationalizing Zone because they do not have a Heartland.

respective populations live in the Nationalizing Zone. They have had the most influence in this zone along with the Fang and have had the most interest in participating in a government located there.

Table III lastly indicates that it is not only in the cities that comparatively intensive intertribal contact is probable. Of 22,600 Fang in the Nationalizing Zone, 6,600 live in Libreville, 850 in Port-Gentil, and 360 in Lambaréné. This means that 14,790, or 65 per cent, live outside the cities. Census data show there is more intermarriage in the three regions part of which make up the Nationalizing Zone than elsewhere — 8.3 per cent of all marriages in Estuaire, 11.0 per cent in Ogooué-Maritime, and 12.5 per cent in Moyen-Ogooué — and that there is more intermarriage outside the cities than inside them.[40] Mobilization and assimilation are not exclusively urban processes.

Assimilation

People may be assimilated by one another, or everyone may be assimilated into a culture that did not previously exist. In Gabon both processes are going on simultaneously. On the one hand, some small tribes without Heartlands are forgetting their history and adopting the language and customs of their neighbors. On the other hand, all tribes have certain shared experiences and are sharing more and more as communication improves and as they live through the problems of development together. They are sharing in the growth of an industrial civilization which is neutral to tribal identity.

Mobilization is a physical process, and assimilation is a question of beliefs and attitudes which vary according to Heartland, Contact, and Nationalizing Zones.

A Heartland

People in Heartlands remember their particularistic histories best. In every village someone can always be found who remembers The Beginning; this same person can usually relate several generations of his own ancestors. The Fang of Woleu-Ntem remember their history best of all.

---

40 Service de Statistique, ftn. 28, pp. 74–78.

The Fang are intensely proud of their history and enjoy telling it. In his tour of Gabon, Governor Deschamps found that Fang informants could relate as many as nineteen generations of their ancestors.[41] They have an advantage over other Gabonese in that they have a written version of their history.

The story of the migration of the children of Afrikara appears in little pamphlets published in the southern Cameroun.[42] It is accepted by most Fang of Woleu-Ntem as their standard history. According to Dr. Fernandez of Dartmouth, it has helped the Fang maintain their sense of identity by explaining why they live where they do and how they are all kin.[43] Non-Fang are barely mentioned in this history. They are, like all men, the sons of *Hamata* and like all Africans the sons of *Afrikara*. When the dispersion of Africans is explained and when the various Fang move into Gabon, there is not a word about non-Fang. The history reflects indifference rather than hostility toward non-Fang. Because there are so few non-Fang in the Heartland, people are not always aware or conscious of tribal differences, and this is reflected in their considerations of the past.

A certain Fang hostility to "outsiders" is reflected, however, in the problems of placement of civil servants in Fang territory. Prefects and other administrators who are not obliged to live in very close daily contact with the Fang of Woleu-Ntem are often Omyènè or members of other ethnic groups. Teachers who live with the people in their villages and also some sub-prefects are Fang. If they are not, they may have trouble in accomplishing their work because of Fang hostility. This is true in most Heartlands, but some people are compelled to accept "outsiders" as teachers because they have no one qualified for the job.

The people of Woleu-Ntem are very much aware of differences between themselves and other Fang; this consciousness is sometimes accompanied by intense feelings of hostility. The Heartland Fang claim they have kept the "pure customs" but their relatives in the Nationalizing Zone have been corrupted by contact with "foreigners." By "foreigners" they generally mean the coastal

---

41 Hubert Deschamps, ftn. 17, p. 92.

42 Ondoua Engute, *Dulu Bon be Afri Kara* (Elat, Ebolowa, Cameroun, Mission Presbytérienne, 1948, 1954, and 1956).

43 James W. Fernandez, "Folklore as an Agent of Nationalism," *African Studies Bulletin*, 5, May 1962, p. 5.

Omyènè. The Fang of Woleu-Ntem associated the political party B.D.G. with the Fang of Libreville and the Omyènè; they preferred to support the opposition party, U.D.S.G. (Union Démocratique et Sociale du Gabon) of Jean-Hilaire Aubame, while it existed. There are examples of this hostility developing into open violence between groups of Fang from Woleu-Ntem and groups of Fang from Libreville. In spite of this there is a tendency today for Fang to call themselves "Fang" without reference to the Woleu-Ntem or to their tribe or clan.

The only languages spoken in Woleu-Ntem are French and Fang. Non-Fang are obliged to learn the predominant language of the Heartland; if they marry a Fang and remain the Woleu-Ntem, they are more or less absorbed. In one Fang village, for example, two men from southern Gabon settled after they were released from the French army, which fought in Woleu-Ntem during World War I. They were not Fang but had married Fang women and had what were considered Fang children. The two had been accepted as Fang, and it was with reluctance that the chief admitted they had once been something else.

Small groups of Bakwélé have been absorbed in the Bakota Heartland. During a 1959 census of villages in Ogooué-Ivindo an administrator discovered that the Bakota of the village of Mekouka in the District of Makokou used to be Bakwélé; two Bakwélé clans left the Heartland of the Bakwélé and dislodged some Bakota where they wanted to settle: "[They] chased away the Bakota who left for Libreville (Benga). The newest village . . . was born between the Liboumba and the Mouniangui Rivers during the 1880–1890 migration. They found the Bakota . . . more numerous than themselves and they were absorbed. All except the old people have forgotten their language; they speak and call themselves Bakota."[44] Bakota leaders say that non-Bakota might as well become Bakota to decrease the number of different groups.

The Bapounou in the south remember their history as well as the Fang, but they are reluctant about telling it because they believe it is dangerous for non-Bapounou to know their history. They are particularly suspicious of anyone from the north, such

[44] Village Census Report for village of Mekouka, Makokou, 1959. The word Benga in parenthesis means the administrator accepted the Bakota idea that the people on the coast who call themselves Benga are really Bakota.

as the Omyènè or the Fang, whom they tend to group together. The Bapounou of Nyanga don't always get on with their neighbors in the southern part of Ngounié. The latter consider their Nyanga relatives as backward, and the Nyanga Bapounou believe that the Ngounié Bapounou have come under the influence of the Bandjabi. Nyanga was the only region of Gabon to vote *non* in the referendum of September 1958 to ratify the constitution of the Fifth French Republic and did so under the leadership of a third political party, P.U.N.G.A. (Parti d'Unité Nationale Gabonaise).

A Contact Zone

People may remember their histories in Contact Zones, but such histories show remarkable resemblances with those of the tribes with which they have the most contact. These other tribes are given a role more important than that given them in the Heartland; the part they play appears to be strongly influenced by what the present relations between the two groups are.

For example, Nze in the Contact Zone near Makokou is a regrouped village that used to be five villages — one Shaké and four Bakota. Making a detailed map, I saw that there were two clearly defined quarters — Shaké and Bakota; this enabled me to establish the tribal identity of each resident by putting names beside the picture of his house and asking questions. Before I did this I inquired whether or not any Shaké men were married to non-Shaké women. Informants mentioned one or two. Once I had written the names of the heads of each household next to the house and asked the question about each person, many more non-Shaké women were named. About one third of the wives were non-Shaké even though they did not always want to admit it.

A map and a tour of the village disclosed there were actually three quarters rather than two. The third section was about twenty minutes' walk up the road. Only Bakota were living here; they used to live with the other Bakota alongside the Shaké but moved out two years before because a Shaké had shot one of their sheep which was destroying a cocoa tree. The administration still recognizes only one chief and one village, but the isolated Bakota have their own chief now and have very little contact with the Shaké. In effect, these Bakota have become demobilized and differentiated from the Shaké and the other Bakota. Oral history reflects such relationships.

In the histories of the Bakota and Shaké, who were still living together, each tribe has an important place for the other: They had been allies in wars, they had almost always lived together, they were close relatives descended from the same ancestors. Those Bakota who were living by themselves first announced proudly that *they* were the "pure" Bakota. They said they could not understand the Shaké accent very well and claimed they were never allied with the Shaké, nor were they descended from the same ancestors. The Shaké were, in fact, not mentioned in their history.

People are more conscious of tribal differences in Contact Zones than in Heartlands; the Bakota and Shaké who were living together, although conscious of differences, tried to minimize them. In normal times such consciousness does not lead to open antagonism or violence, but during economic difficulties people associate their neighbors with their troubles. Coffee prices were down and the sub-prefect had not been sending the truck to collect coffee beans from the Bakota and Shaké villages. The people charged that the sub-prefect, a Fang, preferred to buy from his relatives — this was the reason they had no money.

On the other side of Makokou the Fang live with the Makina who have been practically all absorbed by the Fang. There is some question about who the Makina or Osyeba or Bichiwa really are. Some people say they are a separate tribe, and others say they are a clan of the Fang which arrived in Gabon before the others. The Marquis de Compiègne wrote that he thought the Osyeba were part of the Fang family. De Brazza wrote about people he called the Fans Makey as if they were different from those he called the "Ossyeba."[45] Professor Deschamps, who interviewed many Makina, regards them as a separate tribe but makes the suggestion that they may originally have been Bakwélé who were partly absorbed by the Fang.[46]

Historical records do show that the Makina or Maké or Osyeba or Bichiwa, whether they are Fang or not, arrived in Gabon before

[45] Marquis de Compiègne, *L'Afrique équatoriale: Okanda, Bangouens, Osyeba* (Paris, Plon, 1885), pp. 145–154. "Rapport de P. Savorgnan de Brazza," ftn. 26, pp. 672–674, 686–688.
[46] Hubert Deschamps, ftn. 17, pp. 78–81.

the people who now call themselves Fang; they were later surrounded by the Fang and eventually overcome by them. Today the Makina are not differentiated from the Fang in the census. Until 1951 the chief of one Fang canton, an extension of the Woleu-Ntem Fang Heartland, was half Makina and half Fang. He was replaced by a "pure" Fang.

Makina live with the Fang in a village near Makokou; it is called "Alarmintang" which means "grouped by or near the Whites." The Makina claim that they were here first and that the Fang came down from Woleu-Ntem later; the Fang moved close to them, and then some leapfrogged over their village, they say, to get closer to Makokou. The Makina were thus surrounded. In 1925, at the time of the great famine, the Fang and the Makina were regrouped into one large village. Now the village is divided roughly into two parts, Fang and Makina. The chief is Makina and the sub-chief is Fang; the chief has a Fang mother and is married to a Fang. Everyone in this village refers to the Makina as the "Fang Makina." The Makina recounted a history of origin different from that of their Fang neighbors, although they had forgotten most of it.

In another village there are only Makina. These people do not call themselves Fang Makina, although the Fang do. The chief of this village is an elderly man who says he speaks Makina or Bichiwa: "We are Bichiwa or Makina, not Fang." He said it was the Fang who started calling the Makina Fang. He blamed the canton chief who, according to him, was always asked by the administration how many Fang there were in the canton and who always included the Makina in his totals. (This canton chief was also one of the leaders in the Fang *alar ayong* or clan regroupment movement.) At that moment in our conversation a nearby Fang was heard to say "Fang Makina," and the old chief shouted: "Stop that! You gave us the name Fang; we are just Bichiwa or Makina!"

The register of marriages in Makokou makes no distinction between the Fang and the Makina, although in 1949 many Fang sub-groups and others are listed which (like the Boumouéllé) later disappeared. About seventeen different tribes are listed in 1949, including members of the same tribe but called by different names (Bakwélé and Bakouel, Ikota and Bakota); by 1962 only eight different tribes are listed. It is true that in the meantime the frontiers of the district changed but this does not explain the decrease; many peoples previously listed separately have been assimilated into other groups in the administrative records.[47]

The patterns in intermarriage indicated in the census data are confirmed by attitudes. The Fang say that a Fang woman would never marry a Bakota man because Bakota are considered inferior; marriages between Fang men and Bakota women are, however, acceptable. There do not appear to be any rules with regard to Bakota-Shaké marriages, although Bakota leaders indicate they would prefer to see Bakota men marry Shaké women rather than Shaké men marry Bakota women, so that the children would become Bakota.

Members of any tribe in Gabon are more or less acceptable as civil servants in the Contact Zone. Civil servants who come into the Contact Zone do not necessarily learn any of the local languages because there is no single dominant African language there. Each people prefers to speak its own language and French (in the Makokou area the Bakwélé speak Fang too); they say they communicate with other tribes in French or in the "few words" they know of the other language.

Tribal consciousness has contributed to small-scale violence during the unsettling and insecure times of elections or other forms of political change. When it has occurred, it has been localized around Makokou and was of short duration.

A Nationalizing Zone

In the Nationalizing Zone some people appear to have completely forgotten their histories, but they are not alarmed about it. Here people from other tribes are most visible and everyone is most conscious of differences, but there is often a desire to get along and build something new called Gabon or Africa. Questions of "purity" and "true customs" are not posed here. People appear to adopt different customs most rapidly in this area; they speak many languages and accept teachers in their villages from any tribe in the country.

The village of Dakar with some 200 people is located not far

47 Département Ogooué-Ivindo, Makokou, "Régistre des Actes de Mariage," 2 August 1949 to 21 April 1958; and Région d'Ogooué-Ivindo, Makokou, "Régistre des Mariages, Année 1962."

from Lambaréné. Séké, Nkomi (Omyènè), Fang, Bapounou, Bapindji, and Mitsogo live in two contiguous quarters. The Mitsogo live in two different quarters according to their geographical origins. These various tribes have not been living together very long (except for the Séké and Nkomi-Omyènè), and intermarriage is still rare (except between Séké and Nkomi).

The Séké came here first, then the Nkomi, and then the others after the logging camps to which they had been attracted closed down. The Séké are becoming part of the prestigious coastal Omyènè ethnic group. Their chief says he knows nothing about any particular Séké history, nor is he concerned about it; it is the same as that of the "rest of the Omyènè," but he is not even sure about the details of Omyènè history. These people speak the Omyènè tongue, but their neighbors say that when the Séké are by themselves, they speak Séké. Almost everyone in the Nationalizing Zone speaks Fang and/or Omyènè.

The Fang of Dakar outwardly accept the Séké chief as the leader for the whole village, but they have their own leaders who have more authority among the Fang themselves. They arrived last and tend to disdain the non-Fang. There are no examples of intermarriage with other ethnic groups. The Fang as well as the other people in Dakar send their children to one school which is staffed by a teacher from another region.

The workers in various industrial enterprises and private companies in Libreville and Port-Gentil are as conscious of tribal differences as are the villagers, but there is an added element: a conscious desire to get along with other workers for the good of all. The Gabonese sociologist Laurent Biffot found in a sample taken from three different enterprises that only 27 per cent of the workers interviewed thought workers tended to group themselves according to ethnogeographic affinities; 65.2 per cent said workers tried to build an *esprit de corps* and to sympathize with other workers irrespective of tribe.[48] In spite of this there are examples of members of one tribe becoming predominant in a certain office or section of an enterprise and then more or less driving members of other tribes out.

[48] 6.8 per cent gave no response. Laurent Biffot, *Facteurs d'intégration et de désintégration du travailleur gabonais à son entreprise* (Paris, Office de la Recherche Scientifique et Technique Outre-Mer, 1960), p. 96.

In industrial enterprises outside the Nationalizing Zone workers say they want to get along. In Haut-Ogooué the uranium company C.M.U.F. (Compagnie Minière de l'Uranium de Franceville) and the manganese company COMILOG (Compagnie Minière de l'Ogooué) have workers from all of the regions of the country and from foreign countries, but there appears to be a comparatively high turnover of workers. At the site of the great iron ore deposit in Ogooué-Ivindo the workers are divided by tribe into two main residential groups which were named Brazzaville and Léopoldville. Company officials thought it best to separate the Fang from the non-Fang, but soon after the camp was set up people moved from one area to another so that, in the end, there was no tribal difference. Workers pointed out that the man they had elected to represent them before the company came from a small tribe, but it is true that this man was "suggested" to the workers by officials of the company.

Several industrial enterprises outside the Nationalizing Zone appear to create conditions for extensive contact among different tribes, but the contact is often very brief and unstable, and the companies themselves are trying to mechanize as much as possible so that few Gabonese might be actually affected by living and working together.

It is in the villages and cities of the Nationalizing Zone as well as in the industrial enterprises outside the zone that one finds the least resistance to change and the most desire for innovation. Everyone now realizes the importance of at least a primary-school diploma. This Nationalizing Zone is the nucleus of the developing Gabonese nation. Shared experience is most accessible and most intense in this area, although it is still possible for people from different tribes to be isolated. Also it is in everyone's interest in this area to build a supratribal community because one has a job, material possessions, and because one cannot necessarily count on the help of members of one's own tribe in times of insecurity and violence.

Heartland residents have few dealings with "foreigners" and have a degree of security that comes with the ownership of land and the sense of continuity of living in one place for a long time with one's own family. In Contact Zones strangers may move into villages with people who speak languages different from their

106

own. The newcomers, however, may not possess *fallow* land around the village — a type of investment that indicates a long period of residence and a definite economic interest in getting along with neighbors.[49]

In the Nationalizing Zone there is more possibility of inter-tribal violence that could lead to the destruction of the developing community than in the other two zones. It is here for example that Fang dynamism is most clearly perceived and feared. The Omyènè considered much of what today is the Nationalizing Zone and particularly Libreville as their property which has been usurped by the Europeans and the other Gabonese, particularly the Fang. They resented non-Omyènè presence. They formed their own organization to fight for their land rights and to protect themselves against the Fang. In 1937 when the Mpongouè were organizing a *Comité Pongouè* to protect their interest and install a Grand Chief, they tried to do something about the infiltration of the Fang. They wrote to the Mayor of Libreville, who was also the chief administrative officer in the Estuaire region, and proposed a reorganization of the city. They wanted fewer chiefs. For example, in one quarter they suggested one Mpongouè who would take the place of six Mpongouè and in another they suggested putting in one Benga to take the place of three Fang and one Oroungou chief. For the villages near Libreville (which were getting closer to the capital) they wanted only Omyènè or Benga chiefs who were allied with the Mpongouè.[50]

In the 1920's Omyènè administrators who wrote in *L'Echo Gabonais* occasionally felt they had to defend the Omyènè against comparisons with the Fang. For example, a letter had been written about the bravery of Fang soldiers in Morocco during World War I; these men had been recruited in the Estuaire region. The Omyènè defended Omyènè soldiers who, they said, didn't have to be recruited; they joined voluntarily and were just as brave as the Fang if not more so. In another issue they lamented the fact

---

49 Mademoiselle Jean of the Bureau pour le Développement de la Production Agricole (B.D.P.A.) suggested the factor of fallow land to me. If one had data on who owned fallow land in every village, one could make a better judgment about the attitudes of people.

50 Letter from Le Comité Pongoué à Monsieur l'Administrateur en Chef des Colonies, Administrateur-Maire de la Commune de Libreville, Libreville, 4 August 1937.

that there was an increase in antiwitchcraft movements among the Fang: "For the past few years there has been in the interior of Gabon a recrudescence of fetishism, particularly among the Fang. After most have abandoned the *bieri* of their ancestors there they are hurling themselves into the *bouiti* of the races of the Ogooué."[51] The Fang disliked Mpongouè and Omyènè arrogance and vowed they would not be controlled by them. They too demanded a Grand Chief and wrote to the administration: "The Fang never accept and never will accept being ruled by the Mpongouè.[52] Léon Mba formed Fang organizations to counter the Omyènè. The Fang objected to the *internat* school which was reserved for the Eurafricans and deeply resented the *Cercle des Métis,* a club which admitted only Omyènè and Eurafricans to its dances and parties prior to independence. It was the Fang leader Jean-Hilaire Aubame who often protested against Omyènè discrimination against other Africans.

During the elections in October 1945 for a Constituent Assembly the Omyènè and the Fang fought in Libreville, and martial law was declared; but since that time there has not been any significant violence between the two groups. Intellectual, religious, and political organizations have often been quite mixed since that time.

In the Nationalizing Zone there has been the most conscious attempt to form supratribal groupings. *Bwiti* in the Libreville area is not a Fang organization but is composed of members of several ethnic groups. Organizations such as the *Comité Pongouè* and the Fang *La Voix du Pays,* founded in 1935, were formed on the basis of tribal allegiance. But in the 1940's an organization founded by a Fang, François Mèyè, supported a Libreville Mpongouè for office. A *Groupe d'Etudes Communistes* had Fang, Omyènè, and Bapounou members. In the late 1940's a *Comité Mixte Gabonais* was formed by Fang and Omyènè, but these organizations and the subsequent political parties were localized in the Nationalizing Zone until the 1950's.[53]

---

51 *L'Echo Gabonais,* Dakar, Numbers 6, 7, March, April 1923.

52 Letter cited by Georges Balandier, *Sociologie actuelle de l'Afrique noire* (Paris, Presses Universitaires de France, 1955), p. 201.

53 For a detailed account of Gabonese party politics see John A. Ballard, *The Development of Political Parties in French Equatorial Africa,* unpublished thesis, Fletcher School of Law and Diplomacy, December 1963.

CHAPTER 5

A Developing National Culture

National Culture

Culture, as the complex of ideas, symbols, tools, ways of doing things of a society, provides standards of belief and behavior for members of that society and distinguishes it from all others. It is the cultural system linked with the social system which provides the ways to maintain order, which restrains men, and which gives them goals and directions to reach them. Members of the same society who have had similar experiences are more likely to share the same culture than do people of different societies, and people who share the same culture are more likely to have the same experiences than are people with different cultures. Members of most unified groups share the same culture; but the question of what comes first — unity or shared culture — is less clear.

A national culture is a cultural system that has become coterminous with the borders of an independent geographical entity (or one whose members would like to be independent) which I have designated as a nation-state. It is necessary to emphasize the word state, for there can be no national culture without a state. Without a state or the goal of one a people becomes a mere ethnic group dispersed among other ethnic groups within nations. The Negroes of America share certain racial characteristics with Africans, and Jews of the Diaspora share certain cultural characteristics with Israelis, but both the Africans and the Israelis have built or are building supreme loyalty groups whose cultural systems are different from those to which Negroes and Jews give their supreme loyalty. People who live outside the nation-state may share the national culture, but if they live for a long time beyond its frontiers and if they take part in different national processes, they become part of different nation-states.

A completely standardized national culture does not exist, but some nations are further along than others toward standardization. For some nations it is a conscious goal, the attainment of some aspects of which determines the survival of the nation-state as presently constituted. The dominance of one material and spiritual culture over a politically defined area means that a majority accepts particular norms for behavior, symbols, and traditions; cultural differences continue to exist but they are small and shared by just a few people. Those groups that have a strikingly different culture must be small if they do not or will not change, for otherwise the political unity of the state would be considered as threatened. People who possess the standards or who regard certain norms, symbols, and traditions as the standards for the nation-state must have political power in the country. Leaders like Napoleon and Stalin were born into cultural traditions that were not the same as the developing national culture, but this did not prevent them from adopting and furthering the development of the national culture rather than their own regional cultures.

A completely distinctive national culture does not exist either. Nation-states share languages, religions, and some of the same customs. But there is something other than different governments and inhabitation of different territories which distinguishes nations. Distinctiveness of the developing standard national culture must be recognized as such by the people and by other nations. In part this is accomplished by the writer and artist.

Shared distinctive culture does not mean that political unity will continue or that people will necessarily live in peace forever. Internal strife is possible in any nation just as the threat of disorder is present for every nation. An attempt to reach a goal of national culture will be one factor that will contribute to national unity, but it will not guarantee it.

Development of a national culture is probably easier between people who belong to pre-national cultural systems that are already similar. In Gabon most pre-national cultures are similar. It is not like in Guinea where there are four different zones — coastal, mountains, savanna, forest — with people varying as widely as the Fulani and the Kissi; nor is it like Nigeria with people as different as the Hausa/Fulani and the Ibo. Almost everyone in Gabon comes from the clearings of the same equatorial forest.

In the isolated small villages of the forest clearings the ways of living are quite similar and the social organization is the same. The agricultural cycle is almost the same and so is the diet. Plantains and manioc, which are the two major foods (plus fish), are grown practically everywhere, as are taro, sugar cane, some corn, peanuts, pineapples, and rice in the south where a few spots of savanna country dot the map. Coffee and cocoa have been introduced into practically every region, but most is grown in the north.

Houses used to be made of bark when the tribes were on the move, but now they are built of wattling. On the coast the houses are more likely to be made of split bamboo woven into walls. In Haut-Ogooué one sees an occasional Congolese-type house but most still look the same.

The simple tools are the same in the villages: iron hoes, axes made by blacksmiths, and machetes purchased from the Europeans.

North of the Ogooué the Fang calculate descent on the male line, as do the Mpongouè. South of the Ogooué the descent system is matrilineal. The other tribes of the Omyènè group calculate descent along the female line and south of the Ogooué the Omyènè descent system is generally also matrilineal. The bridewealth has been an important part of marriage although the Omyènè say that it is relatively unimportant for them.

Religious movements and ideas of the supernatural are similar. The Revival affected most Gabonese; missionaries have long noted that what they called fetishes made the rounds from one tribe to another. *Bwiti* on the coast is an organization to which all tribes belong. The Gabonese recognize the similarity among them: An Omyènè has written, for example, that the *evus* of the Fang is what the Omyènè call *ignemba* and that the society called *mwiri* is what the Fang call *ngil*. He also states that some Omyènè societies are also parallel and similar to Eshira organizations.[1] Louis Bigmann, Omyènè president of the Supreme Court, told me he believes that Gabonese have more of a standardized culture than they are aware. He is interested, for example, in dietary laws which he believes are similar for most tribes. These, he says, are signs of brotherhood, common origin, or some kind of historical alliance.

It is possible to extend comparisons of pre-national cultures in Gabon to musical instruments, foods, or ways of living. In spite of the similarity there are always certain differences that are significant — even small differences. In one Fang village, for example, a woman had just divorced her husband and left his village. She was a Bakwélé who had always lived on the Ivindo River. She said she could not stand living ten miles away from it among a people who did not particularly like the water.

Standardization of a New Culture

More than a century of French rule subjected the Gabonese of all groups to common experiences. Contact with the administrator, the businessman, and the missionary changed the lives of all and weakened the pre-national cultures. Africans in French-speaking territories had probably more contact with Frenchmen than those in the average British colony had with Englishmen; for every British administrator there were three Frenchmen.[2] Even if the official policy vacillated between that of assimilation or a desire to mold Frenchmen out of the Africans in a centralized system and that of association or a more decentralized system in which autonomous African development was recognized, the French national culture has become an eternal part of a developing Gabonese national culture. Educated Gabonese feel close ties with France even though they may not always agree with its policies in Gabon or elsewhere in the world. The administrator and military man made the African submit to a system of organization that often took little account of local realities. Africans were to work in ways and with tools and on projects that were completely

1 J. Ambouroué Avaro, "Le Bas-Ogowe au XIX siècle," unpublished thesis, Faculté des Lettres et Sciences Humaines de l'Université de Paris, May 1964, pp. 40–43.

2 Raymond Leslie Buell, The Native Problem in Africa (New York, Macmillan, 1928), Vol. I, p. 983.

foreign. Most important is that the administration organized a territorial and geographical Gabon through which people were supposed to have loyalty to France, a foreign territorial and geographical entity. The idea of a country that demands loyalty was new for most Gabonese whose loyalties were based on kinship.

The administrator built urban centers, reorganized villages, named chiefs, judged litigation. Above all he represented the power of the French government and in principle had control over the activities of the other Whites from whom the Africans learned the ways of white folks.

Missionaries attacked African views of the supernatural and today claim to have converted more than half of the population to Christianity. Protestants say there are about 20,000 Gabonese in their Church. The missionaries, like the administrators and businessmen, said they were convinced that the African way of life was inferior to the European way of life. The Africans might have been able to resist had they been Muslims with a rigid system of beliefs, but they were flexible and, according to what the missionaries believed, became convinced of the superiority of the White and his culture. One missionary claimed he had been so successful in his condemnation of African religious practices that an African came to him and supposedly said: "I am a savage and all the Nkomi are savages; the Whites have come and shown us the right ways. The past is finished; I no longer want to live in the forest. All my children will learn the ways of the missionaries. In a few days I shall bring two man children and a woman child; our Whites will wash them with water from a little glass and my children will keep their skin like ebony, but their hearts will be white as milk."[3]

Roman Catholic missionaries in their flowing white cassocks and their beards were often impressive figures who, often with very modest resources, built large establishments that resembled fortresses in spirit if not in physical appearance. They considered these establishments as centers for the diffusion of new beliefs and customs. Outside the area of the lower Ogooué the Roman Catholics controlled all primary schools until the 1930's. In 1963 almost 33,000 children were in primary schools run by Roman Catholic

[3] Eugène Le Garrec, *Au Fernan Vaz: la rencontre de deux civilisations* (Abbeville, C. Paillart, 1896), p. 58.

and Protestant missions, compared with 28,500 in government primary schools.[4]

One of the Gabonese customs which missionaries did not understand and combated was the matrilineal descent system. They preached against it among the Nkomi people as being "unnatural" and "un-Christian"; it was called an "anomaly against which we must fight. It has in a way broken all the liaison that nature has established between a father and his children; they do not seem to exist in relation to each other. The child does not have the name of his father, he does not belong to his family, he has no right to his heritage. . . . Unfortunate Nkomi!"[5]

Although most missionaries learned African languages, they did most of their teaching in French. A decree, mainly to discourage American missionaries, indicated that "no teacher will be able to practice in the establishments if he is not a French subject and if he does not speak French and the dialect of the region where he works. . . ."[6] In fact, the emphasis was soon put on the French language exclusively, and much attention was given to the study of French history. Justification for French was that, the administration said, there were so many different languages (or dialects as they were called) that one language was needed as a lingua franca and also that African languages were poor in vocabulary and too simple in structure to be used in commerce and in the development of the country. (This is still the view of many Europeans, and even some Africans claim to believe the same thing.) After World War I and in the early 1920's the use of African languages in the schools was forbidden. Gabon had the highest rate of primary-school registration in A.E.F., but a decree of 28 December 1920 indicated that children over fourteen could not attend school. Today with an 80-per cent rate of scholarization and a principle of universal free primary education almost everyone under the age of thirty seems to speak French. Official data indicate that 46.8 per cent of all Gabonese over fifteen can at least speak French and 12.3 per cent of all Gabonese can read and write French.[7]

4 *Patrie Gabonaise*, 15 November 1963.

5 Le Garrec, ftn. 3, p. 37.

6 Article 2 of Decree, 19 October 1917, cited in Gouvernement Général de l'Afrique Equatoriale Française, "Histoire et organisation générale de l'enseignement en AEF" (Paris, Agence économique de l'AEF, 1931), p. 9.

7 Service National de la Statistique, "Rapport annuel sur la situation économique,

The businessman contributed to the standardization of culture and the introduction of French civilization through the goods he sold and the ways in which he undermined local production. Africans who turned from subsistence agriculture to industrial crops and Africans who had been recruited to work far from home were obliged to purchase canned foods to supplement their diet. On the shelf next to the canned sardines was the cheap Algerian wine. Africans were discouraged from making their own tools, cloth, and household goods by the scorn heaped on them. How often the African has heard: "You made that paint? How crude, uncivilized, ugly! Buy some paint from the shop." It is also true that purchasing something made out of plastic was more convenient than making it out of wood oneself.

The combination of contacts and submission to the White led to a great urge to accept French national culture in Gabon as in many other parts of the French empire. This urge to be French has been most apparent in the Nationalizing Zone where the French were concentrated and where churches, schools, businesses, and the administration were located. One section of Libreville called Glass is also called *Akawun' Amenga* or "where we change customs after the fashion of the Whites."[8] The Omyéné administrators led in the early 1920's by Laurent Anchouey called for more education, appealed to the great people of France for greater integration of the colonies with France to bring true French civilization to Gabon and to protect Africans against colonial administrators. Anchouey, who knew of Marcus Garvey, rejected the idea of an independent Africa under his leadership or in league with the Communists: "Frenchmen of France — we appeal to you; answer us! . . . France of our missionaries, France of our benefactors, great and noble nation, have you ceased to personify justice and humanity?"[9] Thirty years later another Gabonese intellectual elite, the Gabonese students in France, wrote: "France, the heart and brain of western civilization" and "Gabonese civilization up until now is an illusion or, more precisely, a very distant

---

financière, et sociale de la République Gabonaise — Fin 1963," Libreville, July 1964, p. 174.

[8] A. Raponda-Walker, "Toponymie de l'estuaire du Gabon et de ses environs," *Bulletin de l'Institut de Recherches Scientifiques au Congo,* Tome 2, 1962, p. 97.

[9] *L'Echo Gabonais,* No. 1, July 1922.

hope."[10] This attitude is shared today by many Gabonese who desire their own assimilation into French culture. In an informal survey taken by a teacher of English in one of the secondary schools (where to learn English one studies such topics as the Anglo-Saxon conquest, the Christianization of the Anglo-Saxons, a translation of a selection from Shakespeare, etc.) found that 80 per cent of the students thought that of all their courses the study of the French language would be particularly important later in life. Gabonese schoolchildren are no longer supposed to learn that their ancestors were the Gauls, but the organization of schools and the subjects studied are about the same as in France.

Gabonese organizations have until the present emphasized the French way of doing things. For example, the *Organisation Nationale des Femmes Gabonaises* sponsors social centers where French ideas of hygiene, sewing, and new cooking techniques are taught to women. In their publication, *Femmes Gabonaises,* women are told that they should take their meals with their husbands, that they should make their babies sleep alone in a bed, and that family means "father, mother, children." New Year's Day dinner is suggested, the latest French fashions are shown, and directions are given concerning preparations for the birth of a child, preparations for a marriage — as if Gabonese customs in these matters were nonexistent or completely invalid. Gabon's intellectual elite has been trained in France, and there have been no signs that this will soon change. Some of this elite change their names to European-type names; for example, one may observe a change from the Fang Mèyè to Meyer.

The French thus encouraged standardization of a culture in Gabon by introducing their own culture or a colonial version of it, particularly in urban areas and industrial enterprises which the European built and to which the African moved in great numbers. In addition, they encouraged the development of regional elites. They favored certain peoples over others for positions and promoted the spread of their languages. It may very well be that the peoples they favored were already in an advantageous position compared with the other tribes in the area, but the White contributed to their cultural predominance and elite status. The White needed Africans to work for him and often preferred to

10 *Jeunesse Gabonaise*, No. 1, December 1953.

bring in workers from different regions because it was believed they would work better far from their families. He used the Africans with whom he had been in contact the longest time, the Senegalese, for example. Then, he used the coastal peoples to investigate the interior and, once in the interior, the members of the tribe in a given place which cooperated best would be given prestigious positions.

In the Haut-Ogooué the concessionary company S.H.O. (Société du Haut-Ogooué) favored the Mindoumou: "We have already said and we repeat it again: the Mindoumou workers are docile, excellent . . . and relatively intelligent. We can get a lot out of them. The Bavoumbou, Akanigui, and the Obamba have about the same qualities but are certainly less intelligent and more lazy."[11] In 1913, the year this was written, the company had as African traders four Mindoumou of the Franceville area, two Fang they had recruited in Lambaréné, and a Loango who had come from Libreville. Even today the Mindoumou have a great deal of prestige in the region although they are a tiny group without a real Heartland. Most Africans around Franceville speak Mindoumou.

The missionaries who took charge began with African languages in their schools and in their catechism work. The early American arrivals worked among some of the numerically most insignificant people such as the Benga and the Bakwélé. These people were on the coast, and the missionaries really had no idea how many there were. They learned their languages along with Omyènè and published small books and brochures. A Presbyterian missionary, Mr. Nassau who worked from 1860 to 1906 in Gabon, translated the Gospels into Benga (the Presbyterians took over the work from the interdenominational A.B.C.F.M. of Boston in 1870). The A.B.C.F.M. had a printing press at their Baraka station on the edge of what is now Libreville in 1844.

The Protestants began printing prayers, language books, the Gospels, and stories in Mpongouè and in English. The first year of operation they published 2,000 brochures and the next year 8,000 brochures of eight different titles. (One suspects that many were shipped out of the country.) They chose Mpongouè as the

---

[11] "Rapport général sur la Société du Haut-Ogooué pour l'année 1913," Colonie du Gabon, Franceville, 30 November 1913, Section X, *Main d'œuvre*.

language for their work because they thought it must be spoken from the estuary to the River Congo. It was not until 1881 that they published something in Fang.[12]

The earliest publication by the French Roman Catholics I have found was a catechism in Mpongouè published in 1847. All the early publications by the Fathers of the Congrégation du Saint-Esprit were in Mpongouè, and the first Fang catechism appeared late in 1891. But after 1900 over half the publications in Gabonese languages were in Fang.[13]

Missionaries had limited funds, and they did not learn every language. Smaller groups would have to learn the languages of the larger and more important tribes if they did not know them already. Interior tribes would be served by catechists from the coast or from tribes that aleady had a number of converts. For example, in the Ogooué-Ivindo region the Fathers taught the Okandé tribe their catechism in their own language, but this is a small tribe and the missionaries found that reliable Okandé catechists could not be found and that Okandé were decreasing in numbers anyway. Fang catechists were then named and taught the Okandé catechism in Fang; they still do. The Bakwélé who live along the Ivindo River used to be taught a Bakwélé catechism, but the Fathers decided to standardize the catechisms in the area and chose Fang as the standard.

In Haut-Ogooué the missionaries, like the businessmen and administrators, were attracted to the Mindoumou who had clustered around the mission and in whose territory the mission was located. They thus started with Mindoumou catechisms, and representatives from this very small tribe went out to teach others. Today Ambamba is also used, for the Ambamba are the most important numerically, but most people can now speak Mindoumou. Around Mbigou the Boumouéllé who have been assimilated to the Bandjabi in administrative records are taught their catechism and prayers in Bandjabi.

This type of regional standardization was far less important than the introduction of the French language of other cultural or

12 Excerpts from "Missionary Herald Reports 1844–1870" (Boston, Library of the United Church Board for World Ministries, Reports for 1844), pp. 82, 88.

13 Secrétariat général, Congrégation du Saint-Esprit et du Saint Cœur de Marie, "Bibliographie," Paris, 1930, pp. 17–21.

economic ties with Europe, of Christianity, or of the experiences Africans shared in a colonial situation. The confidence the French colonialists had in their national culture plus the apparent lack of confidence the Africans had in their own culture seemed to mean that the Gabonese would become black Frenchmen. But some changes, such as for example the apparent adoption of a patrilineal descent system, are deceiving. I have met important men who have taken their sisters' children into their own homes and have more or less adopted them in order that they could inherit the property of their maternal uncle. (That a man inherits his maternal uncle's property is an important characteristic of the matrilineal system.) It is impossible to forget the past, and every nation must have its own distinctive culture. Some Gabonese have begun to realize this and write about it; most often such Gabonese have been Fang or Omyènè.

Distinctiveness of a New Culture

A Fang who later became a high-ranking civil servant wrote in 1958 that it would be incorrect to adopt French civilization completely because pre-national cultures link the Africans and possess their own wisdom. He writes that some bad customs must be forgotten but others can be adapted to the modern world so that a developing Gabonese culture would become a combination of what is judged useful from French civilization and what is still valid from pre-national cultures. He terminates his discussion by warning that an attempt to adopt either French culture or pre-national cultures in toto would lead to the "disappearance of the Gabonese soul."[14]

An essay contest was held in 1960 on the meaning of a Franco-African community; a Fang *lycéen*, who won the contest, wrote: "A strong civilization is not a slavish imitation; it is a solid construction of its own values along with elements offered by the civilizations with which it lives."[15] If aspects of African culture that do not prevent modernization or technical progress nor pre-

---

[14] Jules Mbah, "Coutumes gabonaises et civilisation française," unpublished mémoire (Paris, Institut des Hautes Etudes d'Outre-Mer, 1958–1959), p. 36.
[15] Mba Ndong, "Un devoir d'élève," *Réalités Gabonaises*, January-February 1960.

vent man from leading a good life in a new order are to be kept, the question is: What aspects of whose culture?

The most important pre-national culture in Gabon, in the sense that it contributed to some cultural unity and gave a developing national culture a certain distinctiveness, was that of the Omyènè. Their language was the lingua franca of the Ogooué River because they controlled trade with the coast and were the intermediaries between the White and the other Africans. An administrator noted that some Omyènè was used all the way down the Gabonese coast to Mayumba, a slave port. The leading Gabonese intellectual during the twentieth century is Monsignor André Raponda-Walker who has frequently written about the customs and history of all the Gabonese, but he has concentrated on his own group, the Omyènè and more specifically the Mpongouè. His well-known *Notes d'Histoire du Gabon* is primarily about the Mpongouè and other Omyènè. The image one used to have of a distinctive Gabonese culture was most often Omyènè. This, however, is changing, it appears.

As the Fang got closer to the coast, they began to adopt Omyènè dress, learned the Omyènè language, built houses like the Omyènè, that is, like the Mpongouè of Libreville, the Galoa of Lambaréné, the Oroungou of Port-Gentil. An Omyènè scholar has written not without irony: "If the Galoa 'aped' the European, the Fang admired the Galoa and copied his ways, including his vices. The colonizer who had so much hope for these new peoples was therefore disappointed."[16]

When the Fang sensed the disorder and the weakening of their pre-national systems and turned to various methods of reorganization, one of the methods by which they tried to re-establish order was an assertion of Fang cultural values. These values had been "threatened" by contact with the Omyènè, Mitsogo, for example, and the White, but the attempt to rejuvenate the customs took place within a Gabonese framework and has contributed to the distinctive Gabonese national culture. This it has done in five ways: First, the Fang are interested in the revitalization of an African culture; second, they have a deep pride in their own culture; third, they have intellectuals with a command of French who

---

16 Ambouroué Avaro, ftn. 1, p. 108.

can communicate about the Fang to the outside world; fourth, Fang dynamism has resulted in a certain Fang control over media of communication; fifth, they have an openness of spirit about themselves that has encouraged social scientists and Africanists to write about them.

Just outside of Oyem in the Fang Heartland lives Chief Mendame Ndong, son of a clan chief and deputy in the Gabonese legislative assembly from 1947 to 1961. The Germans took control of Woleu-Ntem in 1911 after an agreement with the French, and in the same year they sent Ndong to their school for sons of chiefs in Berlin; he studied in the German capital from 1912 to 1919, at which time he returned to Gabon. In 1947 he participated in the Fang Congress of Mitzic and claims he is trying to preserve Fang culture: "The Fang used to be united with one set of customs, but the people became dispersed and the customs have changed in different places. The idea of the Fang Congress in the minds of those who attended was a standardization of Fang custom and an attempt to re-establish some kind of Fang unity. Now we are forgetting our art and our customs; I must remind my people of them." He was opposed to new forms of organization for the Fang: "The false Fang dance *Bwiti; Bwiti* is a corruption of Fang customs." Ndong was to be named a counsellor to the President on questions of Fang custom, and a decree to that effect was drawn up, but other events have prevented the realization of this project.

In a report on the origins of the Fang and their real customs, he describes how the descendants of Afrikara were dispersed: "After Daamboga the Fang spread out in three directions: Cameroun, Gabon, Guinea. In spite of their involuntary dispersion, the Fang of these three areas have always guarded an ideal of their true custom. You will find below all the customs of the Fang."[17]

At the 1947 Congress, Fang leaders like Ndong called upon the administration and the elected officials in the Gabonese territory to protect what they considered to be the true Fang custom by laws and regulations made by the state. For example, they wanted the administration to fix the bridewealth at two thousand francs, to fix the fine for adultery at five hundred francs, to forbid the

17 Mendame Ndong, *Origine et vraie coutume fang* (Oyem, 1962).

sale of *iboga,* a drug used by members of *Bwiti,* and to modify the decree which abolished the levirate, in accordance with Fang customs.[18] ". . . the text of 14 July 1938 abolishing the levirate [is to] be altered in the following way: The widow [who remarries] is free to divorce but on condition that she reimburse the bride-wealth . . . the children of a divorced family are given back [to the family of the father] after the age of ten without obligation or indemnization of the woman's family for the care of the children . . . the obligation for the family of the deceased wife to reimburse the bridewealth or any part of it [is to] be suppressed."

In 1962 the government organized a contest to gather as many collections of stories and explanations of tribal customs as possible. Everywhere in the Woleu-Ntem region one found that people had written summaries of the "true" Fang custom and collections of Fang sayings and proverbs. At Mitzic Moïse Nkogho-Mvé, then director of a government school in a regrouped village and now a writer in the capital, wrote an "Abrégé des coutumes Fang." He was particularly concerned about the corruption of the idea of the bridewealth. At Bitam M. Ekogha Mengue, a man who has served for many years in the civil service, wrote several essays about the Fang. In "Histoire, institutions sociales et agricoles d'un groupe éthnique du pays — amélioration" he describes the true rites of the Fang: *bieri* for example. He concludes: "the Fang's central value, his only concern, is love for his own people."

Fang outside Woleu-Ntem were less interested in the "true customs" and wrote historical sketches. Southern peoples sent in collections of fables; the Omyènè did not appear to be interested in the contest, which was eventually won by a Fang who wrote on Fang customs. The newspaper published in Woleu-Ntem, *Actualités culturelles au Woleu-Ntem,* indicated many of the same concerns about Fang culture.

The traditional way to maintain the records of Fang history and Fang culture has been through oral literature. The archives exist in the head of the man who plays the *mvet,* a stringed musical instrument which is now found in most regions of the country.

18 Sources for the wishes: "Le Congrès Fang réuni le 26, le 27, et le 28 février 1947 à Mitzic émet les voeux suivants," unpublished transcript. The version published by the colonial administration was called the *"Congrès pahouin,"* Brazzaville, 1947. In addition to several resolutions on Fang customs the delegates, most of whom were chiefs of cantons, called for an amelioration of the position of chief.

It is used in a special way by the Fang. Most of the old *mvet* players are dead but there are some young Fang who have concerned themselves with the preservation of the traditions of the *mvet*. The man who was most directly concerned with the preservation of this literature, Philippe Ndong, had an important place in the Ministry of Education and represented Gabon at UNESCO. He was in charge of a magazine called *Realités Gabonaises* which was published for teachers of the country. This periodical represented Gabon to the outside world. Founded as a cultural review in 1959 when the A.E.F. review, *Liaison,* ceased publication, it has been published irregularly.

Réalités Gabonaises was divided into four parts: "Pages Africaines," with articles on Fang customs except for frequent articles by Monsignor Raponda-Walker on the Omyènè or other Gabonese; "Variétés" or Fang fables; "Vie de l'enseignement," written by local French teachers about the structure of education with considerable attention to what was going on in Woleu-Ntem; and lastly "Pages pédagogiques" which offered advice to teachers. Several articles about the *mvet* appeared in the review; these were written by Philippe Ndong. Cultural clubs have been promoted in all regions to preserve certain aspects of pre-national cultures. In June 1965 a review to take the place of *Réalités* was started to report on the activities of the cultural societies. It is called *l'Animateur culturel Gabonais* and is directed by three Fang, including one who had formerly published a small periodical in Woleu-Ntem.

Most examples of traditional cultures seen by the visitor to Libreville or to French museums are Fang. In 1962 the French government research institute, O.R.S.T.O.M. (Office de la Recherche Scientifique et Technique Outre-Mer), arranged an exhibit of Fang cultural objects in Libreville and had Fang music performed. Fang art also had a place in the exhibition of African art at the 1966 Festival Mondial des Arts Nègres; according to the descriptive labels on the objects, certain Fang masks influenced the work of Picasso and others.

The Gabonese radio has produced a series of broadcasts for the purpose of adult education, and the fables and proverbs used have been most usually Fang. The use of Fang has increased. Since the attempted coup d'état in February 1964, President Mba has begun to speak over the national radio in Fang, and the Vice President in Bapounou, in order to make sure that people understood them. Prior to that, broadcasts in national languages were unheard of, although in some other African states national languages are used for broadcasts and in public speeches. One also hears occasionally, more in 1966 than in 1962, a teacher say that a Fang student asked for permission to do his classwork and write out his examinations in the Fang language. The President said in 1962 he hoped French would become the maternal language of all Gabonese, but this is more and more unlikely.

The image of Gabon is partly a Fang image because of the Fang openness of spirit. As a group that does not regard itself as an exclusive caste, they will accept any Africans into the tribe who speak their language. Also, they have been willing to open their society to study by European and African social scientists; in fact they have encouraged this. Before World War I Professor Günter Tessmann from Lübeck published a comprehensive study on the Fang, *Die Pangwe*; forty years later Professor Georges Balandier wrote his important book, *Sociologie actuelle de l'Afrique Noire,* about the Fang and the Bacongo; and in America Dr. James Fernandez has more recently written about the Fang in *The Elder Brother's Forest.* Most Spanish writing about the peoples of Rio Muni has been about the Fang, or Pamué, as they call them. Today a collection of Gabonese music is being made, and this music will be primarily Fang and Omyènè.

Standardization of culture is occurring largely because Gabon was ruled by Frenchmen, not all of whom, it is true, were very good representatives of French culture, and because Gabon was brought into the mainstream of the processes of industrialization and urbanization during the colonial period. The Fang who sensed the threat of disorder to their own system have contributed to a growing distinctiveness to Gabonese national culture in their attempts to reorganize and advance materially. In contributing aspects of their own culture to the developing national culture they are also contributing the cultures they have absorbed from other Gabonese, like the Omyènè.

The Fang are, however, ambivalent toward their traditional culture — particularly those who live in the Nationalizing Zone. They are not sure whether to accept all of French culture or to reject some parts. The Fang of the Heartland are less unsure about this question and have more confidence in the value of their customs if they are rejuvenated. It is the rejuvenation of African cultures and their adaptation to the exigencies of industrialization and urbanization that is difficult. Even French-speaking societies which call themselves revolutionary remain culturally very close to France and hesitate to innovate in this area. Innovation requires self-confidence, and this is something Fang have more than their neighbors.

CHAPTER 6

A Developing National History

National History

Every nation must have its national history, just as it must have a standard and distinctive culture. Every people building a nation must find its national history. Those who discover the history find the racial, religious, or tribal factors that link all members of this community of order and which determine that the community should, by the logical course of history, become an independent nation-state.

A national history must explain the origins of what is called the nation: How did the national process start, from what peoples and from what territories? Who were the heroes of the nation and how did they suffer? Who were the enemies of the nation and how were they combatted?

A national history must explain why the nation developed: The nation is unique, it has been chosen by God, the Fates, or Spirits of the Universe to do something that no other nation could do. It thus has goals and purpose for existing; the nation in its form of nation has a special destiny and a special grandeur.

National history shows that nothing is fortuitous: This nation was always meant to be, all historical forces naturally and logically culminated in the start of the national process, and what it does it must do because of these same forces of history. Lastly, a national history must be written by a member of the nation, because it is found in the soul of the nation and no foreigner can know this soul.

Pre-national or tribal history is Genesis. It starts with God, the story of the creation, how peoples were divided, and why they live where they do. It explains in Contact Zones and in Nationalizing Zones why they live alongside certain other people and why the latter are enemies or friends.

The Bawandji of the district of Moanda live near the Bandjabi, Badouma, and Batsangui peoples, all of whom are considered to be their relatives. They learn their genealogies: Their common ancestor is called Dzabi or Nzabi. Dzabi had seven sons, one of whom was called Mvouka; he too had seven sons, each of whom became the father of a clan. One of these founded the Moanda clan, whose members were separated by wars; their ways of speaking changed, and they met members of other clans who were also descendants of Dzabi. Members from these different clans began to live together in four different areas; eventually four different tribes evolved: Bawandji, Bandjabi, Badouma, and Batsangui. The members of these tribes consider themselves related because of common descent explained by history and by the fact that members of different tribes belong to the same clans.

History explains and justifies the status quo: Why people hold power and others do not, why a certain category of people is considered inferior. It changes with the situation it is supposed to explain, and when history is oral as it is for the peoples of Gabon it changes more readily. It was changed by the coming of the White. If pre-national history were to explain everything in the present, it would have to explain why the White was so materially powerful, why the Black was materially weak. According to Père Trilles, a missionary who wrote extensively about the Fang, one Fang legend explained the division of the world into an apparently rich white part and an apparently poor black part on the basis of a supposed decision by God that Whites were superior.[1]

1 H. Trilles, "Proverbes, légendes et contes fang," extract from the *Bulletin de la société neuchâteloise de géographie*, Tome XVI, 1905, pp. 93–104.

When Whites began to write about Africa, they wrote colonial history which was really part of European history; the Whites did not believe the Africans had any history before their arrival, because in Gabon African history was not written. (It is true that a study on Mpongoué history was published by Monsignor Raponda-Walker, but this is out of print and is either unknown or mistrusted by many non-Omyènè.) In other countries histories that integrate the prehistoric, the pre-colonial, colonial, and independent periods have been written. Father Mveng's history of Cameroun is an example of this,[2] and Professor Hubert Deschamps of the Sorbonne has been writing an integrated history of Gabon.

National history will be influenced by the nature of tribal history; it may for example explain how all the tribes within the political frontiers of the modern nation-state were descended from the same ancestor. Second, it will explain how the tribes were dispersed and how languages became different. Third, it must relate how the tribes came together or how they must come together again. Fourth, it must explain the coming of the White and what the colonial situation was all about. The legend of God dividing the earth into two parts and the success of the White in winning the richer part because of his so-called superiority will not be acceptable, because it is false and because any national history must tell the nation's people that they are not inferior.

Such a history must be standardized for the whole country just like the national culture. It must not exclude important groups or imply that some peoples are better than others. It must be distinctive and not a part of European history; it must be different from histories of other countries. It means that the national history must show that the people of the nation-state share a past of experiences different from those of other peoples, and that this past helps to indicate what the goals for future development must be. Knowledge of the past thus helps in the process of national consolidation but, like all other separate forces, it is no guarantee of it.

Standardization of a New History

Oral histories reflect attitudes toward other peoples in Heartlands, Contact Zones, and Nationalizing Zones and are thus a way

2 Engelbert P. Mveng, *Histoire du Cameroun* (Paris, Présence Africaine, 1963). E. P. Mveng is, by the way, Bulu.

to observe or estimate trends in assimilation. Assimilation of one tribe by another means that the first is forgetting its own separate history. Assimilation as part of a process of standardization means a denial of the importance of some particularistic tribal histories.

The Séké chief of the village of Dakar in the Nationalizing Zone was able to recount the history of the village, but when his visitor asked who was the first Séké or who were the ancestors of the Séké, Chief Bomé looked shocked: "I am not *that* old! Our ancestors lived a long time ago, and no one remembers who they were."

The Bississiou, like other small tribes, are disappearing, and they increasingly accept the history of people around them. They appear to be really part of the widely dispersed Bakèlè tribe which has no Heartland. There are now less than one hundred Bississiou, and they are counted with the Ambamba in the census; those who live among the Badouma at Lastoursville are considered Badouma. Near Boundji Falls in the district of Lastoursville Bississiou live with some Ambamba and Bakota people.

The oldest living Bississiou is M. Tembo. He claims that the Bississiou were the first to live here and that the Ambamba and Bakota came later. The Bississiou have always lived with the Ambamba, he said; they speak the same language. He claimed he knew the history of the Ambamba better than that of the Bississiou and began to tell it; then he interrupted himself to say he had known Pierre Savorgnan de Brazza and other French explorers and could tell me more about them than about the Ambamba.

Some African writers have used the explorers and colonial officials to prove that historically certain ethnic groups were once united. Because according to this view the divisions are superficial and imposed, unity should not be difficult.

In a study of the Baluba and Lulua of Congo, a Congolese blamed the Belgians for dividing the two peoples and for creating antagonisms that led to open violence at the time of independence. He traces the origins of the Baluba people up to the time when the Lulua became separated from them by migration. At the end of the nineteenth century they began to call themselves Lulua but still considered the Baluba their brothers. The Belgians came and set up a separate Lulua king, regrouped villages strictly according to Lulua or Baluba lines, and created antagonisms between the two groups by favoring the Lulua, he wrote. The divisions deepened until brother turned against brother.[3]

In Gabon the Badouma say that the Bawandji are really Badouma who live far from the River Ogooué. When the White came he asked who the people were and was told "those who live near the river," or Badouma, and "those who live far from the river," or Bawandji. He took the two words as meaning separate tribes. Thus he contributed toward the division of these peoples, according to the view of many Badouma.

The peoples of Gabon shared much of the same colonial history. Many of their memories are identical. Their lives were greatly influenced by the actions of colonial administrators, and pre-independence colonial history is defined by the names of the administrators and certain events associated with the French administration. For example, census takers refer to administrators' names when determining years of birth. In the district of Libreville the following (partially reproduced) "calendar of historic events" is used by the Service de Statistique in census-taking:

Event	Local Language	Date
Halley's Comet	Mekoheakoneu	1911
Great War	Alouma en 1914	1914
M. Louvel, Head of District	Louvelé Nguema	1923–1925
The Great Famine	Mbou Nzé	1925
M. Vuillaume, District Head		1930
Construction of the road to Kango	Ongoure ekoume	1932–1935
M. Pelieu, District Head		1936
Léon Mba, Prime Minister		1957

Since independence Gabonese, particularly those in the Nationalizing Zone, have shared two important experiences: the expulsion of citizens from the neighboring Republic of Congo and

[3] Mabika Kalanda, "Baluba et Lulua: une ethnie à la recherche d'un nouvel équilibre," in *Collection Etudes Congolaises*, No. 2, 1959, pp. 68ff.

the violence that accompanied it, and the attempted coup d'état and the arrival of French-controlled paratroopers to restore the President to his position. They have lived through elections, the beginnings of industrialization, attempts to organize a single party, the suppression of civil liberties, and growing concern about the nature of independence and the place of Gabon in the world.

Distinctiveness of a New History

At the end of 1963 a Gabonese Prehistoric and Protohistoric Society was set up. Members of this society have discovered potsherds, tools, and stone weapons that indicate the presence of people in the estuary in prehistoric times.[4] Such discoveries will serve as part of a distinctive history for Gabon. Fang history may also serve to give distinctiveness to Gabonese national history.

The Fang recall their history better than other Gabonese, and they are proud to tell it; the fact that they have a written history in the Fang language gives them added confidence. The story of the migration of the children of Afrikara was written in the 1930's at the time when the Fang were attempting to reorganize their tribe along clan lines and escape the threat of disorder. It was originally written by a Bulu and published at the American Presbyterian press near Ebolowa in southern Cameroun.[5]

It was first accepted by the Fang Ntoumou in northern Woleu-Ntem and then spread south and east in Ogooué-Ivindo. Fang who come to Libreville from the Heartland Zone carry the history of the Fang with them. I met a Bulu from southern Cameroun who was working as an agricultural agent at Lastoursville far from Fang country; he had the history which he had brought from home and showed it to other Fang civil servants.

When Edouard Trezenem wrote his reports to the Governor of Gabon about *alar ayong*, the attempt to regroup the clans, he blamed this history as a basis for the regroupment movement: "With the aid of documents collected by the first observers of the Fang the American missionaries may have taught their Fang students the history of the Fang nation. . . . Once returned to the

---

4 *Gabon d'Aujourd'hui*, 23 January 1965, and B. Farine, "Sites préhistoriques gabonais" (Libreville, Ministère de l'Information, 1963).
5 Ondoua Engute, *Dulu bon be Afri Kara* (Elat, Ebolowa, Cameroun, Mission Presbytérienne, 1948, 1954, and 1956).

village, the interested students incited their parents to rebuild the traditional organization."[6] Fang students today use this history when they write about Fang or Gabonese history. A student at one French institute in Paris wrote a history of the Fang which he says was quoted at the meetings held during the regroupment movement: "In order to show that all the Blacks had come from a single ancestor, the elders and tellers of stories went back in history during the meetings from generation to generation to a man called Hamata."[7]

Hamata is portrayed as the father of all mankind. In the sixth generation after Hamata, Afrikara was born; as his name implies he is the father of all Africans. Afrikara had several wives, and the children of the different wives could not understand each other because their father had prepared a special "fetish." Afrikara's youngest wife was called Nangô'ô II, and she had borne seven children: Fang-Afiri, Ok'Afiri, Mevu-Mafiri, Nden-Afiri, Bul'Afiri, Ngue-Afiri (a daughter), and Ntum-Afiri.

One day the family of Afrikara was attacked by the people called redskins — who might have been Arabs, the author suggests. Some people allied themselves with the invaders, but they feared that one day the sons of Afrikara would seek revenge and dig a protective ditch between them. This ditch linked two oceans, and the water flowed over the banks to threaten the village of Afrikara. The whole family fled from this place, and they ran so fast that they left everything behind — their tools, weapons, food, seed, and domestic animals. Only the dog accompanied the villagers.

As they fled they broke up into different groups. The seven children of Nangô'ô II moved toward what is now Gabon, Cameroun, and Rio Muni and became the ancestors of the Fang-Bulu-Betsi groups: The descendants of Fang-Afiri live in the estuary, along the coast, around Lambaréné and in Ogooué-Ivindo, the history indicates; the descendants of Ok'Afiri live in Rio Muni along with the children of Mevu-Mafiri who eventually disappeared, as did the children of Nden-Afiri. The southern Camerounese Bulu are the descendants of Bul'Afiri; the children of Ngue-Afiri live in

---

[6] E. Trezenem, "Rapport à Monsieur le Gouverneur," 29 March 1948.
[7] Mvone-Obiang Thomas, "Les Fang (des origines à nos jours)," unpublished mémoire (Paris, Institut des Hautes Etudes d'Outre-Mer, 1958–1959).

the same region and are called the Ewondo. The youngest child was Ntum-Afiri and became the father of the Fang who live in northern Woleu-Ntem; his first daughter married a son of Fang-Afiri (the father of the coastal Fang), and the son of this union became the ancestor of the Fang who live in the northeastern part of Woleu-Ntem. Thus was the Fang people born.

This pre-national history links the Fang to all Africans and to Egypt where there were domesticated animals, tools, and farms. They had to leave Egypt in a great hurry; what could they do but leave these things behind? This is the Fang answer to the European accusation that Africans have never invented anything and never knew how to cultivate crops before the coming of the European. This history shows how all Fang are related even though they may live in different places and have somewhat different accents. Other Gabonese believe that they originally came from Egypt. Louis Bigmann, a leader among the Omyènè and currently president of the Supreme Court, believes that all Gabonese were once one group in Egypt,[8] and a Bapounou leader has stated he believes all Gabonese to come from the Nile Valley. In one of his famous books, Cheikh Anta Diop traces the dispersion of the peoples of Africa from the upper Nile Valley toward Egypt and Black Africa. The only Gabonese group discussed by him is the Fang who are shown on a map moving from the Nile to what is today the region of southern Cameroun, Rio Muni, and Gabon.[9]

Père Trilles, who worked for several years in Gabon, states that the Fang had connections with the Nile; this was used as a source by Cheikh Anta Diop. Trilles also wrote that the Fang were related to several other peoples in Gabon, such as the Batéké in the south. Because Fang legends are similar to those of other peoples in Congo, Trilles wrote, they must be all related.[10]

Since the Fang have a written history and since several peoples believe they came from the Nile Valley, Fang history might be an important basis for a general national history and thus provide some distinctive elements of such a history. There is proof that the Fang have used history to point out to their non-Fang neigh-

8 Louis E. Bigmann, personal communication.
9 Cheikh Anta Diop, *L'Afrique noire pré-coloniale* (Paris, Présence Africaine, 1960), p. 173.
10 H. Trilles, *Le totémisme chez les Fans* (Münster, Bibliothèque-Anthropos, 1912), pp. 16–18.

bors that the latter are really Fang. They tell the Makina in the Contact Zone they are really Fang, and during the regroupment movement they were reportedly telling the Bakota and Bakwélé they were relatives and proving it by history.

Trezenem adds to his study on the Fang regroupment movement that not only were the Fang trying to re-establish clan lines and eventually reorganize their whole tribe and ethnic group; they were also, according to him, trying to absorb other Gabonese. He claims to have information that Fang leaders had told people like the Bakota and the Okandé, who lived with them in a Contact Zone, that they were really sons of Fang who had left the fold. He was suspicious of all Gabonese leaders, and this might have influenced his report in which he credits one of them with an attempt to absorb the Bakota into the Fang. He reports the following interview with a Bakota chief:

– Do the Bakota listen to A?

– Now, yes, but before I wouldn't give a hut or food to the Pahouin because I did not know then that I am also a Pahouin of the Suke family.

– How do you know that now?

– A. has sent us the news that I myself and Etumbye and Moapa are in the same family as Andum Nze [cantonal chief at Makokou] and as the Mbue.

– I don't understand how it is that you Bakota and Mahongoué are also Pahouin.

– A long time ago we were all Pahouin and lived far from here. Men who were strong made war against us. We fled; some stopped at the Ivindo, and these are the Pahouin. My fathers and the fathers of Etumbye and the Mbue passed the river. They married the Bakota who were here, and now we are Bakota also. But before we were Pahouin.[11]

It is surprising that these Bakota would accept another identity so readily, but the clan Iseke of the Bakota tribe claims today it is related to the clan Esoke of the Fang.[12] Bigmann says that the Akara clan of the Omyènè is related to the Essamekes clan of the Fang.[13]

11 E. Trezenem, "Second Rapport," 25 September 1948.
12 Hubert Deschamps, *Traditions orales et archives au Gabon* (Paris, Berger-Levrault, 1962), p. 69.
13 *Jeunesse Gabonaise*, No. 2, January 1954.

That many Gabonese are really kin and perhaps really Fang might become part of Gabon's national history, but some people remain proud of their traditional histories and struggle against their assimilation. They do not want people to forget differences. A young Bakèlè writes: "I am no longer surprised, but I am disturbed to witness a spectacle as poignant as that of the slow absorption of a people. . . . I shall see it disappear without warning, without war and treaties."[14] People other than the Fang are also writing their histories, but they remain far more secretive about them as if knowledge of the history of a people could be used to harm it.

It is certain that the Fang pre-national history will contribute much to a standard and distinctive national history for Gabon because of the belief of many people in it, because of Fang dynamism, and because of the form in which the history is. More important is the fact that the Gabonese have been sharing experiences that become recent national history. The Fang in positions of power are the ones who make recent history. A growing system of beliefs based on current shared experiences will influence a view of the pre-national past and will be a factor in national consolidation.

14 Marc-Aurelieu Tonjokoué, "La famille — son aspect juridique chez les Bakèlè," unpublished Mémoire de stage (Paris, Institut des Hautes Études d'Outre-Mer, 1963), p. 30.

CHAPTER 7

A Developing National Belief System

National Belief Systems

People who are conscious of their common membership in a level of community share certain beliefs about the nature of the system, what it is doing, and what their relationship to it is. Not everyone has the same beliefs; some people who live within the system do not think about it and may even regard it as an outside threat to their supreme loyalty groups, which may be smaller or larger than the system.

Each system must ensure that most people agree with the standards and support them, to maintain internal order and to protect its external freedom. It therefore tries to inculcate some beliefs into the minds of the citizens and to get their support. In a nation-state they must be conscious of its existence and know their duties for its maintenance. Learning how to be a citizen is the process of political socialization or politicization. By using the mass media of communication and by school lessons, trips around the country to deliver speeches, and various other methods, an official belief system is promoted and policies are justified by it.

In some countries this belief system has been codified by the leaders and is called "Consciencism," or the "Philosophy of the Revolution." The government of the nation-state also wants to maintain its power and will try to promote certain beliefs that may or may not have something to do with the nation; the government has power, and because it may be fearful of losing it, it may try to prevent the expression of the nonofficial variable beliefs that may possibly express lack of confidence or opposition to it or to the government's leaders. Governmental control of means of communication will then mean that only an official belief system is given publicity — particularly in the Nationalizing Zone where the official means of communication are comparatively efficient. If those who hold different beliefs wish to express them, they must use unusual means of communication. Outside the Nationalizing Zone expression of different views might be easier, depending on what other means of control the government possesses. In spite of poor means of communication between Heartlands, nonofficial belief systems might be essentially identical. The greater the extent to which different peoples in different parts of a country sense the contradictions between the official and the nonofficial variable beliefs, the greater the danger of conflict between the leaders and the masses, and the greater the threat to national consolidation.

An African national belief system has most of the same functions as a belief system anywhere else; it must tell people who the Africans are in general, and who the Nigerians, Togolese, and Kenyans are in particular. The national belief system explains internal and external policies to the people within the nation and to the people without the nation. Why taxes, why expulsions, why conferences, why wars? It may be used to camouflage the real reasons for actions. It must also explain in Africa how the Africans were colonized, under what conditions, and by whom; what were the goals of those who colonized us? There must be an official version of the colonial situation; what was it like, how were we treated, what did the White do for us and take from us? The official belief system must explain each historical phase in the memory of the citizens: How and why did we become independent? Most important — the belief systems tell people what they must do now to maintain a meaningful national order. Within the national order citizens must know what their relationships with other citizens are, what the relationship between Blacks and Whites is or should be, and what the relationship between the country and other countries in Africa or elsewhere is.

Each country has certain types of beliefs peculiar to it, which reflect its own struggle to maintain order. In France a core belief is that the French Republic is a cornerstone of western civilization and that it deserves an important independent place in the world among the most powerful nations. In Africa one core belief is that Africans are not inferior, that their cultures have much to contribute to the world. Core beliefs remain in spite of changes of regime; variable beliefs depend more on the regime and on immediate problems.

Core Beliefs

Core beliefs and the variable beliefs in which the government is interested are promoted by Gabon's mass media of communication, although inadequate, by official speeches, and by tours of the country such as one taken by President Mba before the elections in April 1964. It was the President's custom to visit each of the nine regions at least once each year, while the ministers visited their home territory several times, but since the beginning of 1963, when Sylvanus Olympio was assassinated, Mba's travels within the country have decreased and he appears to have made himself much less accessible to the Gabonese. Eventually a large wall was built around the President's mansion, and entrance was restricted to one area. In 1961 he delivered thirty-eight speeches which were noted by the national press agency, and in 1964 about the same. This does not include all the one hundred or one hundred fifty speeches he appears to have given on a tour.

The radio is used and so is television for an explanation of beliefs. Special programs have been set up by a representative from UNESCO to re-enforce some themes. During the dry season a truck from the Ministry of Information and two trucks from the French embassy or other embassies such as that of the German Federal Republic travel about the country to show films for entertainment and to promote the belief system.

138

Gabon d'Abord

Gabon First is an important core belief shared by most Gabonese. Everyone believes that the federation of French Equatorial Africa, A.E.F., exploited the riches of Gabon for the benefit of the development of other countries like Congo. Gabon must be developed first, and Gabonese resources must be exploited for the benefit of its own people and territory, everyone agrees.

Ever since A.E.F. was organized, both Whites and Blacks in Gabon struggled against it. In 1937, for example, the white Chamber of Commerce requested Marius Moutet, the Minister for Colonies, to give Gabon increased autonomy, but this was denied.[1] In 1953 Gabonese students in France refused an invitation sent by the Governor General of the federation to join a delegation of other Africans in Paris; in an open letter they said: "Gabonese students, conscious of the particularly painful fate reserved to their country since its integration into the A.E.F., regret that they are unable to accept your invitation. They believe that in spite of the great economic potential, in spite of an immutable loyalty to France, Gabon has been permitted to become a Cinderella."[2]

Gabonese politicians and the masses believed Gabon was discriminated against and should resist all attempts to integrate the territory further into the federation. In 1953 Jean-Hilaire Aubame proclaimed during a session of the Gabonese Territorial Assembly: "We must resist the intrigues of Brazzaville, above all with regard to education. We are the descendants of those who permitted France to obtain Middle Congo. Our development should not be retarded; we should progress like everyone else."[3] In 1962 President Léon Mba said that, when Gabon was part of the federation, "our territory saw a large part of its resources of men and money serve for the development of what was then Moyen-Congo."[4] Students in Paris took exception to the federation but blamed the French for the disadvantageous position of Gabon within it: "We were the first to denounce the tricks of

1 *Bulletin de la Chambre de Commerce d'Agriculture et d'Industrie du Gabon* (Douala), No. 1, January-April 1938, p. 6.
2 *Jeunesse Gabonaise*, Nos. 3 and 4, February-March 1954.
3 Assemblée Territoriale du Gabon, *Journal des Débats*, 15 April 1953. p. 26.
4 *L'Effort Gabonais*, 11 October 1962, p. 3.

139

Chauvet, the High Commissioner in Brazzaville, when he tried to make our country into the milch cow for an artificial federation."[5] In other words — now that Gabon is independent, let us think of ourselves first.

Government buildings display little signs that read "Gabon d'abord," and all groups in the country agree that the country must be developed before its resources contribute toward the development of any other African state. At a 1963 congress of his political party, the Bloc Démocratique Gabonais (B.D.G.), the President said: "We cannot build elsewhere before we have built our own country."[6] It is therefore necessary to avoid close alliances with other states and to insist that every independent African state has full sovereignty over its territory. In another speech addressed to Gabonese in France he said: "Think Gabon in the morning, think Gabon when you eat, think Gabon even when you embrace a beautiful woman. I had a sign made: Gabon d'abord, and they accused me of racism. No. It is our duty. We must remember that we are Gabonese before everything else, because we forget it at times."[7] Organizations like the Union Africaine et Malgache (U.A.M.) and its successors like the Organisation Commune Africaine et Malgache (O.C.A.M.) are favored over larger organizations which include countries with regimes different from that of Gabon. Many Gabonese also feared that an African development bank might lead to interference in Gabonese affairs or to the use of Gabonese money for projects of which Gabon does not approve.

We Need National Unity; Tribalism Is Bad

The motto *Gabon d'abord* means Gabon before Africa, and it means Gabon before the pre-national kinship groups. The loyalty must be directed primarily to Gabon, not to Africa and not to ethnic groups or tribes. The President speaks most eloquently about this theme. He says Gabon is small but rich; Gabon has neighbors who covet its wealth. In order to develop and in order to protect the country, unity is necessary: "We are here for the construction of Gabon, to create a Gabonese nationality." And,

[5] *L'Etudiant du Gabon,* November 1961.
[6] *La Semaine Africaine,* 8 September 1963.
[7] *Gabon d'Aujourd'hui,* 26 June 1965.

"in Gabon we must exclude any tribal or racist feeling so that a Gabonese of Fougamou or from Okondja can present himself as a candidate in Bitam or at Cocobeach and vice versa."[8] Student groups have long agreed that tribalism is evil even though they, like everyone else, have not forgotten all their prejudices; in 1953 students wrote that the idea of ethnic differences must be buried once and for all: "Let Fang, Omyènè, Eshira no longer be Fang, Omyènè, Eshira but simply and only sons of Gabon: Gabonese. For the *Jeunesse Gabonaise* there is only Gabon and the Gabonese."[9] Those students who oppose most of the policies of the government do support for the most part the idea of national unity: We must form a united front against the exploitation of man by man; we must "cure ourselves of our complexes . . . by a supratribal awareness, a national consciousness. Our ridiculous divisions are profitable only to the great powers, which exploit our weaknesses."[10] On trips to their home regions and into other areas, ministers often say that the people ought to think in terms of the region from which they come and not of their tribe or ethnic group. A cabinet member speaking in Woleu-Ntem told the people they must consider themselves first as Gabonese and then as northerners, but never as Fang. A theme not mentioned in public but sometimes in smaller groups is the claim that tribal antagonisms are a result of a colonial policy of divide and rule.

Gabon for the Gabonese

Africans from other countries are not completely welcome in Gabon. Violence against other Africans is never what it has been in countries like Congo-Brazzaville, but there are occasional outbreaks against foreigners. These foreigners who are identified by the nation-state they come from rather than by the ethnic group to which they belong are accused of getting the best jobs, of marrying Gabonese women, of being arrogant toward the Gabonese, of controlling petty commerce.

In 1953 Gabonese, most of whom were reported to be Omyènè, rioted against the "Popos" or Dahomeans and Togolese in Port-

---

[8] *Bulletin Quotidien de l'Agence Gabonaise d'Information,* 24 April 1961, and *Gabon d'Aujourd'hui,* 26 June 1965.

[9] *Jeunesse Gabonaise,* No. 1, December 1953.

[10] Pierre-Louis Agondjo "Les complexes de papa," *L'Etudiant du Gabon,* July 1964, pp. 19–20.

Gentil. The Togolese had higher positions in the administration than most Gabonese, and they were merchants. After a soccer game in late June a few insulting remarks were reportedly exchanged, and disorder reigned from the 20th to the 22nd. A Dahomean newspaper, furious against the Gabonese, reported that 190 shops and houses had been pillaged and burned, that 32 people had been wounded and that 10 women had been raped.[11] Paul Gondjout, then an important Gabonese leader in Port-Gentil, explained that one basis for the trouble was that in one commercial enterprise, for example, the Popos held one third of the positions open to Africans and that in one other large company out of thirty-five positions open to Africans only two were held by Gabonese.[12] Anonymous letters were sent to the administration from something called the "A.E.F. Death Squad Against the Dahomeans"; the administration was enjoined to expel the West Africans: "the Popos and Dahomeans must be chased from Libreville and from all Gabon; they must be sent home as the Jews were chased from France [sic] and sent to Jerusalem. Then Gabon will be purified."

The West Africans have never been formally expelled as they were in some other countries but they have seen increasing restrictions put on their commercial activities. In 1964 they were called upon to support the President after the attempted coup d'état. In March they paraded in Libreville to support the President after some Gabonese had manifested their opposition to him. As a result they were attacked and had to seek refuge in police stations. Included in the group that was attacked were Camerounese related to the Fang.

Antagonism between Gabonese and Camerounese is sharp but restrained in Woleu-Ntem. The Fang are very conscious of the fact that Camerounese used to occupy most of the favored positions in European-owned shops and other enterprises. In addition, there were Camerounese, such as agricultural experts and teachers, in the civil service. They were quietly being advised to go home, and by 1965 there were practically no Camerounese left in the civil service. Camerounese and other *Aefiens* (residents of the

---

[11] *L'Etoile du Dahomey*, July 1953.
[12] Sénateur Paul Gondjout, "Rapport sur les événements de Port-Gentil," 20-22 June 1953, mimeo.

former A.E.F. federation) still come to Libreville from countries where unemployment increases from year to year, but their positions are very insecure, and the antagonism toward them is clear. Southern Gabonese have been most conscious of the presence of Congolese.

Congolese held the best positions in the mining companies and in commerce south of the Ogooué until 1962. In the SOMIFER iron-ore mining company they held positions as topographers and mechanics and were paid from 20,000 to 35,000 francs a month while Gabonese employed as unskilled laborers got but half that amount. At COMILOG, the manganese mining company, practically all workers were Congolese. All companies were informed by 1962 they must begin to replace Congolese with Gabonese.

In September 1962 Gabon's soccer team played against the Congolese team in Brazzaville and lost; there were garbled reports and rumors of violence on the part of the Congolese toward someone (the Central African referee, as it later turned out). Rumors of the slaughter of Gabonese in Brazzaville became more and more gruesome, and finally the Gabonese and Congolese fought each other in the streets of Libreville the 19th and 20th of September, three days after the game. About nine people were killed, and all Congolese were ordered expelled. In return, Congolese attacked the Gabonese and other foreigners in Brazzaville and Pointe-Noire.

To justify the expulsion order, the President said that the Congo was jealous of Gabonese wealth, they had tried to seize part of Gabonese territory: "They sent into our country emissaries carrying funds and hunting arms in order to bribe Gabonese of certain regions, mainly those of Haut-Ogooué, Ngounié, and Nyanga." In 1962 he stated that of about 4,000 Congolese in Gabon more than half had slipped in without proper notification and were agitating against Gabonese unity. The Congolese were, he said, also discourteous to their hosts.[13] By 1965 the Congolese were invited to return if they cared to do so; among those who did so was the assistant mayor of Libreville, but others were hesitant.

At the beginning of June 1965 the government reported that Congolese troops had crossed the frontier and had advanced five

13 *L'Effort Gabonais*, 11 October 1962; also Léon Mba, personal communication, 8 November 1962.

miles into the country. Gabonese were told to remain calm, and the President's *directeur du cabinet* made an investigation. Gabonese were told that their country desired friendly relations with all countries but that they should be prepared to defend their sovereignty. The result of this was increased distrust of other African states.[14]

We Need the Whites

Gabon for the Gabonese does not mean that Whites are not wanted; they are still regarded as the key to Gabonese development. All Gabonese are proud of what they call their traditional hospitality and friendliness to white foreigners: "In our country brotherhood and hospitality are not just themes of speeches and platform techniques: we live them every day because these virtues are the most precious part of Gabonese tradition and heritage."[15] Whites are necessary because they have the techniques needed for material development. Mitsogo who were leaving their Heartland to move toward the Contact Zone near the town of Fougamou said they moved because they needed some Whites to give them jobs.

It was of course French policy to prove to the African that he needed to depend on the Frenchman. In a letter in 1910 a French administrator wrote his superior that the colonial administration could become indispensable to the Africans if it could prove its efficacy in the settlement of disputes: "The life of a native revolves around the settlement of palavers; resolute action in this area is a powerful lever in the hands of the administration which must not be neglected if it wants to accomplish what it proposes. It will benefit doubly by providing a service to the natives and by molding their customs and their country more readily. Once it has thus shown its utility and once it has become indispensable, the administration will be able to ask for payment for its services."[16]

Even today Gabonese, like many other French-speaking Africans, demonstrate surprising diffidence before abstract white

14 *Gabon d'Aujourd'hui,* 21 June 1965.
15 *L'Effort Gabonais,* 11 October 1962.
16 "Livre de Correspondence," Booué, 1910–1911, "Rapport de l'administrateur au gouverneur," 1 April 1910.

The Ogooué River
Courtesy of the Information Services of Gabon

Ferry across the Ogooué
Courtesy of the Information Services of Gabon

President Léon Mba at Independence Day parade
Courtesy of the Information Services of Gabon

Official portrait of
Léon Mba
*Courtesy of the
Information Services
of Gabon*

National Assembly
building, Libreville
*Courtesy of the
Information Services
of Gabon*

Legislative assembly in session
Courtesy of the Information Services of Gabon

Waterfalls of an
Ogooué tributary
Courtesy of the
Information Services
of Gabon

An okoumé tree
Courtesy of the
Information Services
of Gabon

A regional sawmill
Courtesy of the Information Services of Gabon

Preparing okoumé for shipment
Courtesy of the Information Services of Gabon

Open-pit uranium mine
Courtesy of the Information Services of Gabon

Manganese ore transport into Congo
Courtesy of the Information Services of Gabon

Gabonese mask
Collection Princesse Gourielli, Paris

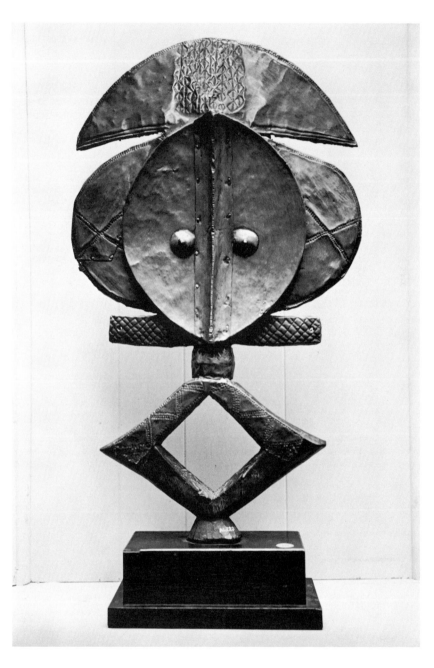

Gabonese Art: funerary object
From the collection of Mr. & Mrs. David Lloyd Kreeger,
at the Museum of African Art, Washington, D.C.

power. (This has not, however, always prevented attacks against Whites considered offensive.) The President continues to praise the White and his power to develop the country but de-emphasizes the role of the French, as non-French companies start to invest in Gabon and as several other countries now have diplomatic relations with Gabon. Until recently Gabon had direct diplomatic relations only with France, the United States, Great Britain, Belgium, Israel, and the Federal Republic of Germany. Along with many other African countries, Gabon is associated with the European Common Market. The first president said that his country was not ready for official contact with the Communist nations. Opposition groups attack certain Frenchmen and certain French policies but still insist, as did the Gabonese civil servants of the 1920's, that they like the "true" Frenchmen and that a bad Frenchman is not a true Frenchman. There are French imperialists but, as one antigovernment tract said, "when we are victorious, we shall raise up on our shoulders the true Frenchmen, those who aid us, who guide our steps, who believe that they can build with us a sincere and disinterested friendship."

Gabon Can be Developed; We Want to be Modern

Gabonese in the government and out believe that with the proper pushes in the right direction by the Whites Gabon could start on a period of self-sustained growth in ten or fifteen years. Development and Civilization mean the machine, they say. Development and Civilization mean material goods. Monsignor Raponda-Walker traveled throughout much of Gabon as a missionary and wrote that in 1907 everyone in one region thought he was a merchant: "Everywhere their first question is the same: Where are you going to set up a trading station? . . . we want to engage in commerce (*motete*). I had all the difficulties in the world to make them understand that I was not concerned with *motete*. This went completely beyond their comprehension because for the Mitsogo, *motete* is the ideal, *motete* is a magic word, the key to all happiness."[17]

All Gabonese are aware of the mineral resources of the country, which they realize can be exploited. At the same time it is be-

[17] A. Raponda-Walker, "Voyage au pays des Ishogos, 1907," unpublished manuscript, Library of Chamber of Commerce, Libreville.

lieved that modernity or material development which is often considered to be nation-building will help the Gabonese become more "civilized" or *"évolués."*

Variable Beliefs, 1963–1966

The widest divisions in the variable aspects of the belief system are between the government and its supporters on the one hand and the younger educated, the Fang (particularly in Woleu-Ntem), the churches, and, it appeared in 1966, over one half of all Gabonese on the other hand. What is more serious for the government is that in the legislative elections of April 1964 voters in the Nationalizing Zone showed their distrust of the incumbent President more strongly than those of any other area with the exception of Woleu-Ntem.

From 1963 to 1966 the number of variable beliefs increased, and the differences in the official and the nonofficial belief systems clearly augmented. Differences in the nonofficial system are based on self-interest and ethnic identity. The official beliefs have fewer internal differences.

Official Beliefs

1. One nation, a single people, a single party. In 1961 the government favored the abolition of parties and the three Gabonese parties formed a slate designated "National Union" for the elections. At that time the official theme was national union and the abolition of parties which only cause dissension. In the period from February 1963 to February 1964 and starting again about October 1964, the theme was that a single party is necessary. Now the theme is that one party is necessary for development but that many parties are a source of discord which opens the way for Communism. Communism is already a threat in Central Africa, the theme continues, because of the presence of Chinese Communists nearby.[18] Members of the government very seldom speak about the need for a single party, but government publications and the people who support the government refer to the Presi-

18 *Le Patriote,* No. 5, 24 November 1964. This pro-government newspaper is run by close associates of the President.

146

dent's party as the National Party and call for everyone to adhere to it.

2. *Order is necessary for development.* Gabon needs peace and order; those who create disorder threaten Gabonese development. Revolution is dangerous. A minister, speaking to student groups which had been engaging in antigovernment activities, said: "Calm, respect, order, and work must from now on reign in all schools. We shall not tolerate a minority of irresponsible young people who compromise the education of Gabonese children."[19] Anyone who causes disorder threatens development because investors will not put money into places where there is turmoil. "Private investors hesitate," said the president of the National Assembly. "They are not going to invest where there is insecurity and where there are unstable political regimes. Rich as it is, our country will be able to develop only when there is peace and political stability."[20]

3. *The attempted coup d'état was made by tribalists, ambitious people, and egoists like Aubame who threaten order and development.* In the first speech after his return to power the President said he would investigate the causes of this horrible event "which led us to the edge of the abyss, anarchy, despair. . . . The affair that we have just experienced represents the upsetting of the established order by those who are traditionally supposed to defend it; it represents the unleashing of violence and the humiliating spectacle of disorder in Africa."[21] When he announced the verdict of the special court set up to try those who led the attempted overthrow of the government, the President said: "The stability of the State has been shaken, its economic future compromised, and partisan quarrels have divided the population."[22]

After the trial of the conspirators the President and the official press began a campaign to put the whole blame on Jean-Hilaire Aubame. It was Aubame, his nephew, and even his wife who with money and lies convinced the military to act.[23] Two condemned leaders of the Provisional Government were released a few months after the trial when they issued a statement putting all the blame

19 Minister of Education, *Patrie Gabonaise,* May 1964.
20 *La Semaine Africaine,* 28 June 1964.
21 *Bulletin Quotidien,* 21 February 1964.
22 *Gabon d'Aujourd'hui,* 12 September 1964.
23 *Ibid.,* 27 April 1965.

on Aubame and a small group of other Fang. The government newspaper published a special number in which these declarations were printed. The editor added after their statements that "Aubame and Eyeghet [Aubame's nephew] wanted to set up a family-run government, limited to the clan and destined to promote the future of their sons and grandsons."[24]

4. But the page of history has turned. Let us forget about the past and think about the construction of a new and prosperous Gabon. Back to normalcy. A prefect visited the schools of his region and told the students "to forget the events of February 18th and their consequences and to try with all your force . . . to make up for the time lost."[25] And the President said after he announced the sentences: "An unfortunate page of our History has turned. Gabonese, let us turn toward the future so that our country will continue the road to a better future in independence, stability, prosperity, and concord."[26]

A newspaper controlled by a Frenchman and some colleagues of the President, *Le Patriote,* called for extreme measures against traitors and denounced the churches of Gabon. This is something the President had done only in speeches in Gabonese national languages. *Le Patriote* also denounced other "traitors" who weaken the country by stealing from the government.

5. Léon Mba is our Leader; he knows what is best for us. He is Papa, the father of the country; he is older than we, and we should respect our elders. The President himself said: "They have called me the Father of the Gabonese country. At present the Father is thinking what will be done for his family and for his sons, some of whom have gone astray."[27] We must be solidly behind our President and we must submit peacefully to the powers that be. (The French archbishop of Libreville in support of this theme said: "The Church can in no way approve the use of force and violence. It teaches to all respect for authority and submission to established powers."[28])

24 *Ibid.,* supplement to number 46, 1 June 1965.
25 *Bulletin Quotidien,* 23 October 1964.
26 *Gabon d'Aujourd'hui,* 12 September 1964.
27 *Bulletin Quotidien,* 24 February 1964.
28 Statement by Monsignor Adam in *L'Effort Gabonais,* 6 March 1964. The head of the Protestant Church also made a statement but he only called for calm and reconciliation.

6. France is our elder brother who has helped us for over one hundred years. We need our elder brother. The emphasis of this theme has changed since France sent troops on 19 February 1964 to restore the deposed President to power. Prior to that intervention it was said that Gabon could become a projection of France in Africa, just as the United States has become a projection of European civilization in America. "French Africa (Gabon included) could likewise be an excellent projection of France, an image which would fill each Frenchman with pride."[29] In 1934 Léon Mba wrote that the "Pahouins" were on the road to civilization, a road that has already been followed by the French, our elder brothers, who came to Gabon in 1839 because of their liberal and humanitarian spirit.[30]

According to this view treaties were signed between equals, and mutual benefit was the result. In 1960 the descendant of one of the early Omyènè kings and a colleague of the President wrote: "A king of France and an African monarch signed a pact of friendship, a solemn affirmation of mutual assistance. On one side force, kindness, humanity; on the other the desire for evolution, confidence, loyalty."[31] Gabonese soldiers who fought for France in World War II are honored. A statue has been erected to Captain Charles Ntchorere who died in 1940. The inscription reads "Mort pour la Patrie," and a stamp to honor his memory issued in 1964 indicated he gave his life for France: "Mort pour la France."

Of all the French, General de Gaulle is considered to be the best friend of the African. He is admired for his nationalism and for what is considered to be his decision to permit the Africans to become independent: "France and particularly General de Gaulle have always been the champions of the black man and of a new Africa."[32] Since the February 1964 intervention there has been more emphasis on an attempt to clarify the French position. It is explained by the government that the French came to Gabon after the Vice-President called upon them in conformity with

---

[29] Memorandum to Albert Sarraut, President of the Assembly of the Union Française, presented by a delegation of distinguished Gabonese, Libreville, 8 September 1952.

[30] Léon Mba, "Essai de droit coutumier pahouin," preface, mimeographed version, n.d. p. 3.

[31] Louis Bigmann in *Union Gabonaise,* February-March 1960.

[32] Léon Mba in *Union Gabonaise,* February-March 1960.

certain agreements signed between Gabon and France. The troops were really troops of the Communauté; they did not intervene to save individuals like the President. They came to Gabon to prevent disorder and anarchy, fomented by a few ambitious soldiers and politicians but unsupported by the masses, which threatened the development of the country.[33] The French remain to help us and guide us in the peaceful orderly development of our country.

Nonofficial Beliefs

Since the expulsion of the Congolese in 1962 the political consciousness of the Gabonese increased, and more Gabonese appear to be interested in politics. Also there appeared to be a certain unity in opposition to the government of Léon Mba, although on other matters there is widespread disunity among the various opposition groups and between various parts of the Gabonese population.

1. An opposition party should be permitted; B.D.G. is bad. Some Gabonese political leaders who belonged to the opposition say they now believe that any single-party system, whether made up of their own party or another, is bad. It is perhaps easy for them to say this because they are out of power, but they indicated a belief that a single party is dangerous because power eventually goes to one man who can make mistakes (like the mistakes Léon Mba has made, they said) and can weaken the country. When westerners say that one-party states are "natural" in Africa and that western democracy is not to be expected there, certain Gabonese retort that such a statement indicates prejudice. Some student groups, however, call for a "united democratic front" based on an "alliance of workers and peasants." Their projects designed to build a socialist state would also imply a one-party state, but a party not controlled by neo-colonialist and capitalist forces in Europe and America, according to them.[34] People in villages outside the Nationalizing Zone do not appear to consider the pros and cons of single-party or multiparty government but are disturbed that members of the opposition whom they know or

[33] President's press conference, reported in *Bulletin Quotidien*, 24 February 1964.
[34] J. Rendjambe-Issany, "Pour un état de démocratie nationale par un front démocratique uni," *L'Etudiant du Gabon*, July 1964, pp. 12–13.

have known and supported are in prison. People south of the Ogooué say that whatever government exists is controlled by the Fang and Omyènè.

2. *Gabon is not independent; revolution is desirable.* Gabon is controlled by the White. We need the White but do not want to be controlled by him or by the international trusts. The present order cannot last. We have had a war with Congo and a war with France, but it is not over yet. Tracts have called for the formation of a front of national liberation, and the Gabonese students' association in Paris, l'Association Générale des Etudiants du Gabon (A.G.E.G.), which is affiliated with the radical Fédération des Etudiants d'Afrique Noire en France (F.E.A.N.F.), issued a memorandum at the end of 1964 in which the Gabonese were called to action and the Organisation de l'Unité Africaine (O.A.U.) was denounced: "We call our people to greater vigilance, to an intense mobilization because the silence of O.A.U. on the French intervention in Gabon shows that their [the people's] action alone will lead to complete liberation and to a unification of the African fatherland."[35] There have been rumors that the Fang of Woleu-Ntem would march on Libreville, and indeed some Fang were talking about digging up guns they had buried. Violence is not feared and is increasingly regarded as a way to sweep the undesirable leaders away.

3. *The coup.* There is the most confusion about this. Most agree that the military men overthrew the President and called on Jean-Hilaire Aubame to take over the government. There was no violence, and the people remained calm: The day of the coup was really our Revolution and should be celebrated as Independence Day. The Gabonese who were killed by French soldiers are our heroes, and their memories will be vindicated.

What confuses the ideas about the coup is that some people believe the United States was behind it in order to take over Gabon, to get revenge on France for France's current policies in Europe and for France's criticisms of American policies in various parts of the world, or in order to get control of the uranium mines so as to prevent France from building an atomic bomb. Many

---

35 A.G.E.G.–F.E.A.N.F., "Mémorandum: La situation au Gabon après la réinstallation de Léon Mba au pouvoir par les parachutistes français," Paris, 17 November 1964, p. 6.

government officials profess to believe a report that guns were stored in the American ambassador's residence.

At their trial the leaders of the attempt to overthrow the President testified they did not agree with the policies of the government and were fearful that oppression would be intensified if scheduled elections with only a Bloc Démocratique Gabonais (B.D.G.) slate of candidates were permitted, as planned for 23 February. They denied that America had any role in the affair. Second Lieutenant Daniel Mbene, one of the military leaders of the coup, said during his trial: "The 18th of February was the most complete act of national liberation since Gabon's independence. My action was dictated not only by the discontent within the army but also by that of the people who lived in fear of arbitrary arrests. . . . As an officer of the gendarmerie I could no longer bear arresting old and young people for simple political reasons."[36]

Another aspect of beliefs about the coup that confuses things is a tendency by some people toward depoliticization or withdrawal from political matters. The peasant says that this is the affair of the big politicians; it does not concern me. Let them fight it out! Even those responsible for some tracts distributed around Libreville wrote in one: "The combat of these two men, Mba and Aubame, is over. Let them go to the moon to have it out if they want, but we shall struggle for the combat of ideas. . . . We are therefore in favor of any party that enlists in the Revolution begun at dawn on the 18th of February." Whereas people did not talk much about politics in 1962, by 1964 many were saying that politics is a dirty business. It is commonly believed the French intervened only to protect their own economic interests.

4. Léon Mba must go; the French troops must go. The first President has always, it seems, been a focus for unity. Until about the middle of 1963 the unity was around him; by 1966 it was against him. In some areas he was never liked, but now people come out more openly — in spite of the danger involved — against him, and others who were his allies turn against him now or entertain doubts about him and his policies. Student groups and tracts have one thing in common: They say the President should resign and

[36] *Jeune Afrique,* 14 September 1964.

foreign troops should be recalled. Leaders of the opposition say he has destroyed the chances for development in Gabon, that he has created deep antagonism; that he is a stooge for international economic interests. He is pictured as a tyrant who has brought in mercenaries from Rio Muni, the Central African Republic, and France to protect him, to torture anyone who speaks against him. In spite of this he is grudgingly admired for his ability to maintain himself in power; the Whites, who are believed to tell him what to do in economic affairs, are blamed as ultimately responsible for bad policies.

The allies of Mba are being denounced. The churches and Frenchmen around the President are in important economic positions, and the Gabonese who support him find places in the cabinet or elsewhere. After the archbishop called upon the people to support the powers that be, the A.G.E.G. met at the end of March 1964 to condemn the "cynical collusion between the archbishopric, certain members of the Evangelical Church, and the puppet government of Léon Mba."[37] The Church is labeled as obscurantist and as part of the neo-colonial plot against the nation. Most priests in the Roman Catholic Church and most pastors of the Protestant Church are opposed to the President — often for quite different reasons, however. The President is distrusted because he is not a good Catholic, for example, and he in turn has accused the Churches of supporting Revolution.[38] Fang in Woleu-Ntem dislike him also because they consider him the ally of the coastal Omyènè and because he has forgotten some of the true customs of his people.

Monsignor Raponda-Walker wrote a letter denouncing the Mba regime: "I protest against dictatorship, tyranny, the reign of terror in a democratic State. I protest against the use of violence . . . against a single party . . . against the abuses . . . arbitrary arrests. . . ." In a later letter he called on the President to amnesty the prisoners.

The students claim that they should take over from old, inept politicians. They are young and educated — the elite.

5. *The War with France has weakened Gabon's ties with them.*

37 Le Comité Exécutif de l'A.G.E.G., "Motion des ètudiants Gabonais sur la politique des missions catholiques et l'église évangélique," n.d.
38 Interview with President Mba, reported in *Le Figaro*, 19 August 1966.

At his trial Aubame said: "The children of Gabon will never forget that for unmentionable reasons a fistful of French destroyed in one day [18 February 1964] a friendship woven in 125 years, preferring the friendship of a man to that of a people." We want Whites from all countries to come to Gabon to develop our country. The "French Imperialists" are denounced, but the Gabonese believe as they have always believed that there is a "true Frenchman" who is different from the French they have seen.

We want the true French, the new French, but not the old French. Many villagers also appear to believe that Aubame wanted Americans and English to come to Gabon to help develop it, whereas Mba wanted to stick with the French. Many people feel they would like American help to get a variety of experiences brought to Gabon and because America in their view is a very powerful country. Since independence there has been a definite increase in consciousness about the world beyond French-speaking areas.

This is another indication, however, of the Gabonese sense of dependence on the White. Mba and his supporters are pictured as being backed up by the French who are by some people blamed for everything bad. Aubame and his supporters are pictured as being supported by the Americans who, for a time at least, were credited with much that was good. Once in the Woleu-Ntem a man refused to show me his plantation because he said he would need a place to hide when the French and the Americans fought it out. (He probably had memories of Franco-German battles in the region during World War I.) In spite of the fact that Gabon is more or less independent the Gabonese considers himself a bystander. Bring in the Americans to fight French influence; bring in the Americans to add their techniques to those of the French or to compete with the French! One leader of the opposition believes that if the Americans do not come in, then the Russians or Chinese should be called upon to provide the necessary different experience.

6. *Civil servants are rich; they support the regime.* This theme is recent, and the divisions between the civil service and the masses have become more clearcut; one tract stated: "I protest against the nouveaux riches who fatten themselves off the sweat of the

people. I protest against the salaries of ministers, which are scandalous compared with the meager salaries of the workers." One heard people refer to civil servants as being supporters of the President in order to get better positions; one heard civil servants accused in public of being able to live much better than the average Gabonese. The villagers are increasingly conscious of the difference in living standards between themselves and the Gabonese who work for the government. And, because the higher ranks of the civil servants have been purged of anyone known to be against the President, senior civil servants are believed to support a government that has lost the confidence of the people.

The variable beliefs, official, nonofficial, or antiofficial, are affected by a change in government, but not completely. Government as a device to exploit people unfortunate enough to find themselves under its control is a conception shared by many Africans. The idea derives from the colonial experience and from the experience of many Gabonese in the first years of independence. Because traditional loyalties were to kinship groups, a man with power would naturally be expected to help his own relatives and those with whom he was linked by marriage alliances. Gabonese who have no hope of getting power themselves believe that no matter who is in power he will think of his own family first, and government is a struggle between the big men who do not necessarily think very much about the masses.

Experience with government influences views of the nation-state, and national consolidation is threatened when the variable beliefs greatly outnumber the core beliefs. The goal of economic development is a core belief and thus is the most important goal. It is made specific when the government explains the railroad and mining operations, but many Gabonese feel that the Whites and high-ranking Gabonese get the real benefits.

PART THREE

National Consolidation Through Human Decision-Making

CHAPTER 8

Leadership in Nation-Building

Problems of Leadership

To maintain order — and this does not signify the status quo — leaders must be able to use power efficaciously. They define the goals of the group and internal order; this means combating capricious forces. They are the spokesmen for the core of beliefs in the shared-belief system; they are surrounded by the culture, and the history of the system gives them a prominent role. They direct the defense of the system against outside attack. The order associated with their position and their vigilance may be oppressive, but often the masses will not act against the oppression because they fear a resulting disorder or because those who might direct such a revolt are either in prison or are given jobs with high salaries. Leaders with power also gain more authority than they officially have by dint of the very fact they are called leaders. That is to say, once a powerful person becomes a leader, the power he possesses increases because of the aura about the post of leadership. In all countries there is a tendency to look for a single national leader, particularly in times of crisis. He becomes the human symbol of the nation, and the image of his own people which he is believed to give other countries is a source of personal power.

Bases for personal power are the special abilities of a man before he becomes a national leader. How well he maintained order on a lower level is important. Another basis is the sub-group to which he belongs; this might be an ethnic, religious, geographical, or professional sub-group. It has mattered in America until the election of President Kennedy that candidates for the nation's highest office be Protestants, and until the election of President Johnson it was thought that no southerner could hold the office. At certain times in history Americans believed that men with military training should lead the country, and in Latin America such a profession appears to be an indispensable prerequisite. A special relationship with the supernatural is also a source of personal power.

Threats to the system from inside or from outside will be used as a reason for the increase in power of the national leader once he is in office. He will ask for special emergency powers, investigations, and purges and may be able to eliminate his competitors. He may suppress the attempts of other leaders to gain power for themselves or to form a coalition with him. He will announce that this is imperative in order to prevent the internal quarrels and disorders that might result from collective leadership.

The people must believe that the leader uses part of his power for the benefit of the group. If he does not use at least part of his power to maintain order and to further the development of the group, he will lose the loyalty of the masses. The masses may have more loyalty to his party or another group to which he happens to belong than to him personally, but a leader is most often blamed for the mistakes and praised for the success of policies that may be his own or those of the group he represents.

Leaders may move from one level to another. They may be leaders at some sub-group level and move up to the level of the developing supreme loyalty group on the basis of their previous power position in parties or ethnic groups. Their loyalties to the previous group may continue and they may try to use the larger system for the benefit of the smaller system, but their own views might also change with the assumption of power at a new level, and the experience of leadership at a higher level might train them to be true leaders at that higher level rather than regional, ethnic, or religious leaders. Every nation must have its national leaders whose stated goal is The Nation and its construction and who may be regarded as representatives of the whole geographic area and web of kinship groups that constitute the nation. National leaders are more important for the survival of the nation-state in the early stages of the national process than at later stages because people may not yet have much loyalty to anything other than persons and other ethnic groupings. There is little concept of loyalty to state and nation; and pre-national leaders or patterns of pre-national leadership are still important.

Pre-National Leaders

The limited authority of chiefs in the egalitarian social systems which have been characteristic of Gabon was based on region as well as on kinship. Even if there were but one head of a lineage, once one part of the group moved away into another forest clearing, isolation and problems of communication would change loyalties. The result would be that if a leader were needed, he would have to come from the region where the people lived and he would have to be related to them. This meant that members of one ethnic group might not be satisfied with a leader if he were not closely related to them and if he did not come from their region. There have been exceptions to this in time of great external threat and during periods of disorder.

Opposition to French rule and trading practices was responsible for the rise of some warrior chiefs who built powerful organizations. In 1901, for example, the French were faced with a coalition of thirteen Fang clans led by Chief Emane Tole who had always been a threat to non-Fang traders along the Ogooué. The French were amazed before the danger of Fang unity: "The most serious aspect of this whole affair is the sort of coalition, a union of thirteen tribes [*sic*] that one would never have believed the Pahouin capable of organizing. It has lasted for a month: complete, absolute, without the least dissidence. . . . In the opinion of all those who know the region — merchants, Protestant and Catholic missionaries — this is a disturbing symptom for the future of which it would be imprudent not to take account."[1] The Fang wanted to force out certain French merchants from the Ogooué and block

1 Arch. Nat. Col., Gabon XVI, dossier 13bis, "Rapport," Copy No. 139, Ndjolé, 3 September 1901.

the river to French communication. It took the French from September to December 1901 to defeat this coalition. In the end Emane Tole was handed over to the Whites by the Fang themselves. This indicates how tenuous a leader's hold was in Fang society.

In a revolt of the Massango during 1917 the French blamed people they called sorcerers and fetishers. In September of that year a Massango called Mabiale Mabioko died in a French prison; he had been jailed for engaging in what the administration judged to be slave trade. The administration was then faced with a revolt led by men with supposed supernatural power whose goal, the French believed, was to protect their slave trade: "The fetishers got together and decided to make a medicine called 'Yengue M'Bourou' which was going to have a decisive influence on the start of the revolt. (It is composed of spears put in the ground in an enclosure of palms and designed to call forth the protection of fetishes for the Massango.) From that moment on nothing would stop the natives who were sure they would not be harmed by the White's guns."[2] The Massango leaders organized a total of thirty-six villages to fight the French, and they gained support among the Mitsogo, the Bakèlè and small groups such as the Bassimba. The revolt was suppressed in 1918 and 1919, after the death of its leader, whose name was Mayombo.[3]

The role of the supernatural as a leadership quality, particularly in the case of the Fang, is a basis for an ambivalent view of leadership. *Evus,* the magical being used for witchcraft practices, is assumed to be in the body of successful, rich, and powerful men. It is to be feared, but it can be used for good. "Good" would be defined as good for the group in which the man with *evus* lives or for the group which he leads. As long as he is using his *evus* for the interests of the group, there is no danger. But people still fear him and do not trust him completely. To preserve themselves and their family against a leader who, they feared, would unleash capricious forces for his own benefit they might destroy him and dissolve the group he built.

The French colonial administration needed, however, auxiliaries to work as heads of the lower-level administrative circumscrip-

2 "Rapport de Monsieur Maclatchy sur la subdivision de Mimongo," 1936, p. 7.
3 *Ibid.,* p. 9.

tions they set up, such as *terre* and *canton*. The men chosen as chiefs were selected on the basis of their supposed fidelity to the administration; thus, former secretaries and interpreters were rewarded with positions as chief even in areas that were not their homes. In French West Africa a governor-general sent a circular to his subordinates in which he advised that if they had decided there was no chief capable of commanding, they could bring in a chief from another region and from another tribe who, "well guided by the *commandant de cercle,* would make himself acceptable."[4]

After World War II some changes were brought about. In French Equatorial Africa, Governor-General Félix Eboué wrote that the administration had no choice in the matter of chiefs; it was their duty to recognize chiefs chosen by custom, "to search out the legitimate chiefs."[5] He also believed that new leaders must emerge in Africa and favored the formation of organizations of évolués or people with some French education. In Gabon it was thought expedient to give more power to chiefs or at least to give the appearance that Gabonese had something to say about the way they were ruled: "The current international political situation, the attitude of certain world powers with regard to the policies of the colonial powers are elements which could make necessary the introduction of methods of rule which are more indirect."[6] The idea of grand chiefs was tried.

The Libreville Mpongouè had long wanted a grand chief; their organization, called the Comité Pongouè, was a shorter name for "Comité Provisoire de Gérance, Conseil du Futur Chef-Supérieur." The committee said its role was to regulate palavers, help the administration keep order, study reforms of the society, and to locate witches. Once a grand chief was installed, he was to concern himself with these matters.[7]

The Libreville Fang who swore they would never be ruled by the Mpongouè had set up their own mutual-help organization, a

4 Circulaire du Gouverneur Général de l'A.O.F. du 15 Août 1917, "Le Problème des chefferies en Afrique noire française," La Documentation Française, 10 February 1959, p. 18.
5 "Circulaire du 8 Novembre 1941 sur la nouvelle politique indigène en A.E.F.," *ibid.,* p. 21.
6 Letter from Governor of Gabon to *chefs de régions,* Libreville, 23 April 1948.
7 Letters from Comité to the Governor of Gabon, 26 January 1937 and 23 April 1937.

"Société de Secours Mutuel pour la Race Fang." Administration-appointed chiefs had no power at all, for it was the chiefs named by the *alar ayong* movement who were in real control. At the Fang Congress, Fang of Libreville pushed the idea of a grand chief, and the man they wanted to be named as grand chief was Léon Mba. But, according to Georges Balandier, rivalries between the Woleu-Ntem Fang who did not trust the proposed grand chief and administrative pressure prevented such a project.[8]

The administration did try to install a grand chief south of the Ogooué among the Eshira people. Cyprien Guipieri had come from a family of judges and warriors, it was said; he had worked for a French company, and he was a member of the new territorial assembly. In 1947 the *chef de région* (or *chef de cercle* in the terminology of Afrique Occidentale Française) convoked Eshira chiefs in Ngounié, and they, the administrator reported to Governor Roland Pré, had elected Guipieri grand chief. The governor then officially decreed him chief of the Eshira.

The new grand chief was a source of considerable trouble because older Eshira leaders refused to accept him and because he eventually began to make requests for the improvement of roads, the abolition of certain rites, and a revision of the bridewealth system. Barely two years after Guipieri became chief an administrator wrote that the whole idea had brought nothing but "trouble to a population already quite agitated."[9] At the beginning of 1953 the position of grand chief was abolished by the governor's decree as arbitrarily as it had been established.

With the beginning of politics in Gabon some chiefs became *conseillers* in the Representative Council or chose who would be elected. Just before independence, 30 per cent of the municipal counsellors in Fang-Bulu country of southern Cameroun were known as chiefs,[10] and in the first elected legislature of Gabon in 1946 the Eshira Guipieri, the Fang chief Mendame Ndong, and Chief Tsamba of the Badouma people were among the most important chiefs. After independence, schoolteachers took many of the posts in the National Assembly. Of sixty-seven deputies elected

---

8 Georges Balandier, *Sociologie actuelle*, pp. 200–201.
9 Telegram-letter from *chef de région* to *chef de district* at Fougamou, 1 June 1949.
10 P. Alexandre and J. Binet, "Le groupe dit Pahouin," p. 133.

in 1961, one third were former schoolteachers, sixteen had held other posts in the civil service as clerks, nurses, or secretaries. The rest were businessmen and planters. Only two chiefs were present.[11]

Chiefs who had some traditional power were often consulted by the French administration during the early days of the Assembly in order to make sure that acceptable men were elected. Once candidates acceptable to certain regional leaders were chosen, the French made sure they got elected and of course often chose candidates themselves. Representatives most often came from the areas which elected them and were from the dominant ethnic group.

After the *loi-cadre* reforms of 1957 a growing civil service provided new opportunities. An increasing number of African civil servants did not necessarily serve in their home territories. Because they had power over the lives of people in a particular district, it was often necessary in Heartland Zones to make sure that civil servants who would be in close contact with the people did not belong to an ethnic group or tribe which the heartlanders disliked. Members of groups with an elite status might be acceptable. In the Fang Heartland Omyènè were often in important positions such as that of prefect, and the Fang appeared to respect them for their competence and apparent disinterestedness. (The first African missionary in the Heartland was an Omyènè who was highly respected by the Fang.)

National Leaders

Most of the early national leaders were Omyènè. It was they who stressed the whole country of Gabon and its development over strictly tribal or ethnic interests. It was in their interest to stress the abolition of tribal allegiances because they were a small group which was rapidly losing its Heartland. Their Heartland became the Nationalizing Zone. They had also organized to fight for their land rights and thus already had political experience. The Eurafricans, many of whom were already French citizens, provided some leadership.

The first national leaders were also mainly civil servants or

11 "Institutions d'Afrique Noire: la République Gabonaise: Députés," edited by La Documentation Africaine, Paris, 1961.

employees of private companies who traveled to different countries. Most had received Roman Catholic education at the seminary or the Ecole Montfort in Libreville. The nature of their politics was strongly influenced by family ties, weak party identification, and isolation from the other A.E.F. territories.[12]

In the first elections in October 1945 for the French Constituent Assembly which met to re-establish a French republic, Gabriel d'Arboussier, a Eurafrican and well-known colonial official, was elected to represent Gabon and Moyen-Congo. With the establishment of the Fourth Republic a double-college system of voting — one for French citizens and one for Africans — was set up in Gabon; the Africans who were allowed to vote could elect a deputy, part of a territorial assembly, a senator, and a representative to the Union Française, separate from those of Congo.

The African deputy to the French National Assembly was a Fang, Jean-Hilaire Aubame, the African senator in the French Senate was an Omyènè, first M. Anghiley of Libreville and then Paul Gondjout of Port-Gentil, and the representative to the assembly of the Union Française was a southerner, René-Paul Sousatte. These three men had been civil servants. The first Gabonese president of the legislative assembly was a Eurafrican, part Omyènè; the second was Omyènè, and this position has been reserved to the coastal people from Libreville until the present.

Gondjout had set up two organizations, the more important of which was the Cercle Amical Mutualiste des Evolués which he founded in 1943 in response to encouragement from Governor-General Eboué for organizations that might provide local leadership when the empire would be liberalized. Changes in the structure of the empire had been promised by General de Gaulle.

In elections in November 1946 Gondjout was elected to the representative council from Port-Gentil, along with eight Fang and nine others. French citizens elected twelve members. In 1949 Gondjout was elected senator after the death of the Libreville-born Senator Anghiley. In 1954 he organized the B.D.G.; he became its secretary general and the editor of the party newspaper

---

12 Much of my information on political parties and electoral politics comes from the detailed study by John A. Ballard, "The Development of Political Parties in French Equatorial Africa," unpublished thesis, Fletcher School of Law and Diplomacy, December 1963.

Union Gabonaise. In order to attract support to the B.D.G., Gond-jout made an alliance with Léon Mba who became second in command in the party. They traveled about the country together and preached national unity.[13] The B.D.G. was, however, known as an Omyènè-controlled party. Most of its support came from the Nationalizing Zone, particularly from Libreville. In 1958 Gond-jout became president of the first National Assembly and remained in this position until 1960 when he was jailed after an attempted motion of censure designed to prevent the transformation of the government from a parliamentary to a presidential type.

At the end of 1962, after he was released from prison Gondjout took up a post in the administration of an independent Gabon. A member of the provisional government in 1964, he was tried but acquitted.

When Gondjout was first imprisoned, some people felt it was because he wanted to Gabonize quickly. (This idea was taken up by Ronald Segal in a reference book on Africa.[14]) He used to be popular among some opposition groups but seems to have become less important since he gave some support to the coup d'état and then rallied to support the President against it.

René-Paul Sousatte from the Ngounié region was a civil servant in Moyen-Congo in the late 1930's; he had been a student at the Roman Catholic seminary in Libreville along with Aubame, with whom he worked in Brazzaville. Pro-de Gaulle, he became the head of an organization of civil servants at Brazzaville, the Union Educative et Mutuelle de la Jeunesse de Brazzaville, which published a pro-Gaullist magazine and which advised the governor-general.

Elected to the assembly of the Union Française, he also founded the Comité Gabonais d'Etudes Sociales et Economiques (C.O.G.E.S.) and became active in Franco-African groups and the African sections of de Gaulle's party, Rassemblement du Peuple Français (R.P.F.), along with Omyènè like Louis Bigmann.[15] The

13 Jean-Baptiste Essonghe, "Les partis politiques au Gabon," unpublished mémoire, Ecole Nationale de la France d'Outre-Mer, Paris, No. 63, 1958–1959.
14 Ronald Segal, *Political Africa* (New York, Praeger, 1961), pp. 98–99.
15 Sousatte wrote in the R.P.F. newspaper *L'Etincelle de l'A.E.F.* and published a book *L'A.E.F., berceau de l'Union Française* (Paris, Collection La Voix de l'A.E.F., 1952).

stated purposes of C.O.G.E.S., most of whose members were Eshira from the south and Omyènè, was to foster cooperation among all Gabonese for a modernization of Gabonese society. The Omyènè were able to write about their land rights for which they eventually received compensation, and development of the country was constantly requested in the newspaper of Sousatte's organization.[16] C.O.G.E.S. no longer exists. For the 1958 referendum on the constitution of the Fifth Republic Sousatte formed a regionally based political party called P.U.N.G.A., which he claimed meant Parti d'Union Nationale Gabonaise but which apparently also stands for tornado in the Eshira language.

His party was strongest in the south where it made appeals to southern solidarity against the northern Fang and Omyènè. While both the B.D.G. and the Union Démocratique et Sociale Gabonaise (U.D.S.G.) decided on a *oui* vote, P.U.N.G.A. advocated a *non* and succeeded in Nyanga, part of the Bapounou Heartland, in getting a *non* majority. According to one observer, Sousatte openly proclaimed the ethnic orientation of his party: "It is not necessary for us to hide the fact that our party belongs to the people of the interior as the U.D.S.G. is the party of the Fang and the B.D.G. is the party of the Omyènè."[17]

Sousatte was arrested, after a trip to Moscow, for his opposition to the government. In 1962 he became a minister in the President's cabinet but left it in 1963 when a coalition of three Gabonese parties was ended.

Aubame, who was associated with Sousatte in the Brazzaville days, also rallied quickly to de Gaulle and encouraged other Gabonese to do the same. He had been helped in his youth by a brother of Léon Mba, became an assistant to Governor-General Félix Eboué, and achieved a comparatively high rank in the European cadre of the colonial administration in 1943; in 1944 he was named president of the council of the African quarter of Brazzaville, Poto-Poto, with strong backing by the colonial administration. He returned to Gabon after the war to run for deputy to

16 C.O.G.E.S.' first newspaper was called *La Voix du Coges* in 1948. In 1949 the name was changed to *Réalités Africaines* and again in 1952 to *La Voix de l'A.E.F. et de l'Union Française.*

17 Cited by Alain Mauric, "Le Gabon de la Loi-Cadre au Referendum," unpublished mémoire de stage, Ecole Nationale de la France d'Outre-Mer, Paris, 28 May 1959, p. 78.

the French National Assembly; he was elected in 1946 and served until 1959. The deputy belonged to Léopold Sédar Senghor's Indépendants d'Outre-Mer (I.O.M.). In 1947 he founded the U.D.S.G. and became its secretary general while Léon Mba became its administrative secretary. Most officers of the party were Fang, and U.D.S.G. soon got the reputation of being an instrument of the Fang. Southerners were, however, in the party or at least used the party title.

Aubame's most important colleague was Jean-Marc Ekoh from Bitam in the Fang Heartland, who along with François Mèyè (sometimes of the B.D.G., sometimes of the U.D.S.G.) were the leading Protestants in Gabonese politics. Ekoh had been a leader in youth organizations. In 1957 their party actually won more seats than the B.D.G., but deputies changed parties, and Aubame became leader of the opposition; in the 1961 elections a single slate, made up of Aubame and Mba, was presented to the electorate. A coalition government lasted until 1963 when Aubame left the President's cabinet to become president of the Supreme Court. After the 1964 coup he was called upon by the military to head a provisional government and after the return of President Mba was tried and convicted for his apparent participation in this overthrow. He was imprisoned at the end of 1964.

Among many Omyènè Aubame is feared. He is called a tribalist, as are most of his colleagues in the U.D.S.G. Three of the four most important leaders in recent Gabonese politics, Gondjout, Sousatte, and Aubame, are closely associated with different ethnic groups in the minds of most Gabonese. While they served in roles as representatives of Gabon, they were often pictured as being closely allied with particularistic groups — whether it was so or not. The man who came closest to supratribal national leadership was Léon Mba.

Léon Mba as the first National Leader

President Mba was born in Libreville in 1902; this made him older than all other important leaders in Gabon. He worked for the administration as an interpreter and became a *chef de canton*. He was known as a judge capable of settling disputes among Fang and among some Omyènè as well, and he was known for his expertise in questions involving witchcraft accusations. He is reported to have joined secret organizations like *Bwiti* and the Freemasons with the aid of the administrators from the Antilles who worked in Gabon. Unlike Aubame he was not favored by the colonial administration and appears to have made many enemies in the Libreville district where he also worked for a private company as an accountant and labor recruiter. He often wrote letters for illiterate Fang who wished to protest against certain administrative practices or make requests of various kinds, and the administration became suspicious of him. In 1922 he was condemned for an offense on apparently slim evidence and had to pay a fine. In December of the same year, under the *indigénat,* he was arbitrarily put in prison for fifteen days where someone reportedly tried to poison him. The Governor-General of A.E.F., Victor Augagneur, wrote that the Lieutenant Governor of Gabon disliked Mba and was responsible for his early troubles. Citing an old Frenchman, he wrote that Mba was considered "a sweet little boy, and this is also the opinion of the superiors of the kid once he became an adult." The Augagneur defense of Léon Mba against the administration was described in the Omyènè-controlled newspaper *Echo Gabonais* in 1923 (23 June).

In 1933 he was tried, convicted, and exiled from Gabon to Oubangui-Chari until 1946 for reasons that are not very clear. The story some people like to tell is that he was accused of having engaged in occult activities which involved acts of cannibalism. In the 1920's supporters of the *Echo Gabonais* and members of the League of the Rights of Man which had a chapter in Libreville were frequently harassed by the colonial administration. One affair called the *Affaire Tambani* involved a leader considered an agitator by the administration which claimed to have found a skull in his house; the supposed discovery of the skull was used as a pretext to jail him, it was said.

After Mba's return to Gabon he became president of the Gabon Groupe d'Etudes Communistes (G.E.C.) which, as in several other countries, was sponsored by French or Antilles civil servants who had been sent overseas during the Popular Front government in France. The membership was open to all ethnic groups, and it appears that several different ethnic groups did belong in addition to a few Congolese residents in Libreville. The purpose of G.E.C.

was the political education of members, and methods of protest were discussed, but members of the group were not necessarily members of the Communist party.

In the late 1940's Mba founded the Comité Mixte Gabonais (C.M.G.) on the basis of a previous all-Fang organization. He broke his alliance with Aubame and in 1951 ran against him for the post of deputy to the National Assembly. After a defeat he was elected in 1952 to the Gabonese Territorial Assembly. In 1954 the B.D.G. was organized, and he became its secretary under Paul Gondjout; in 1956 he was elected mayor of Libreville. The following year his party gained a majority of seats in the assembly and became a section of the West African Rassemblement Démocratique Africain (R.D.A.). Mba was named Vice-President of the government. After the 1958 referendum and the granting of autonomy to all overseas territories, Mba became the Prime Minister of his country. With the gradual elimination of rivals he became the only real national leader with power, and with a 1961 constitutional change he became Gabon's first President.

The bases for his power from the time he became President until the attempted coup d'état in February 1964 were the following: In the first place, he came from the Nationalizing Zone and had for a long time worked with the so-called *bilop-bilop*. (This is the Fang expression for people who do not speak Fang. The epithet is apparently meant to imitate the way in which other Gabonese seem to the Fang to talk. It was long regarded as highly uncomplimentary, and the President forbade the Fang to use it.) Because he had worked with representatives of several tribes in a party and in organizations like *Bwiti* and the earlier Study Group (G.E.C.), people had less fear that he would be partial to the Fang. The Fang of Woleu-Ntem in fact considered that he was the servant of the coastal Omyènè and the southerners, but he still had some support in Woleu-Ntem. Whenever an Omyènè leader was arrested, the coastal people feared the Fang would turn against them, but the President has been able to quiet their apprehension.

Also, Mba has long promoted the idea that he above everyone else was willing to work with all Gabonese for a new united nation, while his major opponent, Aubame, has been pictured as a tribalist. In his 1951 attempt to unseat Aubame he sent out election propaganda which appealed to all: "Whatever your color, whatever your race or tribe, whatever your religion" you should vote for Léon Mba, because "Léon Mba is the Gabonese leader who by his courage, his far-reaching and generous ideas, by the personal relations he has maintained since 1922 with the diverse ethnic groups of Gabon is capable of forging a union of all Africans and Metropolitans in order to prepare a prosperous Gabon within the French Union."[18]

Aubame was constantly attacked in the B.D.G. newspaper as a person who thought only of the Fang, and writers implied that violence and bloodshed would result if Aubame maintained his position. In an open letter to one of Aubame's colleagues a new recruit to the B.D.G., who claimed to be an old friend of Aubame, said that Aubame had become a racist because of his association with Fang tribalists: "If your political bureau, called Aubame's bureau, . . . had not given my friend this idea of racism, this idea of division, my friend Aubame would never have been hated by all those who struggle for the evolution of Gabon."[19] The former deputy has long been accused of hating the Omyènè, some of whom had supported the Vichy regime when Aubame struggled to win support for de Gaulle in 1940.

During his 1964 trial, Aubame was accused of harboring ill feelings toward the Omyènè; the prosecutor in a statement which had really nothing to do with the issues said in the courtroom that Aubame hated him: "He knew my father very well, but he disliked the son." Then he accused Aubame of having stolen some money and said that there were personal conflicts between Aubame and him while the prosecutor was ambassador to France.[20]

Aubame was pictured as anti-White and anti-French, while Mba has always claimed to support the idea of close relations between the Whites and the Blacks as well as between the various tribes. To this end he has encouraged Frenchmen to take out Gabonese citizenship, and they have always been encouraged to vote [for him] in elections. (It has not always been clear whether or not the Frenchmen who voted were already Gabonese citizens

18 Election handout for legislative elections of 17 June 1951, "Candidature Léon M'Ba."

19 *Union Gabonaise,* No. 21, February 1956. Aubame has always denied the accusation of tribalism or racism, and as early as 1949 his newspaper spoke of the need for unity above tribal or ethnic groups. See *Le Pilote,* No. 1, December 1949.

20 Dispatch of Agence France Presse, No. 5470, Libreville, 6–7 September 1964.

or not.) Careful of his relationship with southerners, the President ensured that those who received the longest sentences at the trial of plotters against him were Fang; most of the southerners were not brought to trial at all or else were acquitted.

A third basis for his personal power was a special spiritual puissance. He has *evus*, according to the Fang; he must have it, they say, to have achieved the powerful position of President. Many Gabonese regarded him as a witch who could use his special power to help the country or to threaten the people with capricious forces and disorder. For this reason they feared him.

The story that his supposed connection with strange and occult rites was the reason for his exile from Gabon is widely believed by Gabonese. After Mba's return from exile an administrator reported that his supporters were using secret societies and special ceremonies to call on the spirit world to help elect him in 1951. After the attempt in 1960 by the president of the National Assembly to censure the government and thus ensure its fall, many stories were told about a supposed attempt on Mba's life. Gondjout had hired a sorcerer, it was said, to kill the prime minister. This man, a Camerounese, worked for five days in the forest to hex Mba, but nothing happened. The Camerounese was reported to have become worried and was convinced that if his intended victim had survived all his nocturnal machinations, he must have greater powers than himself. He apparently went to Libreville and told Mba the whole story.

During one of his visits in Woleu-Ntem in 1960 he was giving a speech in a Fang town while surrounded by an essentially hostile audience. Suddenly a man in the front row of spectators fainted. Everyone then ran off shouting that Léon Mba had sent a witch to Woleu-Ntem.

After the French troops had brought him back to Libreville in February 1964 and restored him to office, there was an interval of about thirty hours before he addressed the Gabonese people. It was said that he had been directed by a Dahomean spiritual advisor to purify himself.

In speeches he has often talked about "dangerous forces" at work; these dangerous forces threaten order, and those responsible for them must expect the worst. When he returned from one visit to France he complained about those who create disorder and threatened them with spiritual death.

Europeans have long delighted in fanciful tales about African leaders. Such tales were perhaps more indicative of the workings of the European libido than of anything else, but the political style of the first President of Gabon cannot be considered without reference to his use of the occult. Other Gabonese leaders of a different generation and a different educational background may not have the same style.

His fourth basis for power has come from forces outside Gabon — France and the French. Europeans in the Churches and administration had never looked very favorably on Léon Mba; it was Aubame, a devout Catholic, Gaullist, civil servant, who received their support. Mba had been called a Communist for his connections with the G.E.C. and the R.D.A., an anti-French radical, and a "pagan." Aubame wrote in 1949 after the break between him and Mba: "The Gabonese know you and you are even known outside the country as a tyrannical *chef de canton,* as a vain individual afflicted with chronic jealousy, as a perpetual agitator, and a notorious Communist. In our opinion these are not exactly glorious titles. If some young people follow you today, it is that they are ignorant of your past which we know only too well. I won't remind you of it here out of disgust and because, as a Christian, I believe in absolution."[21] Once he became an important political force in Libreville, he got support from some businessmen who were not in agreement with the administration nor with the Church. These forestry men, particularly a certain Roland Bru, began to contribute funds to Mba's campaigns. Such funds appear to have been important in convincing deputies elected on Aubame's list in 1957 to change to Mba's party to insure a B.D.G. majority.

Once he was in power, the French referred to him as the grand old man, the man who could develop Gabon, the true friend of France, the man who could keep stability. Surrounded by technical advisers paid for by France he insisted that if France had one ally left in the world it would be Gabon. The French often

21 Open letter from Aubame to Léon Mba, No. 1.896/CI (from Deputy Aubame's office), 8 August 1949, p. 2.

said that if he were not there, chaos would reign: "another Congo; après lui, le déluge."

Aid from France to Gabon has been considerable in men, money, and materials. Some Gabonese claim that France gets more in return than it invests. Certain businessmen get the economic benefits while aid maintains for the French people as a whole an extension of French civilization in Africa and in other parts of the world where the French language is spoken. (Even if there were no material benefits to be gained, many French leaders and intellectuals would feel close ties to lands where their language is spoken.)

The French government once gave grants to balance the Gabonese budget and has provided technical advisers and teachers whose salaries were paid by France, research missions to improve the economy and to find new mineral resources. In 1962 there were still two French prefects and one sub-prefect, but these men were replaced by Gabonese, so that Gabonization (and the Gabonese never use the word Africanization) has progressed slowly at least at the highest levels in the civil service. Many schools and technical services are still run by Frenchmen.

When Mba, on 18 February 1964, was overthrown by an army group which called itself the Comité Révolutionnaire, driven off toward Lambaréné, and replaced by a provisional government headed by Aubame, one of the Gabonese military leaders spoke to the people over the radio first in French, then in Fang, Omyènè, and Bapounou and explained why the military had taken the initiative. He appealed for calm: "We urgently appeal to the population to maintain calm and not to mistreat anyone. We affirm that the interests of no individuals will be hurt and that agreements with groups of individuals will be respected. In order to preserve our good relations the representatives of technical-assistance programs are requested not to get mixed up in the internal affairs of Gabon."[22] A group of Frenchmen, however, did appeal to General de Gaulle, and France decided to intervene to return Léon Mba to power. French, African, and Antilles troops were flown from military bases in Brazzaville and Dakar. The fact that the British had successfully intervened under different conditions

22 Broadcast over Radio-Libreville, 18 February by Lt. Ebene. Cited in *La Semaine Africaine*, 23 February 1964.

in East Africa shortly before no doubt influenced French policy with regard to Gabon. The provisional government suspected nothing and did not even think to prevent planes from landing at Libreville airport. The French quickly arrived on the 18th and 19th, took over the city, and were obliged to strafe the Gabonese military camp on the edge of the city where the soldiers were holding out against the intervention. There is considerable dispute about how many people were killed, but it is agreed that they were mostly Gabonese. The French colonel in charge of the intervention met Jean-Hilaire Aubame and Jean-Marc Ekoh, who had been named Foreign Minister in the provisional government, at the French embassy. He noted that his orders were to restore Léon Mba to power and pointed out that France had an agreement with Gabon (secret and never ratified by the National Assembly) to intervene in case the government were in danger. He also pointed out that the Vice-President had requested French intervention. This was clearly incorrect, because the Vice-President was not in Libreville at the time.[23]

With the suppression of the coup d'état the Gabonese army was taken over by French forces who, along with African mercenaries, protected the President. It was generally believed that without this protection he would have been overthrown. Another basis for Mba's power which he hoped to make the most important is the single-party apparatus built around himself as President, mayor of Libreville (a post he has maintained), and Secretary General of the Bloc Démocratique Gabonais.

Léon Mba took over control of the B.D.G. with the demise of Paul Gondjout at the end of 1960. For the legislative elections of February 1961 the B.D.G. and the opposition U.D.S.G. formed a Liste d'Union Nationale, and the parties were considered dissolved. A coalition government with Mba as President, Aubame as Minister for Foreign Affairs, Ekoh as Minister of Education, and eventually Sousatte as Minister of Agriculture was formed. Leaders of all factions were absorbed into the government, and everyone — all the ministers and their assistants — insisted that Gabon had no time to waste in sterile political combats. The coalition lasted until 1963.

[23] It may be possible some day to publish the details of the coup and the intervention.

For reasons that are still unclear even to those cabinet ministers who had belonged to the coalition, all opposition U.D.S.G. and P.U.N.G.A. members were removed from the government in February 1963 and the Union Nationale was dissolved, although it was not immediately decided to set up a one-party state. The President indicated in a speech to the people that there were too many disagreements with members of different parties within the cabinet and there was an "excessive cult of the personality": it is the "President who embodies the Nation and directs its destiny." He added that "National Union remained in the hearts and minds of the Gabonese" even if there was no such union at the government level.[24]

Then the President and his close advisers in the B.D.G. began to make the party the only party in Gabon. An attempt was made to remove Aubame from his position as deputy by passing a law that would make it impossible for one man to be both deputy and president of the Supreme Court. All deputies who had been elected in 1961 except those who had originally belonged to the U.D.S.G. were compelled to renounce the U.D.S.G. and join the B.D.G. Statements of adhesion were published in what rapidly became the party newspaper *L'Effort Gabonais* to replace the *Union Gabonaise,* which had ceased publication. In May 1963 deputies from Ogooué-Ivindo declared their fealty to the B.D.G. and to Léon Mba: "Given the present situation and because you want to know exactly the political affiliation of each deputy, it is my duty to accept publicly my responsibilities. By this letter I adhere to the single governmental party headed by His Excellency Léon Mba, President of the Republic."[25]

From 20 to 24 August 1963 the B.D.G. held a large congress in Libreville to proceed with what was labeled its reorganization and further to make official the fact that Gabon was becoming a one-party state. Three hundred delegates attended.

In his opening address the Secretary General of the party said that the "B.D.G. remains an irreplaceable political movement in Gabon because it alone carries within it the seeds of national unity," and that changes in Gabon necessitated a reorganization of the party. The administrative secretary, Louis Bigmann, re-

24 *Patrie Gabonaise,* February 1963.
25 *L'Effort Gabonais,* 9 August 1963.

affirmed that the B.D.G. was a member of the Rassemblement Démocratique Africain (R.D.A.) and words like "comrade," "party militant," and so forth suddenly came into use. In the days when the B.D.G. was fighting the U.D.S.G. for power such words were never used in newspaper articles or speeches.[26]

One month later, on 22 September 1963, municipal elections were held and Léon Mba was re-elected mayor by the new city council of Libreville. Elections to the National Assembly were then scheduled for 23 February 1964. The number of deputies to be elected was reduced from sixty-seven to forty-seven as part of an economy drive and to ensure that all deputies were B.D.G. members. Only one list, that of the B.D.G., was permitted to present itself for that Sunday election. But five days before that election the coup d'état took place. Many Gabonese had been concerned about the quality of the men who were running on the B.D.G. ticket, most of whom were considered party hacks with little formal education. In his opening remarks after Léon Mba had been removed from office, Lt. Ebene said: "Gabonese were supposed to vote next Sunday in an atmosphere of insecurity which constitutes the reigning police regime. We would again have begun the same dangerous life because from day to day the opposition was indicating its discontent . . . in a muted but perceptible way. To avoid any possible outburst of uncontrollable manifestations, the armed forces of Gabon have decided to bring this situation to an end. As a result the Government is dissolved and President Léon Mba and his acolytes are arrested. Civil liberties are re-established and all political prisoners are freed."[27]

After his return to power Léon Mba set new elections for 1 March and then postponed them until 12 April because of continuing unrest, strikes, and demonstrations against him. For these elections any parties could present candidates for election not as individuals but by list, under a regional unit system. About thirty lists were presented in the nine regions. Six of these were organized in Woleu-Ntem alone. The U.D.S.G. presented itself under the name of Défense des Institutions Démocratiques (D.I.D.), and another opposition group under the leadership of

26 "Le IIe Congrès du B.D.G.," *Patrie Gabonaise*, No. 16, 1 August to 15 September 1963 and *La Semaine Africaine*, 8 September 1963.
27 *La Semaine Africaine*, 23 February 1964.

trade-union leader Jean-Fidèle Otandault of Port-Gentil called itself Défense de la Démocratie. In almost every region groups designated themselves defenders of the interests of such and such a region. In only two regions did the B.D.G. appear under its proper name, in the Estuaire and in Ogooué-Ivindo; and in only one region, also Ogooué-Ivindo, did the U.D.S.G. present itself under its proper name. Names of parties were really quite irrelevant; people knew by the names of the candidates which list was Mba's and which was that of the opposition. Although he had planned to run for deputy in the February elections, President Mba wisely chose not to run in April.

The B.D.G. and allied lists won 52 per cent and the opposition 48 per cent of the popular vote. Because of the distribution of the votes, however, the B.D.G. won thirty-one seats in the new National Assembly against the opposition's sixteen. About 263,000 out of 303,000 registered voters went to the polls, and there were only 5,500 blank or void ballots.[28] Seventeen per cent of those who could have voted for one list or another chose not to vote or they submitted blank or invalid ballots. This is not as significant as the fact that an important change has taken place in the Nationalizing Zone.

In the crucial 1957 elections, the results of which were to determine who would become vice-president of the council and eventually Prime Minister, the B.D.G. won more than 50 per cent of the votes in two of the three regions of the Nationalizing Zone: Estuaire and Ogooué-Maritime. (An independent group won in the third region, Moyen-Ogooué.) The U.D.S.G. won more than 70 per cent of Woleu-Ntem's vote but less than 40 per cent of the vote in the Nationalizing Zone. (It won more than 50 per cent of the vote in three non-Fang regions south of the Ogooué.) Seven years later, in April 1964, the opposition won 34,500 of the votes in the three regions, or about 54 per cent of the total, while the B.D.G. won 28,815 or 46 per cent of the total vote in the Nationalizing Zone. The percentage supporting the actual government would have been less if the vote of foreigners — French, Dahomeans, and others — were subtracted, but there is no sure way of knowing how many votes they represent — 4,000 to 5,000 probably.

28 Data from the Agence Gabonaise de Presse.

In the Woleu-Ntem a list of candidates supporting Aubame and Ekoh, neither of whom was permitted to run, won almost 35,000 out of a total of 41,000 votes cast despite the fact that six lists had originally been presented. (One was eliminated for technical reasons.)

After the elections the opposition was recognized for a time, but eventually some of its deputies were arrested on trumped-up charges, a Port-Gentil leader died, and the government again began to talk of "one people, one nation, one party." Deputies were forced to join the B.D.G., whose reorganization continued into 1966.

The form and structure of the B.D.G., which in 1966 was rapidly becoming the single party of a single-party state, was strongly influenced by the average West African section of the R.D.A. and particularly by the Parti Démocratique de la Côte d'Ivoire (P.D.C.I.) which influenced the form of other sections of the R.D.A.[29] The R.D.A. was, of course, strongly influenced by the structure of the Communist party with which it was once linked.

Before independence neither the B.D.G. nor the U.D.S.G. had much organization outside the Nationalizing Zone. Men were chosen in districts on the basis of family connections and friendships to represent the party and to campaign for it, but there was little formal organization. In 1961 and 1962 the controlling organs of the B.D.G. were a directorate, an executive bureau, the political bureau, and a group of men called regional counsellors. The directorate or *comité directeur*, not the political bureau as in other R.D.A. parties, was the center of power. After the ouster of Gondjout, Mba became the head of the directorate and he was assisted by P.-M. Yembit, a Bapounou from Ngounié, who was also the Vice-President of Gabon; the second assistant was P. Avaro, a minister and Omyènè leader from Port-Gentil. The administrative secretary of the directorate was Louis Bigmann, then president of the National Assembly.

The president of the executive bureau was Vincent de Paul Nyonda, an Eshira from Ngounié and a minister. This bureau

<hr />

29 See William J. Foltz, *From French West Africa to the Mali Federation* (New Haven, Yale University Press, 1965), pp. 54–55. Also Ruth Schachter Morgenthau, *Political Parties in French-Speaking West Africa* (London, Oxford University Press, 1964).

was in charge of publicity for the party. An Omyènè of Libreville headed the rather unimportant political bureau. There were nine regional counsellors, one for each region, and in each region a regional committee, but there do not appear to have been organizations at the village level.

In every cabinet from 1957 to 1964 four key ministers were always present; they were all early members of the B.D.G.: Nyonda, Yembit, Vice-President and mayor of Mouila, J.-F. Ondo, a Fang from Woleu-Ntem, and Anguilè, a Eurafrican Omyènè from Libreville. The concern for ethnic distribution of power among particularly the Fang, the Omyènè, and the Bapounou or Eshira was the same as during the colonial period.[30]

As a result of the 1963 congress in Libreville the political bureau became the most important organ of the party. Composed of twenty-three members, it had two leaders from each of six regions plus three from Woleu-Ntem, three from Ngounié, and five from Estuaire. The secretary general remained Léon Mba, the assistant secretary general was Yembit, and the administrative secretary was Bigmann. Each member represented a region and has specific party functions. For example, Nyonda was still in charge of publicity for the party, and several were assigned the titles commissar for research, for youth, for the women's organization, and for trade-union questions. A permanent secretariat of the party was maintained in Libreville. It dealt with ordinary correspondence and applications for party membership. A vigilance committee in Libreville was specially set up to encourage Woleu-Ntem Fang to join the party. The Organisation Nationale des Femmes Gabonaises, a public agency under the office of the President, had as goals the "emancipation of women" and full participation of women in Gabonese national life. Prior to January 1963 the organization was not considered to be politically oriented and was under the Ministry of Health. Since that time, however, it has come under the direct control of the President and was integrated into the party. It remained a government organ and a section of the party at the same time and indicates an attempt to make party and government coterminous.

---

[30] Data on aspects of the structure of B.D.G.–R.D.A. from "Institutions d'Afrique noire: la République Gabonaise, BDG," edited by La Documentation Africaine, Paris, 6 June 1961.

Since the coup d'état and the elections some changes have been made in the officers. Joseph Ngoua, a Fang from the Estuaire, became the administrative secretary of the B.D.G. to replace an Omyènè; he has been a cabinet minister and was head of the national soccer organization. He has been in charge of the permanent secretariat in Libreville. In the course of 1965 party sections have been organized at the level of villages and town sections. For example, Port-Gentil has six residential quarters, each of which has a *groupe,* which is the lowest level of party organization in towns and in villages. Each such *groupe* has a roster of officers: a president, secretary, treasurer, assistant treasurer, and about three commissars. At the cantonal level there are committees. *Groupes* and committees elect sub-sections at the sub-prefecture level, and the sub-sections form one section at the level of a prefecture.[31] Committees were organized under the aegis of deputies to the National Assembly and of civil servants, such as prefects and sub-prefects, who are not permitted to be politically neutral. Party affiliation of civil servants in the 1964 elections is apparently known, and the President has dimissed all functionaries who have indicated support for his opponents. Even in simple questions of discipline the President had wide control over civil servants. Every time there was a question of discipline concerning a functionary, the prefect made a report and sent it to the President, who has a dossier for each person in government service. He sends a copy of the report to the Minister of the Civil Service. If there were further infractions of rules and more cases of irregular behavior on the part of one person, the President told the minister to call a meeting of a Council of Discipline. This council then summoned the guilty party to defend himself. If he was eventually demoted by the council, his case was reviewed by the President, who had the power to dismiss the individual from the service or let him continue on. Civil servants may be dismissed or jailed for supposed infractions of rules or mismanagement of funds even if committed years previously. During the Mba presidency this was merely a pretext used against those who have displeased the President in some way; it is an old colonial technique. However, once civil servants were released from prison,

31 *Gabon d'Aujourd'hui,* 20 July 1965.

they received another well-paying job almost immediately; this discouraged opposition.

By 1965 the civil service in all its aspects appeared to be firmly controlled by the B.D.G. The official newspaper and other publications began calling the B.D.G. the government party and finished by calling it the National Party. For the first time in Gabonese history it seemed in 1965 that a real mass-based party was being built as a basis for power for President Léon Mba and his close associates. The illness of the President and his long absences from Gabon in 1966 weakened the efforts to build one party, however.

Techniques for Maintaining Power

Léon Mba has learned some of his techniques for maintaining power from M. Houphouët-Boigny, President of Ivory Coast. He was unable to attend the 1946 organization meeting of the R.D.A., but the latter sent reports of its meetings to Gabon. For example, African members of the Gabonese legislature received a report written by J. Williams Bayanlin Acka of the political commission of the R.D.A., dated 20 October 1946. The commission denounced the constitution of the French Republic, and among other suggestions African deputies and senators were advised to form an independent party but to seek alliances with any French party that might support pro-African resolutions. As early as 1948 an R.D.A. newspaper, *AEF Nouvelle* was published in Brazzaville, and Gabonese like François Mèyè, a graduate of the Ecole Renard Secondary School wrote in it. Mba traveled to Abidjan in 1949. In the same year an open letter from Aubame, the Gabonese deputy, made allusions to Mba's connections with Ivory Coast: "If you want to avenge yourself against those who have played a role in your detestable past, you will not have our help. And we shall oppose any attempt on your part to put into practice the lessons you have studied in Ivory Coast."[32]

Ivory Coast is like Gabon; it is rich and has long been opposed to larger unions of African states in which all would be required to give up their control over internal development and use of

[32] Ftn. 21, p. 3.

domestic revenue. Also it is a wood-producing state and has close ties with France. Its President, one of the most gifted political leaders in Africa, has been faced with some of the same challenges to his power as Léon Mba.

President Mba met Houphouët-Boigny at the R.D.A. conference again in 1957 but had maintained contact with him ever since 1949; he has followed some of his techniques for dealing with an opposition and furthering the development of the country. In 1960 he sent Louis Bigmann as his emissary to inquire about a court of security which Ivory Coast had just set up. After Bigmann's return a similar court was established in Gabon. Immediately after the coup d'état, Kouan Kanga, a former minister and the mayor of Abidjan, was sent to Libreville to consult with President Mba. Later, the President of Ivory Coast attempted to mediate between Mba and some of his Gabonese opponents.

In January 1957 an address by Houphouët-Boigny was reprinted in the B.D.G. newspaper *Union Gabonaise,* and his speeches on national unity have been occasionally posted at various government offices. A year after the coup President Mba (on his way to a conference in Mauritania) paid a visit to Ivory Coast. The official newspaper *Gabon d'Aujourd'hui* had a series of articles on Ivory Coast in 1965 in which the development of that country was taken for a model; Ivory Coast was called in the newspaper *le plage de la prospérité.*

In dealing with the opposition Mba used some of the techniques that had been perfected in countries like Ivory Coast and also some techniques of his own creation or that of a small group of French advisers who have had wide experience in these matters: a secret police, suppression of strikes by force, public beatings, shaving women's heads, physical attacks on anyone critical of the President or the party, no matter how old or distinguished, and something called "national indignity," which deprives a person of his rights as a citizen. People suspected of opposition or people who made some wrong guesses were sent to the most isolated regions of Gabon, away from their families and sources of support. Okondja at the end of that road of sand and certain posts in Nyanga were favorite choices.

The President could dissolve the National Assembly at will and could have deputies arrested. Deputies have been arrested without going through the procedure of lifting parliamentary immunity. Judges were appointed and removed by presidential *ordonnance* over which no one else had any control. By an *ordonnance* of 17 April 1965 the President could dissolve any political party, trade union, or association.[33] Prefects and sub-prefects cumulated as many functions as the old colonial administrator, and the system of the *indigénat* has been more or less restored.

The President has also had a group of people around him who have always been willing to speak in more extreme terms than he. The purpose of this was to frighten the opposition, to pretend that future radical policies are in response to needs which the masses have expressed, and to test reactions of people. For example, in 1960 a leader of the *Bwiti* church who was also a civil servant and a relative of one of Mba's closest associates, Vincent de Paul Nyonda, proposed in a signed tract that a presidential form of government be established. Léon Mba, the tract states, is the only man who can keep order in Gabon; without him the tribes would kill each other. Léon Mba must, the author continues, take charge of the country after a referendum. The author, Prince Birinda, an Eshira, concludes by threatening all that he has witchcraft powers: "I am Nganga (Oganga) which acts while awake and while asleep. . . . If they kill me, I shall not die. . . . Watch out — I have already said that after my death each globule of my blood will transform itself into a spirit with a thousand heads, a thousand arms."[34] This tract was considered important enough by Gondjout and by Aubame to be discussed in the National Assembly, and the President was asked in a very weak statement to tell the Assembly what he intended to do. The idea of parliamentary government was reaffirmed. Shortly after this a new constitution setting up a presidential regime was promulgated, and some of the previous leaders found themselves in prison.

At the end of 1964 a new newspaper, *Le Patriote*, was started and by 1966 edited by the same Prince Birinda. Articles in the paper suggest that the opposition has been treated too kindly,

33 Ordonnance No. 17/PR, 17 April 1965, *"Journal Officiel de la République Gabonaise,"* 15 May 1965, p. 256.
34 Extract from the minutes of the plenary meeting of the National Assembly 28 October 1960, *Journal des Débats*, Assemblée Nationale de la République Gabonaise, Deuxième Session Ordinaire 1960, Session Budgétaire, 11 October to 4 November.

that certain church leaders are traitors, that Gabon is threatened by international Communism from without and from within its frontiers. "Vigilance! Death to the traitors! And whoever pardons a crime becomes an accomplice of it."[35]

The supposed 10,000 women who belong to the 380 sections of the Organisation Nationale des Femmes Gabonaises received gifts from the President. Their function was to support Léon Mba because "only he cares about the emancipation of women." Before the 1964 elections President Mba proclaimed again his support of female emancipation while tracts supposedly signed by Jean-Hilaire Aubame said the proper place for women was in the home. Forgery of tracts in elections is, however, an old Gabonese custom. Women in the Organisation Nationale served as spies throughout the country· They were encouraged to observe the actions of civil servants; some civil servants have been removed from their jobs because of reports made by the local women's section on their efficiency and their loyalty to the President. The women were encouraged to make reports on the activities of other Gabonese or of foreigners directly to the President. If, however, they transmitted false information, they were warned that they would be "punished severely."

There is also some evidence that President Mba was building a type of civic service organization with police or even military power as an organization parallel with the army. He set up a loyalist student organization, Rassemblement des Etudiants et Stagiaires Gabonais, after the fashion of Houphouët-Boigny and the French government, to compete with the student groups that opposed him. Lastly, he was able to call upon the French government and some other African governments to extradite opponents who have sought refuge.

Gabon's first President has been a new type of leader for all Gabonese at a new level of community. Motivated by Fang dynamism, first to reorganize the tribe by his interest in Fang custom as a Fang judge and *chef de canton,* in an attempt to become grand chief of all Fang, and after having begun in post-World War II politics on the basis of a Fang organization, he turned to Gabon and has proclaimed that he was the "Grand Chief of Modern Gabon."

[35] *Le Patriote*, No. 6, 8 December 1964.

More than ever before, President Mba became the symbol of the nation-state after the intervention of French troops to restore him to power. He became estranged from many Gabonese who are becoming politically conscious, but as the most important Gabonese national leader for ten years he influenced the pattern of politics in Gabon and the way people look at the nation-building process. This pattern and perception of what governmental and nation-building are all about may remain important in Gabon long after the disappearance of President Mba.

CHAPTER 9

Government Nation-Building Policies

Nation-Building Policy

National leaders in all countries are interested in maintaining their power. Nation-building policies are ancillary to policies designed to maintain the positions of political leaders. A government can call anything a nation-building policy: suppression of competing loyalty groups, construction of a single party, concessions to powerful pre-national systems, special privileges to foreign investors, policies of economic development. Such policies may indeed contribute to nation-building and at the same time keep certain leaders in power and provide them with the funds needed to run a government. There is room for idealism, altruism, and dedication of one leader to the idea that the group is more important than his own interests and desires for power. But even such a leader must struggle to maintain his own power and position if he wants to see his program carried out. A regional ethnic leader who thinks only of his area and family and who gets a road built from his home area into another so that his friends and neighbors may trade more easily contributes unconsciously to nation-building.

A program of conscious nation-building might have policies that have an effect different from that intended. It may have policies conflicting with each other, and some groups may take more advantage of nation-building policies than others because of their dynamism or favored position. Such groups might be certain pre-national supreme loyalty groups or perhaps certain professional or special-interest groups.

Unpopular national leaders may attempt to satisfy an oppressed people with what they call a nation-building program. Some regions or peoples, particularly those in the Nationalizing Zone, may be favored, but if the people find themselves subject to new capricious forces, material rewards may not be sufficient to win their loyalty to the national leaders. Because the national leader has attempted to combine the maintenance of his power and his own glorification with nation-building, the whole idea of the nation as the supreme loyalty group may be discredited.

Nation-building policies depend in part on the ideas of what nation-building is all about. It may be considered as material development and modernization. In Gabon, deputies to the National Assembly think first of the economic development and improvement of communications in their own regions as nation-building. During the first ordinary session of the National Assembly in 1959 a great deal of time was spent one day in a discussion of what a deputy should be called: Should he be designated a deputy from Ogooué-Ivindo or should his title be Gabonese deputy? A representative from Woleu-Ntem insisted on the use of the name of the region for "my first nation is the Woleu-Ntem; the second, the adopted one, is Gabon. I am therefore first of all a deputy from Woleu-Ntem and only secondarily a deputy of Gabon, my second nation."[1]

Deputies from Ogooué-Ivindo claim that future exploitation of the huge iron-ore deposits there constitutes nation-building; deputies from Haut-Ogooué consider the mining of manganese ore to be part of the nation-building process and say that the region must have a good road to connect it with the rest of Gabon. They feel that nation-building means that their people will get

1 *Journal des Débats,* Assemblée Nationale de la République Gabonaise, 5 May 1959, p. 8.

benefits from the central government commensurate with the income the government receives from the manganese exploitation.

Nation-building in Ogooué-Lolo means building a road, people say, from Lastoursville to Franceville. Nation-building in Woleu-Ntem means building a railroad and getting year-round roads to Libreville; and for some Fang, nation-building means the absorption of smaller tribes.

For the president of the Supreme Court, nation-building means a realization on the part of the Gabonese that they are all kin because they are all descended from the same Gabonese ancestor. Cabinet ministers have views based on the role of their own ministry; e.g., the minister for the civil service thinks in terms of efficient organization of a civil service. Once there are enough people to Gabonize the civil service completely and to direct a development program, Gabon will be practically a nation.

Jean-Hilaire Aubame once said that nation-building meant the regroupment of villages and development of communications; the disappearance of internal conflict would lead to increased national consolidation. Some leaders believe that nation-building is consolidation around the Fang, but non-Fang say that people will forget their tribal differences and that there can be no question of grouping around the Fang.

The Whites who have been in Gabon for a long time and who in some cases have become Gabonese citizens (without, however, giving up their French citizenship) have different attitudes, depending on their stake in Gabon. Some do not even think about a Gabonese nation, while others, those who appear tired or prejudiced, say there will never be a Gabonese nation, that France is responsible for the existence of the country, and that once the French leave, tribal loyalties will be asserted and violence will result. White technicians in agriculture and education who have come to an independent Gabon think in terms of economic development and education to give the Gabonese a sense of the importance of a community at a national rather than at a kinship level. Education will show them, these French believe, the rationality of the nation or something higher, such as a Eurafrican or Franco-African community.

The President's conception of national unity is one of order and obedience to the laws made by national leaders, emancipation of women, and help from the Whites. He stated that national unity has already been achieved: "Concord, world and universal fraternity, observance of the laws and obedience to the representatives of order and to the administration, emancipation of the Gabonese woman [are the duties of Gabonese]. National union is something already accomplished, but it must be strengthened."[2]

People outside the government, such as villagers with whom one is able to talk, think of nation-building in terms of railroads and jobs for themselves. Some say that only when Gabon manufactures everything that the European nations manufacture will it be a nation. Some, particularly students, claim that Gabon will become an industrial nation only after it frees itself from foreign capitalist control and has younger educated leaders.

Gabonese Government Policies 1960–1966

Ethnic Balance

Ethnic balance to promote confidence is the government policy of first importance. That Mr. Abe Fortas follows Mr. Goldberg on the United States Supreme Court is as fortuitous as one Bapounou following another Bapounou in a presidential cabinet in Gabon. The Gabonese are highly sensitive to the ethnic identity of civil servants and elected officials: "We, the members of such and such a tribe and in such and such a region, have no prefect, we have no deputy, but we do have one *chef de cabinet*." People have the utmost confidence that their interests are being taken care of when they can say they have a very close relative in a high position; this means someone who belongs to the same kinship group and comes from the same area. The Fang of a district like Mitzic would not be satisfied to be represented by a Fang from Oyem; the Bapounou of Ngounié would not feel represented if there were a Bapounou from Nyanga in the President's cabinet, nor would the Bandjabi of Koula-Moutou like to see a Bandjabi from Mbigou in Libreville. Regional and ethnic leaders or their representatives are absorbed into the government and the administration. Even those who are imprisoned and punished for actions or words considered offensive by the President are given high-paying positions after their release.

2 *Bulletin Quotidien*, 20 March 1962.

Between one third and one half of the members of the cabinet are always Fang. During the period of National Union eight out of seventeen seats were held by Fang, and in the first cabinet after the April 1964 elections five out of thirteen posts were held by Fang. The nine regions are always represented, and the Fang, the Omyènè, and the Bapounou control most ministerial jobs — ten out of thirteen in the April 1964 cabinet, for example, and twelve out of seventeen during the period of National Union from 1961 to 1963.

Six of the regions have only one minister, Woleu-Ntem and Ngounié each have two, and Estuaire has three, two of whom are Fang and one Omyènè; the representatives from the two other regions of the Nationalizing Zone, Ogooué-Maritime and Moyen-Ogooué, are both Omyènè. The presence of three Omyènè ministers testifies to the importance of their ethnic group in Gabonese national life in spite of their numerical weakness. A Bapounou and an Eshira represent Ngounié, and another Bapounou represents Nyanga. A Bandjabi represents Ogooué-Lolo, an Ambamba represents Haut-Ogooué, a Fang represents Ogooué-Ivindo, and two Fang represent Woleu-Ntem. Cabinet ministers who represent the dominant tribe or ethnic group in a region frequently appoint representatives from minority tribes in their regions as their assistants.

Concern with ethnic balance influenced the choice of judges for the court before which members of the Revolutionary Committee and the Provisional Government were tried in August and September 1964. The president of the court was a Libreville Omyènè, the only trained Gabonese magistrate. The nine judges represented primarily the Fang, the Bapounou, the Omyènè, the Eshira. The Eshira representative was the former grand chief, Cyprien Guipieri.

The presidency of the National Assembly has been reserved for the Libreville Omyènè. Deputies from the nine regions are generally chosen by the ministers or other important leaders from the region; this encourages the development of regional political groupings, although President Mba had a great influence over the choice of candidates because he was the head of the party. When there were sixty-seven deputies, Woleu-Ntem had twelve, all of them Fang. No other region had deputies from just one tribe.

Ngounié, for example, had eleven: four Bapounou, two Eshira, two Bandjabi, one Bapindji, one Massango, and one Mitsogo. The Bandjabi actually greatly outnumber the Bapounou in the region (about 17,000 adults to 8,000) but the Bapounou have more power in the Nationalizing Zone, and this has influenced the number of deputies they have been allowed. In the National Assembly elected in 1961 and dissolved in 1964 there were twenty-four Fang, eleven Bapounou, seven Omyènè, five Bandjabi, three Bawandji, three Bakota, three Eshira, two Mindoumou, two Bavili, one Batéké, one Ambamba, one Mitsogo, one Massango, one Bapindji, one Badouma, and one Pove.[3] The Fang-Omyènè-Bapounou coalition is as important in the National Assembly as in the President's cabinet. In this National Assembly all cabinet members were also deputies, but in the forty-seven-member National Assembly elected in April 1964 some ministers were present while others, including President Mba, were not.

Ethnic conflicts over elections have not led to widespread violence, although there are many accusations of favoritism and attempts to prevent deputies from seeking office. The Fang have in some instances been accused by neighbors in Contact Zones of attempting to influence non-Fang to vote for Fang candidates. Once a legislative representative complained that Bakota were forced to vote for Fang. Similar accusations have been made against the French and other ethnic groups in Gabon. Fang accused of trying to get Fang elected by non-Fang votes were also leaders of the *alar ayong* regroupment movement.

In 1962 there were seven Gabonese prefects of whom four were Omyènè, two were Fang, and one was Bapounou. By 1964 five out of nine prefects were Fang, and three were Omyènè. Woleu-Ntem has most often had an Omyènè prefect but most sub-prefects are Fang.

Civil servants may be from the same ethnic group as the people in the area where they work, but they are seldom natives of the area. It is believed that if civil servants are far from their families they will not be subject to pressures for favoritism and will be watched more carefully by the local population.

The Gabonese army has been about 40 per cent Fang, 40 per

[3] Calculations from Direction de l'Information de la République Gabonaise, "Assemblée Nationale 1961."

cent Bapounou, and 20 per cent Omyènè and others. The gendarmerie and the police force have tried to maintain the same proportions. The military men who led the Revolutionary Committee which overthrew President Mba were mainly Fang and Bapounou.

Service to People

A second nation-building policy is service to people. Services like an educational system reward the people and inform them of the benefits they can get from the state. The problem is that most services are available only in urban areas and to civil servants. For example, the Banque Gabonaise de Développement was created in 1960 to grant small loans for the purchase of equipment, to help small businesses, for the acquisition of forestry-exploitation gear, to enlarge the development of industrial crops, and to improve public markets. From 1960 to 1963 over 43 per cent of the loans were for small goods, some of which were luxury goods such as motor scooters or radios, about 29 per cent for the financing of public markets, and slightly under 7 per cent went to the agricultural sector.[4] Loans are made to people with regular incomes, but the only Gabonese with regular incomes are civil servants. Therefore, if an applicant is not himself a civil servant he must have a close relative who is. Approximately 69 per cent of all loans were made in Libreville, but the Fang Heartland requested and received more agricultural loans than any other region outside the capital.[5]

To help the African peasant, the colonial administration had set up Sociétés Indigènes de Prévoyance (S.I.P.). All cultivators were members and were supposed to be taught techniques to ameliorate their rates of production, to encourage solidarity among themselves, and to serve as an intermediary between the individual producer and the purchaser, who was most often a European merchant. In fact S.I.P.'s were under the arbitrary and strict control of colonial administrators and the benefits to producers were slight. Their name was later changed to Sociétés Africaines de Prévoyance, and in 1962 the Société Gabonaise de Développement Rural was set up to help cultivators of industrial crops, to purchase

4 *L'Effort Gabonais,* 6 March 1964.
5 Direction de l'Information, "Investissements au Gabon," p. 71.

coffee and peanuts from them, and to run the small coffee factories where the beans are prepared for export.

In 1962 Gabonese peasants were complaining that their cocoa and coffee had not been purchased by the administration as promised, with resultant great losses through rotting. In many areas the Gabonese refused to bother harvesting the industrial crops because they had lost confidence in the government's willingness to purchase it; unless they could sell it themselves, as the Fang did to Spanish purchasers in Rio Muni, all effort would be considered wasted.

Among other social services offered to the people are measures to encourage large families and to help such families financially. Expectant mothers are encouraged to have their children in hospitals, and they are supposed to receive a small sum of money for children so born. In 1956 an expectant mother was supposed to receive 225 francs for each month of a pregnancy; at the time of birth she received 1,125 francs and thereafter 225 francs per month for each child. Starting in April 1964 this was increased to 1,000 francs for each month of pregnancy, 5,000 francs at birth, and 1,000 francs each month after birth. This money is distributed by the Caisse de Prévoyance Sociale.[6] Yet out of an estimated 160,000 children only 27,500 get such allowances, and these come from families of civil servants and salaried workers in the urban areas.[7] Social centers have also been set up in most towns and in smaller sub-prefectures. The purpose of these twenty-six centers is to teach wives and mothers modern techniques; most centers have a nursery school, cooking classes, sewing classes, instruction on child and infant care, home improvement and maintenance. Directors, who are paid by the *collectivités rurales,* are supposed to make visits to the villages, to keep records of newborn children, and to distribute milk, soap, and articles for babies.

Like the other services offered, the social centers are most effective for wives of civil servants in urban areas. There is usually a little building constructed, but the village women have no funds to travel to town, and the director has no way to travel to the

---

[6] Service National de la Statistique, *"Rapport annuel sur la situation économique, financière et sociale de la République Gabonaise — Fin 1963,"* Libreville, July 1964, pp. 189–190.
[7] *Gabon d'Aujourd'hui,* 30 January 1965.

villages. It is often impossible to take time from working the plantations and taking care of children to attend classes in towns or in the village.

The Organisation Nationale des Femmes Gabonaises attempts to do many of the same things, but their publications and the nature of the advice they give are clearly not directed to the village woman. Almost 400 "animators" are supposed to lead Thursday meetings during which suitable subjects are discussed and courses taken.

Another type of service is the arbitrary granting of funds to people. The members of the Organisation Nationale des Femmes Gabonaises received gifts of money from President Mba which they used for the purchase of cloth in the (European-owned) shops, and there are indications that gifts of money were made on special occasions. Such practices were also characteristic of the colonial administration.

Economic Development

Economic development is a key part of government policy, but it is controlled by non-Gabonese.[8] Like most other African states Gabon has a double economy. There is an industrial sector, totally oriented toward countries outside Africa, which is represented by enclaves that take the form of forestry camps, a plywood factory, a manganese mine, a uranium mine, oil wells, and some day an iron mine. There is also an agricultural sector in which most Gabonese work and which is almost totally unaffected by the industrial sector.

Production of wood still accounts for about 50 per cent of all Gabonese exports. Almost half the lumber cut in Gabon's seventeen sawmills belongs to the Consortium Forestier et Maritime (C.F.M.), which provides the French national railway with wood for railroad ties. The French-owned plywood factory in Port-Gentil exports most of its production, which has attained a value of $10,000,000.[9] Mineral production is rapidly increasing. In 1963

---

8 Studies of problems of economic development have been made by Gilles Sautter and Hans-Otto Neuhof. The latter has written a thesis for the University of Munich, *Die Rohstoffwirtschaft Gabuns — Geschichte, Struktur und Probleme,* unpublished, Munich, 1966.

9 "Le bois dans l'économie de l'Afrique noire," *Europe France Outremer,* No. 422, 1965, pp. 26–28.

exports of oil totaled $10,000,000, of gold $1,000,000, of uranium $8,500,000, and of manganese $14,000,000.[10] Along with the Ivory Coast, Gabon always has a favorable balance of trade, which the records of recent years show is about $20–25,000,000 each year. In the last year of the A.E.F. federation, 1959, Gabon had a trade surplus of over four billion CFA francs in 1959 and four billion in 1960, while the Congo had a ten-billion deficit in 1959 and a thirteen-billion deficit in 1960 (250 CFA francs = $1). Oubangui had a 500-million deficit in 1959 and a one-billion-five hundred-million deficit in 1960. Chad's deficit was two billion in 1959 and three billion in 1960.[11] In 1963 Gabon's favorable balance was over five and one half billion CFA francs, or almost $23,000,000.[12] The favorable balance is computed on the basis of the value of minerals exported, but it is not clear how much of this is retained by the Gabonese government. More revealing is the fact that while receipts exceed expenses for the Gabonese budget, the excess in 1961 was 600 million CFA francs while in 1963 it was only about 100 million, in spite of increased mineral production and an increasingly favorable balance of trade.[13]

Most forestry enterprises are owned by Frenchmen whose camps are mainly in the Moyen-Ogooué and Ngounié regions. Okoumé is the wood principally sought. The percentage of Gabonese participation in the exploitation has risen to 18 per cent of the total 1963 production, and most of the Gabonese participating are still Omyènè.[14]

COMILOG, the Compagnie Minière de l'Ogooué, began to exploit the huge manganese deposit in the Haut-Ogooué region in 1962 after construction of a cablecar conveyor system seventy-six kilometers long to the Congolese frontier where the ore is transferred to a railroad connecting with the Congo-Océan. It is estimated that there are 200 million tons of ore at the present location at Moanda. United States Steel Corporation owns 49 per cent of the shares of the company, and three French companies the remaining 51 per cent. Local operation is assured by the French.

10 *L'Effort Gabonais*, 23 March 1964.
11 Banque Centrale des Etats de l'Afrique Equatoriale, "Rapport d'activité," 1960, p. 57.
12 Ftn. 6, p. 65.
13 *Ibid.*, p. 97.
14 "Bilan de l'économie gabonaise," *Information d'Outre-Mer*, 1-15 October 1964.

The uranium reserves, estimated at about 25 million tons, are exploited by the Compagnie Minière de l'Uranium de Franceville (C.M.U.F.). All uranium goes to France.

Oil was discovered near Port-Gentil in 1956 and is now being exploited by the Société de Pétrole de l'Afrique Equatoriale (S.P.A.F.E.), which is mainly controlled by French companies but in which the Shell and Mobil Oil Companies also have an interest. (A Gabonese cabinet minister has been on the Administrative Council of S.P.A.F.E.[15]) In 1957, 143,300 tons, worth $2,000,000, were exported; this total has increased to over one million tons at present. Construction of an oil refinery at Port-Gentil has begun. This refinery will process 700,000 tons of oil each year, of which 400,000 will come from Gabon, 100,000 from Congo, and 200,000 from Nigeria. The refinery is scheduled to produce mainly for consumption in the four states of former A.E.F. and Cameroun.[16]

In 1961 and 1962 the Société des Mines de Fer de Mékambo (SOMIFER) finished its tests of the huge deposit of high-grade iron ore, estimated at one billion tons, in the Ogooué-Ivindo region. A railroad and a port near Libreville are to be constructed for shipment out of Gabon. It is the responsibility of the Gabonese government to build the railroad, and the mining company will have charge of the construction of port facilities. The government has granted SOMIFER the concession for a period of seventy-five years. Over 50 per cent of the shares of SOMIFER belong to Bethlehem Steel Corporation, and the members of the Common Market own the rest.

Gabon has very little small industry. At the end of 1963 a palm-oil plant opened near Lambaréné; it is owned by Unilever. Some paint is produced, there are several metalworking shops, but there is really no Gabonese-owned small industry. The big companies and the commerce of the country are controlled by Europeans or Americans; the government encourages their investments by liberal concessions and suppression of strikes in the name of order and unity.

Attempts have been made to develop Gabonese agriculture, but so far they have been very unsuccessful except in the Woleu-Ntem.

15 "Société des Pétroles d'Afrique Equatoriale, "*Rapport Annuel, 1961*," p. 35.
16 "Les hydrocarbures dans l'économie africaine," *Europe France Outremer*, No. 413, pp. 31–33.

About 86 per cent of the active population are engaged in agriculture, but they produce only 30 per cent of the gross national product.[17] A decrease in production in the agricultural sector since independence has been noted. In 1963, for example, 570 tons of rice were treated by the rice-processing company in Tchibanga, compared with 900 tons in 1962.[18]

Coffee production has not increased since 1959, and Woleu-Ntem has produced about half of the total. Woleu-Ntem also leads in cocoa production. Between October 1963 and April 1964 a special campaign was undertaken to market cocoa. Woleu-Ntem marketed 3,000 tons, compared with 118 from Ogooué-Ivindo.[19] Sixty-four per cent of the people who own plantations are over forty years old,[20] and their incomes in the last ten years have decreased by about 8,000 CFA francs because of falling prices. People refuse to follow instructions about the care of plants, and although the government has distributed thousands of coffee plants, these are not properly cultivated. In the Haut-Ogooué region 122,000 plants were put out in 1954, but by 1962 this number had decreased to 40,000.[21] One possible reason for this decline is the effort on the part of the government to promote the emancipation of women; women are increasingly reluctant to work in the plantations. Another reason is the fluctuation in the price of cocoa and coffee.

An attempt was made to introduce cattle into southern regions, but the people did not take care of them. Gabonese seem to believe that somehow plants and animals can get along by themselves, and very little effort is made at feeding, insect control, and other ways to preserve livestock and plants. The most serious problem appears to be lack of administrative sensitivity to the problems of agriculture. Production is encouraged, but crops are not purchased. Libreville is forced to buy most of its food outside of Gabon and even outside of Africa.

Another problem is the small extent of the agricultural ex-

17 Ministère de la Coopération, République Française, *Economie et plan de développement: République Gabonaise* (Paris, May 1963), p. 8.
18 "Gabon: les industries du bois en tête de la production industrielle," *Le Moniteur Africain*, 26 September 1964.
19 *La Semaine Africaine*, 24 May 1960.
20 Ministère de l'Agriculture, République Gabonaise "*Rapport Annuel, 1962*," Libreville, 1964, p. 67.
21 *Ibid.*, pp. 160–163.

ploitation. About 57 per cent of plantations are two and one-half acres in size or less, 23 per cent are between two and one-half and five acres, and only 5 per cent are over ten acres. The largest farms are in Woleu-Ntem where only 3 per cent cultivate less than one acre and 10 per cent have more than a dozen acres. In Ngounié 36 per cent of the farms are less than one acre and only 3 per cent above a dozen acres.[22] In all regions except Woleu-Ntem the Libreville government has had to provide about two thirds of the regional budgets.

Gabonese cultivators are largely unhappy, as are the 45,000 unskilled workers, for the minimum guaranteed wage, the *salaire minimum interprofessionel garanti,* is only about one dollar per day. In part of the Nationalizing Zone (Libreville, Port-Gentil, Lambaréné, and a five-mile area around each city) the minimum wage was raised on 1 January 1965 from 220 to 266.70 CFA francs per day. For the rest of the country the wages were raised from 192 to 233 francs per day. The difference between minimum wages paid in the urban areas of the Nationalizing Zone and those elsewhere increased from 28 to 33.70. This difference is further accentuated by the rule that urban workers are required to work only six hours and forty minutes each day while agricultural and forestry laborers are required to work eight hours each day.[23]

A planning commission has been working on a development plan for Gabon, but reports of internal conflict over the orientation of the plan and the role of private enterprise may possibly lead to the publication of a plan as poorly conceived and followed as previous attempts.

Mobilization

Mobilization for shared experiences is a fourth government policy to standardize culture, to break down antagonisms between kinship groups, and to facilitate education and construction of hospitals or dispensaries. Jean-Hilaire Aubame's program of village regroupment has been continued. There has been widespread opposition to the program on the part of people who do not want to leave their villages and who do not want to live with

22 J. Bidault, "Résultats provisoires de l'enquête agricole par sondage 1960," Ministère de l'Agriculture, République Gabonaise, n.d., pp. 24–25.
23 *Gabon d'Aujourd'hui,* 19 December 1964.

people they do not know. In some places people fear that the dangers of witchcraft will be greater in large villages.

In 1963 committees were set up in each region in order to plan for regroupment. Although it has not been possible to proceed with regroupment in all regions as quickly as had been hoped, administrators continue to encourage it, particularly because they themselves can benefit from it. The newspaper *Gabon d'Aujour-d'hui* has pointed out to its readers, who are mainly administrators, that their census tasks would be made easier and contact between themselves and the masses would be facilitated by regroupment.[24] Villages are being constructed increasingly along roads leading to Contact or Nationalizing Zones.

In 1962 the Gabonese government began a program to control the labor force. Work cards that indicated the profession of an individual over eighteen were required. The unemployed were supposed to accept any available jobs which the labor office offered them. For this policy and others Gabon was accused by the International Labor Organization of reimposing the system of forced labor used by the colonial regimes.[25] The government has encouraged the development of towns near the Congolese frontier and publicizes activities in these places to make the inhabitants feel part of Gabon and to make other Gabonese aware of these towns. Development of Lambaréné's storage and docking facilities permits provisionment of the entire Ngounié region with imported goods and materials. Only Haut-Ogooué remains almost totally dependent on Congo. In the course of 1965 and 1966 radio-communication network between Libreville and the regions was to be developed.

A radical move to standardize culture was made by the law of 31 May 1963 abolishing the bridewealth. This is one of the bases of the pre-national kinship systems, and the law to abolish it is one attempt to weaken the pre-national kinship systems all over Gabon. Contests were held and a great deal of publicity was given to this program. Bridewealth was called contrary to modernization, and it was said that it had made women articles of merchandise.[26] Men have been arrested for giving goods to the families

24 *Ibid.*, 22 February 1965.
25 Ordonnance No. 50/62, 1 September 1962. Also *The Observer*, 6 May 1962.
26 *L'Effort Gabonais,* 11 October 1963.

of their future wives, but bridewealth remains an important custom just the same. President Mba has also attempted to get a uniform civil code for the country in place of the several traditions used by the traditional district courts. In this code he wanted to establish the patrilineal or bilateral system of descendance as the norm for all Gabonese instead of the matrilineal system current south of the River Ogooué. He felt that Gabon customs are flexible and can be changed and standardized.[27]

The government has also tried to "capture" ethnic differences and encourage their expression within the structure of the state. *Cercles culturels,* or cultural centers, have been set up by civil servants or elected officials in most districts for the purpose of sponsoring what is called "folklore" and traditional ceremonies.

The fact that people want to change helps the government, even though the changes are not always considered with approval after they have been encouraged by the government. There is an urge to be mobilized, not so much into a stream of contacts with people from different ethnic groups but into a new society.

In Gabonese villages the men are bored and the women work very hard. This is apparent to all visitors. Dr. Biffot examined the attitudes of villagers in Heartland and in Contact Zones in Ogooué-Ivindo and found a real consciousness of status among the peasants. Young men want to leave the village; they do not want to live near their parents who demand their submission and whose ways are the old ways. Biffot found that 92.55 per cent of the males in his sample wanted to exercise a profession in which they would be paid once a month.[28]

The government is trying to take advantage of this desire for change in its various programs and in its educational policies, but it does not always provide more than a partial answer, and its administrators sometimes show more naïveté in their dealings with villagers than did the former colonial administrators. For example, a sub-prefect went to one regrouped village in order to examine the construction of a school and to bring a teacher. The two-room school had been started, but the villagers were told it could not be completed because of lack of materials and because

[27] Author's interview with President Mba.
[28] Laurent Biffot, "La jeunesse gabonaise face au monde rural et au monde urbain" (Paris, ORSTOM, April 1964), pp. 11–12.

the workers were needed elsewhere. He promised that it would be completed soon and that a dispensary would be added. No one believed him. Then he called on the women to express their complaints if they had any; since he could not speak the languages of the villages, his words were translated by the chief: "Have you any complaints? Have you anything to discuss? Gabonese women are emancipated. Speak up." The silence was complete.

Civic Education

Civic education to promote a shared belief system is a fifth aspect of the government's program to promote national consciousness. This takes the form of a school program and adult education by use of the radio particularly as well as by symbols and ceremonies.

In 1962 the Ministry of Education published a civic-education manual for use in primary and secondary schools. A special issue of *Réalités Gabonaises,* the cultural and pedogogic review which is no longer published, it was written by a Frenchman.[29] The brochure has nothing to say about the history, the geography, or the population of the country and has now been supplemented by two smaller pamphlets called "Gabon mon Pays" and "Gabon ma Patrie."[30] The first of these has a short section on history, Gabon's place in Africa, Gabon's geography, and a description of the nine administrative regions. The second contains a description of the institutions of Gabon, the constitution, a section on Léon Mba, a part on the various government functions, and one on foreign relations.

Lessons in the civic-education manual consist of three parts: substantive, a résumé, and questions. For the lowest grades the teacher will read just the résumé and ask some questions; higher grades will be expected to read the whole thing. The last few pages are devoted to instructions for the teachers and a series of lessons that they might give their students. These lessons and lectures are an attempt to combine basic education with education about

29 "Notions d'instruction civique," *Réalités Gabonaises,* special number, July-August 1962. Several other francophonic countries, including Senegal, Cameroun, and Ivory Coast, have recently published civic education manuals. The Camerounese manual was written by an African educator.

30 Both published by the Ministère de l'Information et du Tourisme, Libreville, n.d.

citizenship. Children study the family first, according to this outline, then the state or nation, and finally they are supposed to study world organizations and the role of Africa.

The actual manual[31] begins with a letter from President Mba: "This little book will inspire you, Gabonese schoolchildren, with love for your homeland at the same time as it inspires you with the duties of a Citizen." The Minister of Education (then J.-M. Ekoh) adds: "May every young Gabonese discover and acquire, thanks to this manual, noble virtues capable of promoting a Gabonese people which is happy, healthy in body and spirit, animated with love for others and 'capable of dying' for the homeland."

The student then reads or hears descriptions and explanations: What is the Gabonese homeland, its flag, its national anthem, its motto, the national holiday? He is taught about international institutions: the acceptance of Gabon as a member of the United Nations Organization, the meaning of U.N. Day, the text of the Universal Declaration of the Rights of Man, with a special explanation of points relevant for Gabon.

The third part contains the constitution of Gabon with a detailed explanation including tables of who the people who rule are and how they get elected or appointed. The structure of Gabonese administration is outlined. The young are told about "Military Duty (National Defense)," and "The National Army." They are told about financial duties in "Fiscal Civics," "Fiscal Fraud," "The State and Its Fiscal Functionaries," "Professional Conscience."

The principal themes of this manual concern tribalism, laziness, thievery, independence; the reader and student are told what citizenship means and why one must be a good citizen; what must a good citizen know and what must he do, what must a good citizen not do and how can Gabon be like other nations: The nation is like a family; the homeland is our mother and Léon Mba is our father. Children must be good members of their family and citizens must be good members of the nation because they have duties and receive many things from their parents: "Our HOMELAND does for us all that our MOTHER does for us." Résumé: "The Gabonese Republic is my HOMELAND. I love her as I love my MOTHER."

31 "Notions d'instruction civique," ftn. 29.

We must respect all manifestations of the homeland, including the national anthem and the flag: "We must render the same honors and have the same respect and love for this anthem as for the flag. In effect, if the latter is the image, the national anthem is the VOICE of the HOMELAND, it is the VOICE of our MOTHER." All the children work together in union "in order to help the HOME-LAND, to keep her on the right track, that of progress and happiness. This is the way sons and daughters help their mother."

"A mother loves all of her children, no matter if they are boys or girls, big or little, light or dark, quiet or active. The Gabonese MOTHERLAND also loves all her children, no matter whether from the Woleu-Ntem or Nyanga, from the Estuaire or the Haut-Ogooué. She has the same feeling for all Gabonese, Fang or Mpongoué, Vili or Batéké, no matter if they are Catholics or Protestants, cultivators or functionaries, women or men, poor or rich." If the children of the same parents fight among themselves, their parents will be hurt; the mother will be chagrined and so will the father. President Léon Mba says that we must be united: "We have better things to do than to tear ourselves and wear ourselves down by vain, fruitless palavers."

The national holiday is the birthday of our mother; it is the 17th of August and "that day all her children should rejoice together and live in communion with the same feelings."

The Universal Declaration of the Rights of Man condemns tribalism and all forms of racism; "By its admission to the United Nations the Gabonese Republic has dedicated itself to respect these principles; Gabonese who act in a contrary way will be bad citizens and will be disdained by other nations." Lastly, our own Constitution condemns tribalism and racism.

We must know certain things and act in certain ways to be like citizens of other nations, to make our nation modern like others. For example, we must take off our hats when the flag passes and be quiet during official ceremonies. According to the Universal Declaration of the Rights of Man there is no restriction about race, nationality, or religion in marriage, and people get married only with their own consent. "These are the principles accepted by all modern nations." When we respect these principles, we "become the equals of all schoolchildren and of all citizens in the world!"

We must have a sense of honor to protect and to be proud of

our motherland. We must all be willing to serve in the army: "Military service is equal for all and is an HONOR. It lasts for two years." The army has a flag that symbolizes its honor. "The bravest and most experienced soldiers are chosen to carry the flag because it must never fall into the hands of the enemy. That would be a dishonor."

We are an independent nation and must remain so. The fact that we have laws to obey is a proof of liberty. Slaves have no laws because they are forced to do what they do; "if you don't know the laws, you accept the life of a slave." We became independent on 17 August 1960 as the result of certain agreements signed between the French and Gabonese governments. "On 23 August 1960, under sponsorship by France, the Security Council of the United Nations unanimously recommended our admission to the organization." By this we have the same rights as all other nations, even the biggest nations like the United States and France.

As an independent nation we have a constitution which everyone should know. We also have an army which "guarantees the first of all our liberties: *National* Independence." We all work together in unity and obey as soldiers; we must make sacrifices as did our hero Captain Ntchorere who died on the Somme on 7 June 1940. "Let the sacrifice of this Gabonese hero serve as an example and give us the necessary courage and firmness to march without fear to combat if one day the homeland is threatened."

To build the nation strong and independent we must work and be honest. The most important characteristic of those who handle money, such as tax collectors and treasurers, is honesty.

The good citizen must avoid treasonous acts. He must pay his taxes, for "without taxes a nation cannot live: there would be misery for all. He who tries to avoid payment of taxes is not only a COWARD, he is a traitor to his HOMELAND." "All fraud is a crime against JUSTICE. He who falsifies an official act . . . signs a false declaration or a check without backing is a bad citizen who hurts the HOMELAND." Do not waste your food and do not damage schools and property, for this would be to "STEAL from the State which gives them to you."

The student must listen to his teacher and work with professional conscience; if he does not, he robs the state, he fools the teacher, and he fools himself. The book concludes:

Gabonese SCHOOLCHILD, my little friend, you will soon be a CITIZEN. Before leaving school you must know your country, you must love your MOTHERLAND for which no sacrifice is too great. Remember Captain NTCHORERE, killed in war to defend his ideal, and the Gabonese soldiers dead on the Field of Honor. Remember your parents, friends, and chiefs who struggle, who suffer for your happiness and that of the MOTHERLAND. It is the CIVIC SENSE of men, of women, and of children that constitutes the POWER of a nation and it is PATRIOTISM which makes its GRANDEUR. Improve yourself without letup, by struggling against bad instincts and bad habits. And above all: WORK and OBEY. Why? President Léon Mba answers: "Because work is the law of humanity, because it is the condition of all individual and collective progress. Because there is no possible society without government which commands and without governed who obey."

A formal civic-education program for adults was undertaken in 1961 by a French representative from UNESCO and run until the present by a team of Gabonese. Listening groups were organized in the nine regions. Each group is composed of twenty to thirty people, male or female. A problem is presented during each broadcast having to do with life as a peasant and life as a citizen of Gabon. There is one broadcast for men and one for women.

A radio donated by the Ministry of Education is lent to the villagers or to the forestry enterprises, many of which also have listening groups. Each group has a leader; he receives from the central office lists of questions to be discussed after the broadcasts, and he must make a report on the activities of the group. Themes of broadcasts have been about the Gabonese resources, girls at school, the importance of medicine to protect us against diseases, how to plant a tree, what is the meaning of unity.

Most of the groups have been set up among the Fang. There are more in Woleu-Ntem than in any other region — twenty-four compared with six in Ngounié. Even in the Estuaire the groups have been formed almost without exception among the Fang.[32]

In addition to the classroom or radio-lesson experience, there are celebrated all over Gabon certain days, like the Journée de la

---

32 Idrissou Youssouf, "Qu'est ce qu'un groupe d'écoute radiophonique?" and Ango Bie Paul Edouard, "Fonctionnement et constitution des groupes d'écoute radiophonique," *L'Educateur*, No. 5, March-April 1964, pp. 12–13.

Patrie Gabonaise, for which essays must be written about themes such as "unity." There are symbols like the monument to Captain Ntchorere at the end of the Boulevard de l'Indépendance and a monument to the dead where foreign dignitaries place wreaths after their arrival in the country.

The flag of Gabon flies on all public buildings, of course, and, as the civic manual explains, the three horizontal bands, green, gold, and blue, have a particular meaning: Green represents the forest, gold represents the fact that it is rare that a country should be on the equator, and blue is the sea. For a time after the 1958 referendum the flag of Gabon had a little insert of the French tricolor, but this has since been removed. In every prefecture and sub-prefecture the flag is raised with bugle call every morning; all civil servants are present. A seal extolling motherhood, a coat of arms honoring the tree and the explorers from Europe, and the motto, Union, Work, Justice and *Uniti Progrediemur,* complete the official national symbols.

The national anthem is played every time the radio goes on or off the air or whenever the President speaks. It is supposed to be sung every day in school. It is called *La Concorde* and adjures the Gabonese to wake up and welcome the new days dreamed of by their ancestors. The Gabonese should chase away witches and those who trick others in order that Gabon become dignified in the eyes of the world and friendly nations. Everyone must forget internal quarrels and build together "the new edifice of which we are dreaming." It is a truly beautiful national anthem.

In every prefecture the prefect is assigned a large house which once belonged to the French commandant. In Libreville the palace of the President is large and is on a hill overlooking the estuary; even those who do not like the present occupant are proud of his home. Although the presidential palace was formerly quite open and only slightly protected, a large wall was built around it when President Mba began to feel himself threatened; this wall was known as "the wall of shame."

The national holyday for Gabon has changed; it used to be 19 February to celebrate the day on which the treaty between King Denis and Captain Bouët-Willaumez was signed and also on 14 July to honor France. The former is no longer the national day and the latter became the "Day of the Community," during which the French flag flew alongside the Gabonese flag. From 1960 to 1964 the most important day, the national holyday was 17 August, Independence Day.

This day is celebrated with great ceremony each year. In 1964, after the attempted coup d'état, the ceremonies were very restrained and there was no parade. Other years, there is a torchlight parade through Libreville the night of the sixteenth, and on the seventeenth there is a huge parade.

Those ministers who have not gone to home regions for similar celebrations wait in the reviewing stand along the Boulevard de l'Indépendance, by the sea, or now in the Lefebvre Stadium. They wait with the French advisers, deputies, guests, and the diplomatic corps. On one side is the Garde Républicaine band. People have been waiting for two and three hours before the scheduled start of ceremonies. Everyone waits for the chief of state. Suddenly a motorcyclist dressed in white approaches to alert the crowd; everyone is silent, and everyone looks toward the road which the President will take from the palace.

The siren sounds, and people stand to applaud. The band plays the national anthem as his auto drives toward the reviewing stand. The President reviews the troops and takes his place in the stand. The first part of the ceremony is finished.

Next, the President confers on worthy citizens and helpful foreigners different orders of the Equatorial Star, the Gabonese Legion of Honor. Once this ceremony is completed, the parade begins. All the major businesses, clubs, regions, tribes, and schools march with the armed forces. They mainly salute the President. His virtues are extolled and praised; people carry his portrait, and others sing songs about him and Gabon.

The parade finished, the President descends to his car and returns to his palace. Some people then go to church to pray for nation and soul; but a greater number go to the central square, the Place de la République, where dancers from every region of the country perform all afternoon while the Gabonese soccer team plays an opponent from some other African country in Lefebvre Stadium, named after a Roman Catholic missionary. Before the coup the President, standing in his auto, toured the city to wave to the people. In 1965 and 1966 he did not undertake such a tour on Independence Day.

CHAPTER 10

The Formation of National Frontiers

Frontiers

A map of the nation-state is its most important symbol. It is proof that it exists, has existed, and will remain on this earth. The frontiers that define the geographical expression of the nation are defined by members of a nation as natural. They are natural, in their view, because of physical barriers such as mountain ranges or rivers, and because the course of history logically determined that these should be the frontiers. Teachers at the Alliance Française stand before their maps of France and point to the shape of the country as perfect for absorbing all the varied influences that have made the French nation and as inevitable for the development of French culture and French history.

National frontiers may include areas not now occupied by members of the national community; such areas will be slightly pink instead of red and will be called "stolen" or "occupied" by another nation. The ancestors of the nation lived here, and relatives recognized as close relatives live there now; the latter may not realize they belong to the nation, and someone may believe he must convince them of it. Some nationalists then say it is the logical, manifest destiny of the nation to claim these occupied lands as part of the national territory because of history, geography, and kinship.

States that have at one time been controlled by outside powers say that part of the national territory was separated from the nation because of the imperialists' interests. The imperialists divided families, tribes, and these must be reunited with the homeland; in spite of political independence from these imperialist powers these are sometimes blamed for maintaining the divisions and preventing unification.

National frontiers are part of the national culture: "This little island." The image of the national frontiers is another aspect of national distinctiveness. The development and greatness of the country are associated with its frontiers, and leaders say that if they were ever contracted the country would never recover from the blow to its power, its prestige, and its national character.

The older the nations become, the less arbitrary their frontiers seem, but there is no natural geographical reason why Britain should be a nation of one and one-half islands instead of two islands. It is true that in Africa frontiers were drawn as the result of imperialist adventures and agreements, but these were not always made without regard to geography, because the explorer followed rivers or else was blocked by mountain ranges. A river or a mountain range might form a barrier between two explorers such as de Brazza and Stanley, and treaties were signed by representatives of pre-national systems whose frontiers influenced colonial frontiers. The rivers and mountains and treaties might have been crossed, respectively abrogated, or they might be used later to justify national borders as natural and unchangeable.

National frontiers are determined by the course of history, communications, location of ethnic groups, government policies, expansionist desires of neighbors, and the power of the government to withstand pressures from these neighbors. Human decision-making plays an important role in deciding what national frontiers will be.

Tribal frontiers are far more flexible where there has been movement of population, little tradition of permanent settlement, and an egalitaran social structure. Tribes split by national frontiers may provide an excuse for demands for frontier change by the states in which they live, even though the divided peoples may have no desire for the unification which is used to justify territorial claims. *Anschluss* does not always depend on the will of the people most directly concerned.

Gabonese frontiers, which have not changed since the end of 1946, were influenced by the river system. Explorers moved along rivers from the estuary and then along the River Ogooué toward Congo. Ogooué's affluents, like the Ivindo and the Ngounié, served for further exploration, trade, and control. The Cottes mission defined Gabon's northern frontiers after part of the colony had been given to Spain at the turn of the century. Spain claimed it needed workers for its plantations on Fernando Poo and also that it had an older claim than France to the area above the estuary of Muni. The frontier extends from the estuary east along the first parallel north of the equator. The rivers Ntem, Kom, Ayina, Ivindo, and Djouah (or Djouab) define Gabon's frontier with Cameroun and northern Congo. At other places along the national frontiers, rivers correspond with the line that distinguishes Gabonese territory from that of Cameroun, Rio Muni, or Congo. It is the River Ogooué and its two major affluents Ngounié and Ivindo which appear to form the skeletal structure of the country, and Gabon has sometimes been described as the country in the valleys of this river system. The rivers are, however, filled with rapids, making communication difficult and not providing the unity implied by the map. The Cristal Mountains and the Massif du Chaillu are two more barriers, but these geographical expressions are less imposing barriers than are the Mississippi River and the Rocky Mountains.

Like most other African countries an independent Gabon has accepted colonial frontiers as national frontiers, but unlike these countries Gabon has been more outspoken in its rejection of plans to dissolve those frontiers in a larger pan-African grouping.

Assertion of National Frontiers

Gabon had tried to extricate itself from the federation of French Equatorial Africa ever since it had been established. On this issue both French businessmen and Gabonese were in agreement. It was believed in Gabon that the federation was getting the benefits from the exploitation of Gabonese resources — principally wood. It was said that Gabon supplied two thirds of the federation's income and that Brazzaville got all the benefits. Autonomy from the other three colonies, Moyen-Congo, Oubangui-Chari, and Chad was requested, but there was no question of demanding independence from France.

In 1940 Gabon, under French Vichyist leadership, broke away from the pro-de Gaulle A.E.F., and from September to December Libreville was the capital of Vichyist Equatorial Africa. Governor Masson, who had first supported the Free French, gave way under pressures from local French businessmen like René Labat and from the Church hierarchy headed by Bishop Louis Tardy. In a circular to all French citizens in Gabon the Bishop wrote: "I should fail my duty as Bishop and as a Frenchman if I were not to indicate to you the right and loyal way in clarity, in fidelity, and in honor. There is only one right and loyal way: It is fidelity to the MOTHERLAND, it is complete confidence in those great leaders, Marshal PÉTAIN and General WEYGAND."[1]

The forces of Free France moved into the country, General Leclerc briefly annexed the Woleu-Ntem to Cameroun, and the Vichyists were isolated. Some fled into Spanish Guinea and then to France while others, including the bishop, were imprisoned at Lambaréné. After the war there was keen competition and some bitterness between Gabonese and Congolese over the election of the first deputy to the National Assembly who would represent both Gabon and Moyen-Congo. The setting up of Representative Councils in each overseas territory as well as representative institutions at the A.E.F. level increased feelings of a separate identity in Gabon.

The loi-cadre voted by the French National Assembly on 23 June 1956 led to the establishment of territorial executives, gave more power to the territorial assemblies, and abolished the double-college system. Attempts to create federal executives in addition to the Grands Conseils or legislative assemblies in French West Africa and in Equatorial Africa at this time were feared by the Gabonese. Deputy Aubame, who later attended the Parti du

1 Circular, Louis Tardy, Evêque de Libreville, Libreville, 11 September 1940.

Regroupement Africain (P.R.A.) meeting in Cotonou in July 1958 at which demands for independence and African federations were articulated, had previously moved in the Gabonese assembly to express Gabonese disapproval of any kind of federal executive "which will impede the actions of local executive councils. Each territory ought to work out the reforms of the 1956 loi-cadre."[2] The motion was passed unanimously.

A year later members of both the B.D.G. and the U.D.S.G. submitted a motion to the assembly further to denounce any moves toward the establishment of federal executives which would be a step toward unity with the other three states of Equatorial Africa. Creation of executives was considered in opposition to the loi-cadre, "which is a progressive step in the direction of territorial individuality." The resolution insisted that Gabon favored administrative and economic coordination among the territories but that it "refused to give up any part of its acquired rights for the profit of an organism intermediary between the Metropole and the Territories. If its will is not met, it has decided to take advantage of its geographic and economic position which permits its direct integration into the French government."[3]

Although it may be true that the colonial administration in French West Africa did not always favor federation, Paul-Louis Chauvet, Governor-General of A.E.F. from 1951 to February 1958, said in his opening speech to the Grand Conseil in 1957: "It is up to you to make the people understand that their security and their prosperity depend on their union. . . . At the moment when Europe is trying to unite its resources and its forces it would be a catastrophe for Africa to divide itself into a multitude of states, isolated and incapable alone of assuring progress."[4] Chauvet encouraged the establishment of interstate organisms for cooperation and coordination.

The referendum of September 1958 was a time of decision about relations with France and relations with other members of A.E.F. From 21 to 23 August 1958, one month before the referendum, Jean-Hilaire Aubame and Prince Félix Adandé, who

[2] "Débats de l'Assemblée Territoriale du Gabon," Session extraordinaire, 5 October 1956, pp. 75–77.

[3] "Débats de l'Assemblée Territoriale du Gabon," 9 October 1957, pp. 60–61.

[4] "Débats du Grand Conseil," Grand Conseil de l'Afrique Equatoriale Française, 17–18 June 1957, pp. 8–9.

represented Léon Mba, traveled to Brazzaville for an all-A.E.F. meeting and to hear General de Gaulle speak. The declaration emanating from this meeting indicated sensitivity about the fact that English colonies were becoming independent rapidly. The French government was requested to insert in the constitution of the Fifth Republic provision for unilateral declarations of independence by the governments and legislatures of African countries. The day after the last meeting General de Gaulle assured the Africans in his Brazzaville speech that any state could become independent from the proposed Franco-African Communauté once it was set up.[5] Both the U.D.S.G. and B.D.G. then advocated a *oui* vote.

Barthélemy Boganda, leader of Oubangui-Chari and president of the Grand Conseil had favored more than anyone else the establishment of a unified state in place of A.E.F. He even envisaged a great "Latin Africa" made up of Equatorial Africa, Cameroun, Belgium's Congo, and Angola: "I was born a Congolese and I have become an Oubanguian. One part of my tribe is in the Belgian Congo, another in the former territory of Oubangui, and yet another in Chad. But, it is the French language and our common Latin culture which is one of the essential ties for us. That is why I firmly believe in the future of what we must call Latin Africa as one speaks of Latin America."[6] At this time Moyen-Congo leaders indicated that a vague confederation would be desirable, and Chad said it favored something called "flexible federation." Gabon remained suspicious.

On 17 January 1959 the four leaders of Equatorial Africa signed a declaration and two protocols dealing with the fate of the institutions of A.E.F. which would be dissolved, relations with France, and cooperation among the four countries in the future. The declaration indicated that the four countries would not put into their respective constitutions any articles that would create obligations to the Franco-African Communauté set up by the constitution of the Fifth Republic; this meant that independence could come when and if the countries wanted it. Protocol No. 1

5 Jean-Michel Wagret, *Histoire et sociologie politiques de la République du Congo (Brazzaville)* (Paris, Librairie Générale de Droit et de Jurisprudence, 1963), pp. 75–77.
6 *Le Monde*, 22 January 1959.

provided for the establishment of a customs union, a regular meeting of chiefs of state or chiefs of government, and suprastate organisms for cooperation and coordination. Protocol No. 2 provided for the liquidation of A.E.F. On 30 June 1959 Afrique Equatoriale Française was no more.[7]

The 1959 protocols provided for meetings of the heads of government at least twice each year. It was in these meetings that leaders of the four states discussed what they should do after Sudan and Senegal in September 1959 asked for their independence. Out of several meetings in Africa and in Paris Gabon announced in May 1960 that it would ask for independence by itself while Oubangui-Chari, Moyen-Congo, and Chad indicated they would ask for it as an ensemble; on 17 May 1960 representatives of these three countries signed a charter creating the Union des Républiques d'Afrique Centrale (U.R.A.C.). Gabon refused to sign but agreed it would maintain the customs and communications agreements signed in 1959.[8]

Gabon refused to sign because the charter asked for the submission of each state's sovereignty to the Union. Articles nine, ten, and seventeen state: "Foreign policy is the domain of the Union."[9] The Union never really existed, for two months after the charter was signed Congo retired from it; Chad was next, and now only Oubangui-Chari remains as the Central African Republic. Fears of loss of power on the part of leaders in Congo and Chad to Oubangui's powerful party influenced these decisions.[10] The possibility of some kind of union with Congo-Léopoldville may also have influenced Brazzaville. In 1960 the four states became independent separately. Some Frenchmen may also have had a role in the failure of the Union, for they advised each country: "France, always [Gabon's] friend, serves as its counsellor in its public affairs and in its relations with brother countries."[11]

Gabon has preferred arrangements that provide for consultation and some economic coordination and loose organizations of

[7] For the Declaration and Protocols see "Journal Officiel," Afrique Equatoriale Française, 30 June 1959, pp. 1136–1138.

[8] Agence France Presse dispatch, No. 4162, 18 May 1960.

[9] Text in "Journal Officiel du Congo," 1 July 1960, Loi 28–60, pp. 490–491.

[10] Jean-Michel Wagret, p. 79.

[11] M. O. Nkogho-Mvé, "Si Libreville m'était conté," Gabon d'Aujourd'hui, 6 March 1965. "La France, son amie de toujours, lui sert de conseillère dans ses affaires publiques et ses relations avec les Pays Frères."

French-speaking states, such as the Union Africaine et Malgache (U.A.M.) and its last successor, the Organisation Commune Africaine et Malgache (O.C.A.M.). For the former A.E.F. states there was the Conference of Chiefs of State, all of whose decisions on common policies, regulation of tariffs, and control over interstate organisms had to be unanimous. A permanent secretariat was run by French civil servants. The customs union, officially set up in 1959, whose decisions had to be unanimous, had customs offices in all states except Gabon, but Gabon agreed to follow its decisions with regard to customs rules. The customs union was expanded to include Cameroun, and at a conference in Brazzaville in December 1964 a treaty setting up a Union Douanière et Economique de l'Afrique Centrale (U.D.E.A.C.) was signed. The old Conference of Chiefs of State was transformed into a Conseil des Chefs d'Etat, the most important organ of the U.D.E.A.C. Ministers of finance of the five countries form a Committee of Direction. The general secretariat has its headquarters in Bangui. The purposes of the U.D.E.A.C., which began to function on 1 January 1966, are coordination of industrial projects, like the oil refinery in Port-Gentil, a common tariff and fiscal policy, and a standard investment code.[12]

The third interterritorial organism is the Agence Transéquatoriale des Communications (A.T.E.C.), which administers the Congo-Océan Railroad, ports in Congo and the Central African Republic, and some interstate roads and rivers. The French have controlled this agency. The money used in the four states and Cameroun is essentially identical (Cameroun's currency is slightly different but easily interchangeable) and is controlled by the Banque Centrale des Etats de l'Afrique Equatoriale et du Cameroun. Other technical groupings have little political significance.

Further organisms have been set up and later dissolved, like the important Office Equatorial des Postes et Télécommunications which controlled the post offices and issued stamps. Gabon does belong to interstate organisms but insists on much more internal autonomy than the other members. It sends some students to the

12 "Organismes communs aux Etats de l'Afrique équatoriale" and "Organismes communs aux Etats de l'Afrique équatoriale et au Cameroun," in "L'Afrique d'expression française et Madagascar," special edition, No. 421, 1965, *Europe France Outremer*, pp. 243–46; A.-G. Anguilè, and J.-E. David, *L'Afrique sans frontières* (Monaco, Bory, 1965).

Fondation de l'Enseignement Supérieur set up in 1961 to serve as a basis for a university, but like Chad and the Central African Republic it set up its own school of administration even though one was provided by the Fondation in Brazzaville.

Gabon has faithfully supported the French-sponsored organizations of French-speaking states. These organizations have been termed "realistic" by the Gabonese press while the Organization of African Unity has been found wanting. Gabon has found that what it calls the immoderate states of the O.A.U. do not respect the sovereignty of other states, it says. Along with the other members of O.C.A.M. Gabon decided not to send delegates to a 1965 meeting of chiefs of state in Accra, but it insists that the smaller organization can assist the O.A.U.,[13] and that it is a step toward ultimate unification.

Gabon refused to sign the agreement establishing the Banque Africaine de Développement in 1963 because it feared an attempt might be made to control the use of Gabonese funds for its own national projects. The minister of state indicated that Gabon might join the bank at some later date.[14] It is important for Gabon to maintain close relations with France, which is its major source of aid, purchases most Gabonese exports, and furnishes Gabon with most of its imports. In 1963, 59.7 per cent of Gabonese imports came from France, which in turn purchased 51 per cent of Gabon's exports.[15] Cameroun is the only African country that has significant trade with Gabon; it furnished 2.6 per cent of Gabon's total imports — a very low figure — and bought 1 per cent of Gabon's exports. Senegal also buys about 1 per cent of Gabon's exports.[16] The country sells less than 0.5 per cent of its exports to the three countries of the former A.E.F.[17]

Frontiers with Congo

Frontiers with the Congo are the longest frontiers between Gabon and any foreign state, and these frontiers have changed the most. Trade of southern Gabon has been linked with the

[13] *Gabon d'Aujourd'hui,* 1 June 1965.
[14] A. G. Anguillè, *L'Effort Gabonais,* 16 August 1963.
[15] Service de la Statistique, *"Rapport annuel — Fin 1963,"* pp. 33, 47.
[16] *Ibid.*
[17] *Ibid.,* p. 64.

Congo ever since the sixteenth century. The Portuguese had a large trading station at Loango: "The area touched by the trade of Loango was considerable, extending from Cape Lopez to the mouth of the River Congo, covering the whole area between Kongo and Kwilu Nyari, the whole basin of the latter river, and large parts of the mountains and forests of Gabon."[18]

Prior to 1918 the Gabonese frontier extended south of Nyanga to Loango. In order to bring all the territory which the Congo-Océan railroad would traverse under the control of one administration, the southern part of Gabon was attached to the Congo: "It is hardly to be expected that Libreville, chief town of Gabon and too far from these regions, could be a center of direction. . . . The new limits between the two colonies formed by the watershed of the Nyanga and the Kouilou result in an integration into the colony of Moyen-Congo of the whole concession of the Company of the Kouilou-Niari."[19] During both world wars the colonies were short of personnel, and the Nyanga region's frontiers changed, as it was believed necessary to bring both districts under the control of the same administrator. The district of Divenie also used to be part of Gabon.

In 1950 some people from Nyanga wanted to attach their region to Congo. They included one delegate in the Gabonese legislature. Another group opposed this move; they were Bapounou of Nyanga who were working in Brazzaville. In a letter to the Gabonese legislature they wrote: "We have the honor to inform you that we natives of Nyanga who live in Moyen-Congo are unalterably opposed to any proposition to attach . . . this region to Moyen-Congo. In spite of the forgetfulness of the administration toward the region we want to remain Gabonese."[20]

Nyanga is one of the least developed regions of Gabon; it is called the forgotten region. Nyanga has iron-ore deposits which, for the time being, are not to be exploited. To the east in Ngounié bauxite deposits have been reported, and Congo was suspected of exploiting them. The prefecture is linked with the Ngounié

18 J. Vansina, "Long-Distance Trade Routes in Central Africa," *Journal of African History*, No. 3, 1962, p. 380.

19 Arch. Nat. Col., AEF 648, dossier 4, Letter from Secretary General to Minister of Colonies, 16 August 1918.

20 Letter to President of Conseil Représentatif, "Population de la Nyanga à Pointe-Noire," 25 August 1950.

region by one of the most peculiar roads in the world. The road from Ngounié appears to be well-graveled, but it ends suddenly, to be replaced by a track of rocks and gullies. After a few miles of this there is a road about fifty feet long, and then the rocks and gullies continue. This alternation continues into Tchibanga, the prefecture headquarters. According to the French company, there was not enough money to do the whole route, so they did it in parts. The road is being improved, however.

In 1958 the Parti d'Union Nationale Gabonaise (P.U.N.G.A.) succeeded in getting the people to vote *non* 6,055 to 4,697. The B.D.G. newspaper of Léon Mba said that the people of Nyanga wanted to indicate they felt mistreated; by voting *non* they would thus call attention to their feelings.[21] Gabonese from this region often write to the Roman Catholic newspaper *La Semaine Africaine*, published in Brazzaville, to express their opinions about their isolation from the rest of Gabon and the lack of development there. Another source of their opposition to Libreville is the often-expressed view that the government is run by Omyènè and Fang. Some Bapounou leaders from this region say the Bapounou of Congo would like to attach their region to rich Gabon. But Bapounou in Congolese border areas claim that Gabonese want to be part of Congo, which has larger and more exciting cities than Gabon.

Haut-Ogooué secession has been a greater threat to Gabon than that of Nyanga because of its manganese and uranium mines. The people of Haut-Ogooué, mostly Batéké and Ambamba, are closely related to those in the Congo, and there is much visiting back and forth. Many people speak Lingala, the language of the Congo River. The Batéké have little more than a distant historical political connection with their Congolese relatives, however. Even the Congolese Batéké are not united, and they are influenced culturally by the people with whom they live, just as the Batéké of Gabon are influenced by the Ambamba. The Congolese Ambamba, who are called Mbédé, are not united with their relatives either. Attempts to unify them have been used as a means to threaten the government and assert what the people believed to be the rightful importance of the region.

For reasons that are not clear the French administration seems

21 *Union Gabonaise,* October 1958, pp. 8-9.

often to have favored the development of Congo over and sometimes at the expense of Gabon. That the French were conscious
of competition from across the river in Léopoldville is part of the
reason for building up Brazzaville, but there may also have been
competition between administrators serving in the different countries, as there was between those working in Guinea and Senegal.

In 1888 white merchants who had their headquarters in Gabon
complained that the administration was not allowing them to trade
in the area of the upper Ogooué and that as a result commerce
was coming under the control of merchants in Congo. They complained to the lieutenant governor who said they need not bother
about the upper Ogooué: "Merchants don't have to go up beyond
Ndjolé because today canoers from French Congo sell rubber at
Ndjolé."[22] In 1925 the Haut-Ogooué region was made part of
Congo. It is generally believed that the reasons for this change in
frontier were the same as for those made in the southwest in 1918.
Although the Haut-Ogooué region was not to be traversed by the
Congo-Océan railway, workers were to be recruited from this area,
and the principle of unity of command determined the change in
frontier. Although the railroad was completed in 1934, Haut-
Ogooué remained part of Congo until a general post-war reorganization of A.E.F. took place in 1946.

Between 1925 and 1946 the region's ties with Congo were re-
enforced greatly. The Libreville-based trading company Société
du Haut-Ogooué (S.H.O.) was replaced after 1930 by a Congolese-
based company, Compagnie Française du Haut et Bas Congo
(C.F.H.B.C.). In order to move workers to Congo, communications
were improved, and according to one rather anti-Gabonese report
by an anonymous administrator in Franceville only the Ambamba
looked to Gabon as their homeland while "the Ogooué was losing
all its political and economic importance."[23] It was not until 1946,
however, that an all-weather motor route was opened between
Franceville and Dolisie in Congo but "out of a road system of five
hundred kilometers only about twelve kilometers [were] oriented
toward Gabon."[24]

22 Arch. Nat. Col., Gabon XII, 12C, extract from register of Conseil de Commerce et d'Agriculture, 14 February 1888.
23 "Rapport — pourquoi le Haut-Ogooué dépend essentiellement du Moyen-
Congo," Département du Haut-Ogooué, n.d.
24 *Ibid.*

As soon as the region was reattached to Gabon, a movement calling for a return to Congo, led by a representative in the Conseil Représentatif in Libreville, was started. At the beginning of 1949 this representative wrote to the governor and said that Haut-Ogooué had been neglected by the administration and that Gabon, "egoistic territory, which after having slowed down the evolution of the region for forty-eight years, now begins again."[25] He was interested in getting improvements, such as a resident physician and radio communication with the capital, for Okondja.

In the meanwhile letters were written to the president of the Congolese Conseil Représentatif in 1950 demanding the reattachment of the region to Congo; the Congolese did nothing to discourage such requests. The letters were written by Gabonese working in Congo and sometimes by Congolese, as it later turned out. The Gabonese who wrote said they were Batéké related to the descendants of King Makoko: "The population of Franceville is largely . . . Batéké who were part of the realm of this King. . . . The territory of Gabon to which they pretend to attach us has no communications with the region; all our local products are bought by the merchants of Dolisie (Moyen-Congo)."[26]

Governor Pelieu opposed any attempts to change Gabon's frontiers and rejected the complaints of the representative from Okondja and the desires of the Batéké from Franceville. He made a report to the Conseil Représentatif in which he said there was no ethnic division between Haut-Ogooué and the rest of Gabon because everyone except the Batéké had mixed with other Gabonese. He indicated that various attempts to organize a plebiscite on the matter had failed, but that a small group of self-seeking troublemakers kept agitating. He added that underpopulated Gabon could hardly afford to lose any of its territory. (At that time Nigerians were being brought in to work in forestry enterprises because there were not enough Gabonese.[27])

The Conseil Représentatif then set up a commission of investigation including one Frenchman from the first college or group of French citizens of the legislature, Senator Gondjout, a Fang,

---

25 Letter to Conseil Représentatif, Libreville, 13 February 1949.
26 Letter printed in *L'Etincelle de l'A.E.F.*, July-August 1950, p. 4.
27 Letter from Governor Pelieu to the President of the Conseil Représentatif, Libreville, 18 September 1950 and attached "Rapport."

Obame Ange, and M. Migolet, a Bandjabi (the only representative from the first Conseil who was still a deputy in 1966). The last week in October 1951 the commission traveled in the region and asked the opinions of chiefs and local leaders. They found only a minority of the population concerned with the matter of frontiers, and those who desired attachment to Congo took this position because there was a good road into Congo, because Moyen-Congo had set up a school and medical center at Franceville, because merchandise came from Moyen-Congo, and because a bulldozer promised by the governor of Gabon had not yet been sent.[28]

Batéké in Brazzaville were interested in attaching Haut-Ogooué to Congo in order to get more electoral strength, but the Gabonese who remained in Haut-Ogooué were most concerned about material benefits from Libreville. When they saw one town of their region get something like a hospital or school, they became resentful and talked of secession. In July 1964 *La Semaine Africaine* published a letter from some people in Moanda, the third sub-prefecture in Haut-Ogooué after Franceville and Okondja, complaining that Franceville was getting more than Moanda from Libreville. They resented the fact that a radio transmitter set up in 1961 in Moanda had been transferred to Franceville. The deputies from Haut-Ogooué who are from Franceville favor their own town: "The latter, invariably natives of Franceville, want to prevent the development of Moanda and are concerned only with their own district. In sum, there is not much to say for the time being, but we have considered it useful to draw the attention of the Government in order to remedy this situation."[29]

In 1946 the mineral resources had not been really discovered, although some investigations had been made in the region. Between 1951 and 1953 manganese was discovered,[30] and since that time the Congolese have been particularly interested in the region.

Abbé Fulbert Youlou, first President of Congo, never made a secret of his desire to integrate the exploitation of manganese with the construction of a dam and hydroelectric plant on the Kouilou River. The second President, Alphonse Massemba-Débat and his Prime Minister appeared to be more concerned with Congo-

---

28 "Rapport des membres de la mission d'enquête dans la région du Haut-Ogooué," P. Gondjout, rapporteur, Libreville, 2 November 1951.
29 *La Semaine Africaine*, 26 July 1964.
30 "Le livre d'or de Comilog," *Perspectives d'Outre-Mer*, No. 51, January-February 1963, p. 27.

Kinshasa than with Gabon although Congolese soldiers were said to have moved into Gabonese territory in June 1965; and at the end of 1964 secret meetings between Congolese and Gabonese were reportedly held in Libreville on the question of frontiers.[31] Gabonese leaders have warned Congolese that territorial demands on Haut-Ogooué are as justified as Gabonese demands for return of the area south of Nyanga, which would include the important port of Pointe-Noire. In a declaration in 1960 Léon Mba said that France had changed Gabon's frontier for the purpose of getting laborers for construction of the railroad: "At the time Gabon yielded because it was a question of French prestige and grandeur. Are we going to see, as they told me during my recent trip to Paris, the appearance of claims to our manganese or our iron based on this precedent? In the manner of what is going on further to the north, are some people going to discover old rights of sovereignty over Gabonese borderlands?"[32]

Congolese had been expelled from the area for having smuggled guns and for having spoken against the Libreville government. In September 1962 during a conference of chiefs of state of the Union Africaine et Malgache, Abbé Youlou and other members of the Congolese government met with Congolese working in Gabon. President Mba said he believed the goal was to encourage them to action that would undermine the Gabonese government. A demonstration in Libreville had been planned, it was reported.[33]

As long as Congo is poorer than Gabon, the frontier between the two countries might become the source of disputes. As information about Gabonese potential and mineral resources is spread among the peasants, the desire to remain part of Gabon increases. Visitors to isolated Gabonese villages along the frontier have found that peasants are very well informed about the economic development of resources and are keen to develop their regions within Gabon rather than in Congo where unemployment has long been a serious problem and resources are less promising. These border areas are, however, often referred to in the Congolese press as if they were part of Congo, and the Gabonese press has sometimes written in similar fashion about Congolese towns.

---

31 *Le Monde*, 23 December 1964.
32 *Union Gabonaise*, October 1958.
33 Author's interview with President Mba, 7 November 1962.

One important factor in keeping the Haut-Ogooué and the entire south tied to Gabon is the Fang. Fang and Omyènè occupy most civil-service posts in this area, and it often seemed that where there was a Fang sub-prefect there was also a Fang gendarme. In one border district where I happened to be at the end of September 1962 a Fang sub-prefect expelled the Congolese residents in less than twenty-four hours after the order came through from Libreville. He said he had long been waiting for the day when he could do this. In Libreville French commanders of the armed forces lost control of Fang soldiers and Fang police when Congolese were being put aboard ships for Congo. Some Congolese were badly beaten.

Two factors in the Fang dislike of the Congolese are important: First, there could be no efficacious national order without the south, and the Fang know it. The north has iron ore but this will not be exploited until the mid 1970's. Second, the tendency to predominate among the Fang as part of their motive force was hindered when the Congolese controlled commerce and had positions of power and prestige. No Fang could put up with the arrogance and the monopolization of women which Gabonese said were characteristic of the Congolese "invasion."

But while the Fang have been opposed to Congolese influence, there have been tendencies among those Fang who live in Woleu-Ntem to become part of Cameroun.

Frontiers with Cameroun

During his mission into Woleu-Ntem from 1905 to 1908 Captain Cottes found that the region might as well have been part of German Kamerun: "The Germans have made this region a veritable extension of their Cameroun by organizing an administration, by exercising rights of sovereignty, regulating judicial matters among natives, ordering requisitions, and by receiving orders, munitions, and even personnel borrowed from the regular forces of the German colony."[34] By treaties in 1911 and 1912 Woleu-Ntem, almost as far south as Mitzic, became Neu-Kamerun in return for German recognition of French sovereignty over

34 Le Capitaine Cottes, *La Mission Cottes au Sud-Cameroun (1905–1908)* (Paris, Leroux, 1911), pp. iii, iv.

Morocco. The Germans also got territory that connected Kamerun to the Congo River.

Neu-Kamerun lasted until the First World War, when bloody battles were fought between the French and Germans in Woleu-Ntem. By the Treaty of Versailles Woleu-Ntem was restored to Gabon, and Kamerun became Cameroun, a mandate and later a trust territory under French control. Many Camerounese consider their national frontiers to be those of 1911, when Kamerun was larger than ever before. Part of western Cameroun which was under British control has, in Camerounese terms, been restored, but many Camerounese say that Woleu-Ntem is really within their national frontiers.

President Mba has often claimed that many of his Fang opponents are "racists" who want to establish an independent Fang state. Recent attempts to standardize the Fang language across national frontiers have increased his fear of this. At the end of 1959 there was apparently an attempt to detach a part of Woleu-Ntem from Gabon. The president of the National Assembly ordered that two deputies be indicted for illegal possession of weapons.[35] The implication was that the deputies wanted to use the guns to start a movement against Libreville. One of the two had complained a few days before the order for his arrest that "there are not even roads to go to Woleu-Ntem; what good is it to vote money for roads? It is the estuary that makes up the Gabonese state all by itself."[36] A third deputy was accused of holding meetings calling for the attachment of Woleu-Ntem to Cameroun; he was removed from his post and jailed. Jean-Hilaire Aubame defended the deputy in question: "Having said that Minvoul could be attached to Cameroun does not constitute a danger to the security of the State."[37] In the middle of 1960 troops were parachuted into Bitam to suppress reported attempts to attach that district to Cameroun, and troops were also sent to this area at the time of the restoration of President Mba to power in 1964.

Many people in Woleu-Ntem recall with nostalgia the days when the region was part of Kamerun, because the more un-

[35] *"Journal des Débats,"* Assemblée Nationale de la République Gabonaise, 22 December 1959, pp. 298ff.
[36] *Ibid.,* p. 257.
[37] *Ibid.,* p. 300.

pleasant aspects of German colonial rule have been forgotten while their efforts at development are remembered. Fang will often point to a building or to a well that is still in good condition and say that the Germans really knew how to build.

Cameroun is considerably larger than Gabon and has more impressive cities, but the people in Woleu-Ntem are quite conscious of the fact that Gabon now seems to have greater potential for development than its neighbor and that Cameroun has had a rising rate of unemployment while Gabon boasts it has no unemployment at all. Camerounese come to Libreville in increasing numbers to drive taxis or engage in small commerce, and some Gabonese from the frontier area say southern Camerounese are more interested in becoming part of Gabon than the reverse. The Fang realize that if Woleu-Ntem were part of Cameroun, even with some measure of unity with the Bulu and the Betsi, they would still not be as large a percentage of the population as they are in Gabon. For better or for worse Léon Mba is Fang but Ahmadou Ahidjo is not, they said. Camerounese railroads and motor roads are being directed toward the north and northeast, toward Chad and the Central African Republic and between east and west Cameroun rather than toward Gabon; this indicates that Cameroun's interest in annexation is far less than Congo's.

If there is any conflict between Gabon and Cameroun over frontiers, the source might be Rio Muni.

Spanish and Portuguese Colonies

Rio Muni, located between Gabon and Cameroun and a former overseas province of Spain, achieved the status of autonomy as the result of a plebiscite in December 1963. Together with the island of Fernando Poo and a few tiny islands it forms what is now called Equatorial Guinea.

Rio Muni has a population of about 180,000 according to the 1960 census; of these about 27,000 live in Bata, the capital.[38] Probably three fourths of this population are Fang. The coastal people are Benga or Séké but consider themselves closely related to the Omyènè. Many of these have been to Libreville as students. Rivers such as the Woleu flow into Rio Muni from Woleu-Ntem,

[38] Instituto Nacional de Estadistica, *"Boletin de Estadistica,"* No. 214, October 1962, p. 4.

and there has been considerable movement across the frontier. Captain Cottes believed France had made a mistake in ceding this territory to Spain because it was really part of Woleu-Ntem, and Bata could have served as a good port for Woleu-Ntem.[39]

Prior to the change in status of Rio Muni, Gabon insisted the people were suffering under Spanish rule, and it was said that President Mba had given money to rescue some Fang. In a parade on 10 September 1962 at Libreville in honor of the chiefs of state at the U.A.M. meeting, a half-dozen men carried a sign appealing for the liberation of what they called Equatorial Guinea but which was then officially Spanish Guinea. President Mba wrote in his capacity as president of U.A.M.: "We demand the exclusion from the United Nations of impenitent racist countries; we shall ask that questions relating to Spanish Guinea, the island of Fernando Poo, and all dependent territories be discussed."[40]

Since an autonomous status has been achieved, Gabon has refused to comment on what are now considered internal affairs of another country, and maintains very cordial diplomatic relations with Spain. Equatorial Guinea has its own legislative body and a government council or cabinet with four representatives from Fernando Poo and four from Rio Muni. The capital is in Santa Isabel on Fernando Poo. It is also in Fernando Poo where the Spanish High Commissioner has his office.

The first chairman of the cabinet is a Fang, Bonifacio Ondo Edu, and one of the most important members of the opposition is Atanasio Ndong, who submitted a memorandum to the September 1962 meeting which proclaimed that a liberation committee had been formed. Ndong, who used to be a gendarme in Libreville and who, it is said, married a relative of President Mba, is opposed to the present arrangement which in some ways recalls the slow evolution of French-speaking countries toward independence. Spain controls defense, the budget, and foreign affairs.[41]

Ndong founded the Movimiento Nacional de Liberación de la Guinea Ecuatorial and a government in exile located first in Douala and later reported in Algiers.

39 Cottes, pp. 73, 85–86.

40 President Léon Mba, "De Tananarive à Libreville: l'Union Africaine et Malgache a un an," *Communauté France Eurafrique*, September 1962, p. 1.

41 René Pélissier, "Spain's Discreet Decolonization," *Foreign Affairs*, April 1965, p. 527.

In August 1963 Ndong presented a program that did not in-clude independence.[42] But since the plebiscite, the Spanish have retained firm control of the country, while Guinean exiles have begun to demand complete independence. Cameroun has spon-sored a liberation movement which has its headquarters at Ambam near the Gabon and Guinea frontiers.

Many Guineans are concerned about the future unity of their country which they see as becoming independent one day. There is some internal conflict between the coastal people who have had more access to education than the interior Fang (Spain did not move into the interior of the country until the mid 1920's); the latter joined the various Fang attempts to establish a new order through *Bwiti,* which spread from Gabon, and through *alar ayong.* On the island of Fernando Poo the indigenous Boubi have been outnumbered by immigrant Fang and Nigerian workers on cocoa plantations.

At the 1962 meeting of chiefs of state in Libreville there was speculation about the future of the then Spanish Guinea, and some thought Rio Muni could become part of Gabon and Fernando Poo part of Cameroun,[43] but it is clear that Nigeria would have strong claims on the island. Guineans say they are interested in increasing freedom and eventual independence from Spain and from neighbors; people of Rio Muni feel close ties to Fernando Poo, which has many of Guinea's rich plantations.

Since the plebiscite, relations between Guinea and Gabon have been very cordial. Fang ministers have visited Gabon, and Boni-facio Ondo, who was referred to as the President of Guinea Equa-torial in Gabon's newspaper, visited Gabon in May 1965. He toured the country and was given a reception by the Bloc Démo-cratique Gabonais at which the Fang administrative secretary of the party rather than the vice-president of the government wel-comed the guest.[44] (Léon Mba was out of the country.)

Many Guineans claim that Léon Mba was not born in Gabon;

42 "Programa Presentado por el Gobierno Provisional de la Guinea Ecuatorial en Exilio, Sobre la Autonomía Propuesta por el Gobierno Español," Douala, 14 August 1963.

43 Philippe Decraene, "La conférence de Libreville a marqué l'entrée en scène des derniers territoires africains sous dépendance," *Europe France Outremer,* Nos. 391-392, p. 20.

44 *Gabon d'Aujourd'hui,* 1 June 1965.

they say he was born just inside their frontier. Great concern and interest are shown in Gabonese politics, and, at the time of the overthrow of Léon Mba, Fang leaders in Rio Muni were reportedly saying he had been overthrown by a group of Omyènè like the Omyènè in Rio Muni.

Gabonese leaders, including several in opposition, say that Guinea should be allowed to develop in its own way but that Rio Muni might be expected gradually to become closely associated with Gabon. The Fang of Gabon, particularly those of the coast, feel close ties to Rio Muni while they have feelings of antagonism toward the Fang of southern Cameroun. The Camerounese, however, claim Rio Muni as part of their national territory.

Paul Soppo Priso, an important political figure from Douala and formerly the president of the Camerounese legislature, wrote that all Africa would soon be free but that there was no sense in having a great many little states which, economically unviable, would naturally be threatened by neo-colonialism. He stated he was not going to mention what *could be* Cameroun's *legitimate* territorial claims and then added that, by the way, the real Cameroun had once been an area of 750,000 square kilometers but had been reduced to a bare 430,000 after parts of it had been given to Gabon, Oubangui-Chari, Congo, and Chad, with the result that Camerounese tribes had thus been divided. The least the other countries could do is recognize Cameroun's claim to Guinea; once the little country is independent it will be in its own interest, the writer says, to federate with Cameroun. Guinea is the "natural and ethnic prolongation of Cameroun, the continuation of the southern zone of the Fang Ntoumou people of the low region of Ambam, a zone which, by the way, used to include Woleu-Ntem, a former Camerounese region today included in the national territory of Gabon."[45] The opposition and exiled party Union des Populations du Cameroun (U.P.C.) also considers that Rio Muni is part of Cameroun.[46]

When Guinea does become independent it may try to remain so, but there is undoubtedly going to be some competition to draw it into closer relationships with either Gabon or Cameroun. Ga-

[45] Paul Soppo Priso, "Face à l'harmonisation de l'Afrique: le Cameroun et la Guinée Espagnole," *Communauté France-Eurafrique,* September 1962, p. 7.
[46] *Afrique,* January 1963, p. 37.

bon's intentions are not as brutally stated as those of the Camerounese, but it is clear that the Fang would like to see Rio Muni unified into the Gabonese national frontiers; it would mean further Fang unity with the addition of 100,000 relatives and it would mean that the Fang would account for an even greater percentage of the Gabonese population.

Just off the Gabonese coast are two islands which form a so-called overseas province of Portugal. These are the islands of Saint Thomas and Prince, both of which have had a most interesting history. The Portuguese have been here almost continuously since the end of the fifteenth century. Saint Thomas has a population of about 53,000 and Prince one of around 7,000. Most of these people are descendants of slaves from Angola.[47] Since 1961 a liberation committee has had its headquarters in Libreville, with Miguel Treveada as its president. Gabon welcomes this committee and may not even look with disfavor on the idea of attaching the islands, but they are not considered very important now.

Gabon's frontiers could remain fairly stable in the south. There are ethnic ties that could be used to justify invasion and territorial demands, however, and an unstable government in Brazzaville with very serious problems of its own might embark on an expansionist adventure. Frontiers in the north could also change, but for more complex reasons. As long as France remains in close contact with all three countries and continues to play its paternalistic role, it is unlikely that conflict will be serious. If there were any conflict or threat to Gabonese frontiers, it is likely that the Gabonese people would react strongly to protect what are increasingly considered the logical, natural frontiers of the Gabonese nation.

[47] La Documentation Française, "Les territoires portugais d'Afrique," Notes et Etudes Documentaires, 26 January 1962, pp. 44–47.

CHAPTER 11

Threats to a Developing National Order

Threats

The seriousness of some threats to a developing national order depends on how far along in the process of nation-building a nation-state is. No nation is free of threats to its continued existence, although the threats might be more or less rare. In the earlier stages internal antagonisms between kinship and regional groups tend to play a more important role than in later stages, and what might be considered minor disturbances in one country take on a crucial aspect in others. In countries where nation-building is in its earlier stages, conflicts, questions of distribution of power, and prestige positions are more apt to be seen in particularistic terms of tribal membership and region. There are in these countries fewer loyalty groups which cut across kinship lines; working classes are, for example, still small, and problems of communication prevent worker unity.

Second, threats depend on the zone of the country and on certain groups of people. Problems in the Nationalizing Zone differ in some ways from those in Heartland Zones; there is an incipient urban proletariat; there are concentrations of students in Na-

tionalizing Zones; and people of different ethnic groups are mobilized for intensive contacts. Mobilization does not necessarily
mean assimilation, and the gap between these two phenomena
may be large enough to mean that quite different people have
intensive contacts with each other while they maintain their differences. They may turn to violence as a way to resolve their
disputes because they recognize no peaceful ways to do it.

Third, there are both internal threats and external threats.
Invasion by another country can mean the end of a nation-building process within the previous frontiers, and it can mean the end
of the development of a standardized and distinctive national culture, national history, and national belief system. On the other
hand, such an invasion might stimulate those who represent the
motive force to further action in building the nation, and might
encourage others to follow these leaders.

Some of these threats are what might be called core threats; they
have nothing to do with the government in power. They are the
result of the process of nation-building and have little to do with
personalities. They are influenced by the location of the developing nation-state, its economic problems, its problems of inter-ethnic
antagonisms. These problems might be influenced by governments
but they would exist to some extent regardless of the government
in power.

In Gabon there are also threats that arise out of the conflict
between the government and the opposition. These are influenced
by personalities and human decision-making. Such threats would
not necessarily vanish with the disappearance of the personalities,
for certain patterns for behavior to gain and maintain power will
no doubt influence future national leaders and their opponents.
The patterns are sometimes a continuation of a pre-independence
conflict and competition for power.

Core Threats

Threats from the Exterior

The Congolese are regarded as a real menace to Gabon's frontiers. If Haut-Ogooué were attached to Congo, Gabon might be so
weakened economically that it would retreat back to the estuary
area and would once more be Rio Gabon. Because most Gabonese

increasingly share certain beliefs about the possibilities for the development of their own country, the threat of outside attack has tended to encourage at least temporary solidarity.

In September 1962, when it was reported that Gabonese were being killed in Brazzaville after the expulsion of the Congolese from Gabon, there was a great sense of unity on the Ogooué. If a man was beaten up in Brazza, it did not seem to matter whether he was Bapounou, Omyènè, or Fang; he was Gabonese. And if a visitor from Brazza was Bandjabi or Bapounou, it did not seem to matter either; he could be beaten by Bandjabi or Bapounou Gabonese.

During this period I was in the regions of Nyanga and Ngounié along the Congolese frontier. I took a truck from Tchibanga to Mouila on the Sunday after the trouble had begun and the Congolese had been ordered expelled. The driver spread the news from village to village; the information became more and more exaggerated as he received information from other travelers and as we journeyed north: Gabonese killed, Gabonese raped, Gabonese disemboweled, and so forth. The mood of all the southerners who are related to tribes in Congo became increasingly antagonistic to any and all Congolese until stray Congolese who had not succeeded in hiding were attacked and beaten.

In Tchibanga I encountered a government information truck that had been showing films in villages. The driver was a Congolese, and the projectionist was a Fang. They were ordered to return to Libreville but had to drive through Nyanga and Ngounié to get there. Their lives were saved in this Bapounou-Eshira area by their protests that they were really both Fang.

Any government may try to use a real or imaginary threat from outside to gain the support of the people, and accusations that Congolese troops cross Gabonese frontiers or that Congolese are secretly exploiting some Gabonese mine might be considered useful even if they are not totally true.

Threats from Old Internal Divisions

Some Gabonese do not like other Gabonese of the same tribe, of different tribes, and of different regions. This is not a new phenomenon. There are the disputes between the Fang of Woleu-Ntem and the Fang of the coast, between Bapounou of Mouila and Bapounou of Nyanga, between the Fang and the Omyènè, between the Fang and the Omyènè on one hand and the southerners on the other. At Lambaréné, where the two major groups of Fang have met, disputes and open fighting have at times been settled by the calling in of some Galoa (Omyènè).[1]

The Badouma and most Bandjabi in the south have not gotten along. One source of conflict has been the name of the region in which they lived. It used to be called "Région des Adoumas," which was quite flattering to the Badouma but offensive to the more numerous Bandjabi who in 1951 succeeded in having the name changed to Ogooué-Lolo.[2] In 1955 a number of Bandjabi were killed in automobile and canoeing accidents by Badouma, who were invariably exonerated in Badouma-run courts. In the same year a Bandjabi *chef de canton* was not allowed to go to Libreville for a state-wide celebration because a Badouma chief who had influence with the administration had said he was too dirty to appear and could not, as a Bandjabi, represent the supposedly superior Badouma. All this encouraged ill feelings between the two groups, and some Bandjabi tried to secede from the region and become part of a neighboring *canton* in Haut-Ogooué.

In work situations in the Nationalizing Zone or in industrial enterprises there is a tendency for one tribe to predominate over another. For example, Fang and Bakota worked for a while in the woodworking shop of one of the large mining companies, but eventually the Bakota, who were a minority, wanted to get out. The Fang were happiest without any Bakota around, and the Bakota were happiest working in another section. In Libreville one tribe may dominate a specific office and make life difficult for others. In one bureau where I spent considerable time, a solitary Mitsogo found himself surrounded by Fang to whom he referred occasionally as "savages." The Fang thought this was very amusing and told him he could become a Fang if he admired them so. For the solitary non-Fang-speaking Mitsogo, life was very uncomfortable.

---

1 Noted by Georges Balandier, *Sociologie actuelle de l'Afrique noire*, p. 205. This was done in hopes of gaining some advantage because the Omyènè would be unfamiliar with Fang custom, but it is nonetheless an indication of a certain respect for the Omyènè.

2 Letter from governor to president of Conseil Représentatif, Libreville, 11 March 1951.

Whereas conflict used to be pictured in terms of Fang versus Omyènè in the Nationalizing Zone, it is increasingly pictured in terms of Fang and Omyènè versus the southerners led by the Bapounou who, according to my calculations, have over 27 per cent of their total population in the Nationalizing Zone and who probably constitute about 15 per cent of the Gabonese population of Libreville.

Southerners or Mérié who are migrating in increasing numbers to the Nationalizing Zone resent what they call Fang or Fang-Omyènè attempts to control Gabon. Everyone knows the Fang are the largest group, and everyone is aware of the Fang tendency to dominate others. Mérié and Omyènè say that Fang are, however, "barely one quarter of the population" and that they are not a very large group even though they are the largest in Gabon. The Bapounou insist that they are running a close second, even though some data indicate that the Bandjabi outnumber them. Fang estimates of their own numerical strength have been as high as 400,-000; they add, of course, that there are Fang in Cameroun and Rio Muni in such numbers that the whole group is really two millions strong.

After the election of J.-H. Aubame to the French National Assembly he became the subject of attacks by anonymous letters and brochures, some of which no doubt came from other Fang. Many, however, came from non-Fang and attacked Aubame's ethnic group. In an open letter Aubame was obliged to defend the Fang: "They say correctly that racism calls for contrary racism, that calumny calls for calumny, and that one cannot unite in dividing. I shall not lower myself in applying this principle. . . . I suppose that in speaking of 'savages' the author wanted to attack the Fang. Let the races who were not clearly named know that this insult of 'savages' is meant to apply equally to them."[3]

Antagonisms usually remain below the surface or are expressed verbally; they seldom result in violence. Even during the very unsettling times of the coup d'état and the restoration of the government there was little or no intertribal conflict, although many people talked about the possibility of it and some others may have hoped for it. Talk of a Fang march on Libreville created much agitation among the Bapounou.

[3] Letter, J.-H. Aubame, Député du Gabon, Paris, 27 June 1947.

During one day and one night I rode up the Ogooué in a boat with a dozen workers and fishermen. Six were Bandjabi, and the others, including the captain, were Fang. One of the Bandjabi was a foreman on a construction project; as a man with some standing he would be paid even if he were not actually working. The other Bandjabi were laborers who had been waiting for three days for the boat to take them to a new job in Lambaréné; they were not paid when they did not work. Naturally they wanted to get to Lambaréné as soon as possible. The Fang captain of the boat had about the same standing and pay as the foreman, and he was in no hurry to get back to Lambaréné where his boss, the sub-prefect, had plenty of little jobs for him to do. Besides, he had some relatives to pick up along the river so that they could take their fish to Lambaréné to sell. At the beginning of the trip he had also picked up some young Fang in a village.

In Gabon apprentices and the young learn fast when the man who is supposed to be in charge of a job takes advantage of his position to sleep or chat. While the captain slept, the young Fang steered the boat in a meandering sort of way. It was necessary to stop in one village where beer could be bought and, of course, the helmsman's relatives were waiting.

When the trip up the Ogooué had begun everyone was cheerful and glad to be on the way. Passengers were scattered helter-skelter about the boat which must have been thirty feet long. If there were any distribution, it was that the foreman found the helmsman's company more interesting than that of the workers. The Bandjabi foreman even spoke Fang, and the two got along very well talking about old times in Libreville and Lambaréné.

But the Bandjabi workers suddenly became angry. Why wasn't the captain driving, and why were we taking so long to get to Lambaréné? The captain explained that a longer route to Lambaréné had to be taken because the river was still too low. As far as letting the young Fang drive and as far as stopping for his relatives — the workers could go to hell. This was the end of harmony.

Bandjabi occupied the bow and the Fang occupied the stern. The foreman moved into the bow and shouted over the small cabin to the captain who spoke for the Fang.

The rainy season had just begun so that the sky was clear at night, and one could see all those stars visible, it seems, nowhere else on this earth. The moon was reflected in the calm Ogooué, and the boat drifted against a bank as no one took the wheel during the shouting match which had begun.

The battle remained verbal, and the foreman seemed less energetic a leader than his appearance suggested he could be. The Bandjabi accused the Fang of trying to control everyone else, of trying to boss them around and to have their own way which was what, according to them, Fang always try to do. The captain shouted he would run the boat the way he wanted and that Bandjabi were idiots. The forest was filled with human sounds deep into the night. The Fang captain finally got the boat going again amid continuing shouts of approval, disapproval, and sarcasm. The shouting between the two groups decreased in intensity and frequency with an occasional outburst in order to have the satisfaction of the last word, and the two groups remained essentially divided as far as Lambaréné although the foreman and the captain appeared to have re-established their rapport.

Resentment toward the Fang also appears to exist among some of those people who are being assimilated. Tiny tribes which are becoming absorbed by other tribes because they desire to escape the opprobrium attached to their original identity or because separate histories and customs are being forgotten as shared experience draws them increasingly into the orbit of a different people sometimes try to reassert their pre-national distinctiveness. This has not yet been a problem in Gabon although some younger members of small ethnic groups say they deplore the disappearance of old traditions.

Threats from New Internal Divisions

Changes in Gabonese society have led to new conflicts between young and old, between men and women, between civil servants and others.

Younger Gabonese resent being ruled and ordered about by older men whom they consider less educated than themselves and unable to meet the problems posed by economic development. They consider all the older leaders to be too much under the influence of foreigners and to have outmoded ideas. It appears that divisions based on age differences are important within the opposition movement as well.

The revolt of women against submission to men has barely begun but is already responsible for decreases in production, particularly in southern areas where the women do an amazing amount of the total work. The government encourages women to spy on men, particularly on civil servants.

Increasing antagonism between the masses and the civil servants has become evident. The average family in which there are from two to five persons gets over 40,000 CFA francs each month when the leading male is a civil servant. In 1964 about 38 per cent of the Gabonese budget was designed to pay personnel of the administration and the National Assembly.[4] This represented an increase of only 4 per cent over 1963 compared with increases of 10 per cent in Congo, 22 per cent in Chad, and 23 per cent in the Central African Republic.[5] The average family earns about 22,000 francs if the father is in the private sector, 14,700 if a servant, and 14,000 if a laborer.[6] Within the civil service an agricultural agent gets only about 20,000 francs, compared with 40,000 in general administration, and a family of farmers earns less than 4,000 francs each month.[7] Monthly salaries of deputies and ministers have been about 175,000 francs plus the various perquisites that go with such positions. Everyone knows about how much civil servants and government officials earn. The result has been increased antagonism toward this group and a desire to leave agriculture to others.

The resentment of peasants and others toward functionaries in Heartland and Contact Zones is reflected in a growing desire to impede their work and even to attack them. Although villagers have long been exploited by a colonial regime in search of free or almost free labor, they accept such treatment from Gabonese civil servants with decreasing docility. They often refuse, for example, to bring agricultural products to market to sell or to "give" them to the administration; the result has been that civil servants sometimes cannot get food. Insults and attacks on civil servants have

4 Service National de la Statistique, "Rapport annuel — 1963," p. 103.

5 Banque Centrale des Etats de l'Afrique Equatoriale et du Cameroun, *Bulletin Mensuel*, No. 91, June 1964.

6 Ministère de l'Economie Nationale, République Gabonaise, "Note sur l'enquête des conditions de vie au milieu africain, effectueé à Libreville en 1961–1962," Libreville, 1963, pp. 12–15.

7 SOFRED (Société française d'études de développement) "La population active: la politique de l'emploi et de la formation dans le cadre du plan," 1960–1961, Paris, p. 19.

been reported, and in one southern town a gendarme was stoned to death after a local resident whom he had arrested died.

In the Nationalizing Zone there is a new threat in the widening gap between those who are mobilized for intensive contacts and those who are assimilated. The only way to estimate this gap in Gabon is by the criterion of unemployment. Census takers found that in the group fourteen years and older 39 per cent of the people of Libreville were technically unemployed in 1960–1961. Once schoolchildren and housewives were subtracted, 9 per cent of Libreville's population was found to be without employment. Most of these were adolescents who live alone.[8] Although inhabiting the Nationalizing Zone, they are not a part of the system. They constitute a threat to a developing Gabonese nation because they have intensive contacts and yet remain unassimilated.

Threats from Corruption

Many private firms have long overcharged and cheated the Gabonese while for many years paying them very low wages. After independence several foreign companies were engaged in road construction, but it seemed to be general knowledge that they were paying off this civil servant or that government official. Government officials are also accused of using state machinery, for example, to build houses which they then rent to foreigners, and also of thievery of government funds.

Ways have been tried to lower prices that are kept artificially high by expatriate merchants whose goal is to make as much money as possible and then get out of Gabon. One way was the purchase by the government of a series of shops throughout the country. These shops, called *Ceca-Gadis,* have become even for the supporters of the present government the symbol of corruption and robbery of the masses. The prices in the *Ceca-Gadis* shops are just as high as in the privately owned shops, if not higher. For example, pilot farms have been established to reduce the dependence of Libreville on importations of vegetables, but the produce of these farms is sold at the same prices as the imported food. One progovernmental newspaper, *Le Patriote,* reported that mineral water was being sold for 70 francs in private companies

---

[8] Service de la Statistique, "Recensement et enquête démographiques 1960–1961: Résultats pour Libreville," Paris, 1962, p. 5.

and for 80 francs in the state stores.[9] It is commonly suspected that civil servants make a large profit on this chain of shops, but some people accept this as natural.

The idea that government and administration exist to exploit people is an inheritance from the colonial period, but some people say they occasionally look back to that period as a time of greater freedom and honesty in government than at present. Gaining a government post is still regarded as a way to get rich quickly and to help the family. Change in government is thus regarded as giving someone else a chance to get rich.

Threats from a Refusal to Work

The Gabonese ask themselves, what is the point of working if the civil servants and members of the government make all the money and live a life of ease and foreign capitalists are getting most of the benefits of exploitation of Gabonese minerals? They ask themselves when free plants are distributed: "Who will get the benefits from my work?" Few are convinced they will benefit through the construction of a new level of community.

They then ask themselves whether or not they, as Blacks, have the power to take the initiative to invent things. After years of submission to a foreign ruler who claimed to represent civilization and who claimed to be able to do anything while the African was said to be incapable of doing anything, many Gabonese have become docile and submissive before white technology and white initiative. And, as long as there are jobs and advantages for regional leaders and intellectuals, few complain. They say to the Whites: "Come to our country to develop it." Altruism and working for the benefit of the non-kinship group are not understood by all Gabonese. Peace Corps volunteers, for example, were thought of as a private American company, and its members were often offered gold to build private houses for villagers for whom they were only supposed to build schools as part of an American aid effort. Without supervision many Gabonese workers as well as middle- and lower-ranking civil servants refuse to work, with the result that government-service efficiency is declining in some areas.

That part of the national belief system which insists that Gabon

9 *Le Patriote,* 20 March 1965.

needs the White is firmly implanted and leads to widespread passivity. Feelings of African inferiority are assiduously encouraged by many *petits blancs* who have many of the characteristics of lower-class Whites in southern United States.

Government versus Opposition, 1960–1966

A Disloyal Opposition

The type of loyal opposition, as in a country in Europe or America, which respects the basic institutions of the nation-state and follows certain recognized procedures to suggest policies that in its view are better than those of the government in power, has been dismissed as unrealistic in most African countries. Opposition has been called un-African and disruptive. Opposition may be expressed, it is said, within the single party or within the government, but once decisions are made "in an African way" no one criticizes.

There is no reason for the existence of a loyal opposition in Africa just because such a system has worked well in the United Kingdom, and there is no way for an outsider to know just how much free discussion and opposition can be expressed within the ranks of the single party. But the result of the stifling of all opposition has been that the opposition cannot be loyal. The opposition that does exist does so outside any system of rules for behavior. It is by definition lawless and may commit lawless acts.

In Gabon the opposition is characterized by the government in the most extreme terms possible: It is composed of Communists, Chinese agents, warmongers, racists who would stop at nothing to gain power, according to the government and its supporters. "Be Vigilant! Communism is at our doors, it is waiting for a propitious moment; it is ready to steal into our country under all the most tempting promises."[10]

Order as defined by the government is set against Communism and racism, which are called the ultimate opposition and the ultimate disorder. Order thus comes to be associated with oppression and the maintenance in power of the present personalities. Order is thus mocked as a corrupt concept used to justify personal power,

10 *Ibid.*

and disorder becomes attractive to a secret opposition which is increasingly convinced that extreme measures are necessary.

Opposition Outside Gabon

The main opposition groups are those of students and exiles. The Association Générale des Etudiants du Gabon (A.G.E.G.), affiliated with the Fédération des Etudiants d'Afrique Noire en France (F.E.A.N.F.), has long attracted most students who oppose the government of Léon Mba. Drawing heavily on Marxist-Leninist terminology it attacks the regime for oppressing the masses and for submitting to the foreign capitalists-imperialists, as they are called: "The present Gabonese State is not serving the nation and will never do so because it is serving foreign monopolies."[11] Revolution is needed and a union of workers, peasants, and students must establish a new society, they say. Members of A.G.E.G. come from all parts of Gabon, but Fang and Omyènè predominate.

A second student movement is the Mouvement Gabonais d'Action Populaire (M.G.A.P.), which allies itself with the P.U.N.G.A. Most of its members appear to be southerners. M.G.A.P. publications indicate it was founded in 1958 and along with the P.U.N.G.A. favored a *non* vote. Its aspirations were to become a student movement and then to spread its activities to Gabon where they believe revolution is necessary.

A third movement is the Mouvement National de la Révolution Gabonaise, whose leader is Germain Mba, a Fang who was formerly assistant secretary general of the Union Africaine et Malgache. He resigned his position and went into exile after the French intervention in his country.[12] Generally considered to be favorable toward J.-H. Aubame and J.-M. Ekoh, he has written that the present regime is illegal.

With the help of the French government President Léon Mba fought against this external opposition. The student publications in France have at various times been suppressed, scholarships have been canceled, French and Gabonese police have arrested students

[11] J. Rendjambe-Issany, "Pour un état de démocratie nationale par un front démocratique uni," *L'Etudiant du Gabon,* July 1964, p. 10.
[12] Germain Mba, "Occupé, le Gabon lutte, humiliée, l'Afrique se tait," *Jeune Afrique,* 6 April 1964.

at the Cité Universitaire in Paris and have detained Germain Mba and other exiles.

Some of these exiles and students have gone to the Soviet Union and elsewhere to complete their studies when they have not been permitted to remain in France or when they have sought to learn from non-French experience of political and economic development. A few have reportedly studied various techniques of violence for use in overthrowing the regime. They state that the present government is not legal and that the country is occupied by a foreign power: "The Gabonese people consider that since 19 February, owing to its occupation by a foreign army, the Gabonese State has ceased to exist."[13] Attempts to smuggle arms into the country have been reported, and these groups give publicity abroad to what they consider the injustices of the present regime.

Opposition Within Gabon

After the attempted coup d'état and intervention, revolutionary committees were formed in schools. Some schools were closed and the students were sent back home. They have attacked government officials and members of French technical assistance teams; teachers, for example, have been attacked; a few students have been killed by government troops and gendarmes.

Students in Gabonese schools were required to sign statements they would not participate in politics. In one school in Woleu-Ntem, where a few students signed such statements, the sub-prefect's office was invaded and the statements were torn up by a large student group. The sub-prefect escaped through the window to ride to a military camp in order to get soldiers to bolster his authority. The students, who thought he had found asylum in the home of an expatriate teacher, marched to the house and searched it in the presence of the occupants.

Another form of opposition has come from the Church and from Monsignor André Raponda-Walker, whose letters and appeals have been published in foreign magazines and newspapers. "Monsieur le Président, permit me to tell you that you have gone too

13 Adolphe N'Dong M'Bile, "Des prisonniers 'français' devant la justice gabonaise," *Afrique Nouvelle*, No. 891, 4–10 September 1964.

244

far; you have gone beyond your rights; you have abused your authority in face of the whole world. One does not govern a country by violence, by terror."[14] The Monsignor was beaten for this letter.

Former members of the opposition and participants in either the coup or the Provisional Government were put into prison or have received "national indignity." During their trial none of the accused showed the slightest remorse at the attempted coup. Sub-lieutenant Mbene declared: "Whatever your sentence, I regret nothing. The 18th of February constituted the most complete act of national liberation since Gabon's independence."[15]

The most powerful internal opposition among the peasants comes from the Woleu-Ntem; villagers in several other regions have talked of arms they have buried and of the possibility of a march on Libreville. In Libreville two Fang quarters went into open revolt against the government and against French troops in February 1964. In the disturbance that followed the coup, workers went on strike in the Nationalizing Zone, in Libreville, and in Port-Gentil; they demanded higher wages but were also opposed to the government. Because the major industrial enterprises of Libreville, Port-Gentil, the forestry region, and Haut-Ogooué are not connected by a good system of communication, unity among the workers is difficult to achieve, and so far they have not been a very important factor in Gabonese politics. The labor leader, Jean-Fidèle Otandault, who led the opposition list in Ogooué-Maritime in the 1964 elections, died in 1965.

The opposition within Gabon is no more united than that without Gabon. In addition to the differences between groups there are internal dissensions within single opposition groups between the older leaders and the younger leaders, who often have far more radical ideas.

Younger leaders admire the Union des Populations du Cameroun and they admire the change of government in Congo-Brazzaville, while older leaders are not willing to go this far and feel more attachment to France in spite of the intervention. The desire for a choice and the desire to extricate themselves from complete French control and complete French influence is an

14 Letter reprinted in *Croissance de Jeunes Nations*, No. 44, May 1965, p. 28.
15 Reported in *Jeune Afrique*, 14 September 1964.

important motive. Some opposition leaders hoped for greater American influence in Gabon, not necessarily to replace the French but to offer alternatives (and perhaps to compete with the French while the Gabonese watched). They say they want "a choice, not an echo." In the face of America's unwillingness to weaken French influence, some opposition leaders say they will turn to the Soviet Union and China, both of which have embassies in neighboring countries. A desire to have contact with the Russian and Chinese experience is, however, older than the 1964 coup.

Personalization of the Nation-State

This is one of the greatest threats to the development of a cohesive national community. In campaigning for elections, President Mba is reported to have said after the fashion of another leader in another age: "L'Etat, c'est moi," and that he was the "Caesar" of "render unto God that which is God's and unto Caesar that which is Caesar's." As the single national leader he has attempted to associate the nation-state with his own personality as the head of one great family. The result is that symbols and institutions are considered Léon Mba's symbols and Léon Mba's institutions. Or they are considered France's symbols and France's institutions. The implication is that they must be destroyed when the President is gone, or that if they are attacked, the President is attacked. Everyone must be either for or against Léon Mba.

Laws and institutions are used to crush the opposition, and all Gabonese know this. For example, after the end of National Union in 1963 and the installation of Aubame as president of the Supreme Court, Mba had a law passed that forbade the holding of two offices, one in the National Assembly and the other in the administration or judiciary. The purpose of the law was to weaken Aubame.

Deputies have been arrested without following the necessary procedure to lift parliamentary immunity, and President Mba has made surprise appearances before the National Assembly to force passage of a government-sponsored law by means of threats. There appeared no limits to what the President could do. When Mba was apparently summoned to Paris after he had a French citizen beaten in public, many Gabonese hoped that General de Gaulle would somehow force him to change his ways or would remove him from office.

The Penal Code adopted in 1963 has no less than 162 articles out of a total of 347 dealing with crimes against the state, its exterior security, internal security, and rebellion:

> Article 156: There will be punished as meetings of rebels, as defined by the above dispositions, any meetings that will have been formed with or without weapons and accompanied by violence or threats against the administrative authority, the police:
>
> 1. By workers or laborers in workshops, mines, work camps, and in general all public and private enterprises.[16]

By this and similar measures almost any meeting may be banned. The measures and weapons of the government are those of a totalitarian regime in spirit, but they still affect the masses outside the Nationalizing Zone in only minimal ways. In a radio broadcast at the beginning of June 1965, Gabonese were warned not to criticize the President who is watching over all Gabonese, or his government.[17]

The state and its institutions were considered the possessions of Léon Mba. Tracts addressed to the President sometimes referred to "your state." In Woleu-Ntem the Gabonese flag has been torn up, and people of Libreville committed other disrespectful acts at the Monument to the Dead and at the monument to Captain Ntchorere. These acts indicate their total rejection of these symbols for Gabon. Most Gabonese did not celebrate independence day in 1964 because they said Gabon's real national day was 18 February, the date of attempted liberation from France. The President has been called every possible name in a multitude of tracts which mysteriously appeared on the desks of functionaries and in businesses when offices opened in the morning.

The President has encouraged betrayal of the leaders of the coup by forcing declarations of loyalty to him personally. Such declarations were made by some of the accused and were made sometimes at gunpoint, it is reported. The opposition, however, had representatives in very high posts who were very willing to

---

[16] "Code Pénal," République Gabonaise, Law No. 21–63, 31 May 1963, p. 35. Even civil servants have criticized these and other aspects of the Code.

[17] Printed in *Gabon d'Aujourd'hui*, 8 June 1965.

declare their loyalty to the President in oaths they had to take but who passed on information to opposition groups of everything that went on. Intrigue and betrayal encourage the pre-national belief that one can trust only members of one's immediate family.

The Greatest Threat

The greatest threat to a developing national order is the threat of disappointment. The disappointment may first be in terms of material rewards which were expected with independence in 1960. These rewards consist in the construction of a good road, for example, which is something in which all Gabonese are intensely interested. In 1964 the people of Nyanga wrote to the Brazzaville newspaper *La Semaine Africaine* in hopes of getting results from this publicity in a foreign publication: "Oh! Do they want to forget that Moabi is a sub-prefecture? We beg the authorities and particularly our representatives, who have promised us roads, to do something, because for the past year our road network has hardly improved."[18] The Gabonese often had no clear idea of what independence would bring. Used to French paternalism, they expected a paternal government, but they also expected great benefits quickly.

Another expected reward was freedom, but as one Gabonese wrote in *La Semaine Africaine*: "During four years of independence, particularly lately, more injustices and crying abuses have been committed than during more than a century of French occupation."[19] Freedom was also supposed to mean Gabonization of the public and private sectors. In 1960, out of 1,424 top-ranking personnel or cadres only 53 were African (and of these several were non-Gabonese).[20] And postprimary education was totally controlled by the French. By 1964 the private company COMILOG had a mere four Gabonese out of a total of ninety cadres, and the plywood factory had not a single Gabonese in the upper categories.[21] Secondary education was still controlled by

18 *La Semaine Africaine,* 8 November 1964.
19 Editorial by Louis Badila, "Les enfers africains," *La Semaine Africaine,* 8 November 1964.
20 "Les besoins d'encadrement de la République Gabonaise," *La planification de l'encadrement: problèmes et méthodes* (Paris, Institut de science économique appliquée, 1964?) p. 167.
21 *Ibid.,* pp. 164–165.

French teachers and in the highest post, or category A, of the civil service only one third were filled by Gabonese.[22] There is some proof that the President has desired to retard Africanization because the presence of Whites weakens the ability of Africans within the administration, Church, or army to oppose Mba's policies. Not a few Gabonese civil servants have looked for ways to leave the country in order to avoid serving as agents for an oppressive regime.

The third disappointment is seen in terms of order. The government of the nation-state may be able to impose its own brand of order, which is unjust and which subjects people to new, capricious forces. That the government of the first President of Gabon has subjected people to such capricious forces cannot be disputed; as a result the most serious opposition to the government came from the Fang, particularly those of Woleu-Ntem, who regarded the first President as a traitor to the Fang and as a traitor to Gabon.

From 1964 to 1966 action by the Gabonese was difficult because the French army occupied the country, and economic development has been in the hands of investors in Europe and America. The armed forces are controlled by the French, and foreign troops guarded the national leader.

In the face of this inability to act, younger people are increasingly repelled by politics. They say they want to become soldiers to protect the country against invaders from Europe or elsewhere; they say they want to become professors and specialists, but politics is regarded as unclean. There is a growing feeling of "I couldn't care less; leave me in peace to do my work."

A new type of national leader was to replace the first President, but the Fang say they would not accept a non-Fang. Although Léon Mba fashioned himself the sole national leader and effectively convinced many people that he was the only living Fang who could rise above his ethnic group, another Fang could also become the national leader, but he would have to prove his goodwill to the non-Fang. A non-Fang might conceivably become the national leader, or non-Fang might take part in a governing group of leaders, since some of the opposition favor establishment

22 *Ibid.,* pp. 170–171.

of a government like that in Brazzaville, with a president and a prime minister.

These disappointments, the presence of many Whites, the absence of a clear idea of whether Gabon is independent or not, the lack of a spirit of self-sacrifice fostered by a confusion about who gets the benefits, all these threaten the future development of Gabon. The resolution of these problems depends in part on the growth of a nationalist spirit among all Gabonese.

CHAPTER 12

Conclusions

The world still belongs to the nationalists. We, who incorrectly regard ourselves as beyond or in some sense too old for nationalism, cannot deny it to others by pretending it is always outmoded or dangerous. Every person needs the consciousness that he is part of an efficacious order, and that when it is threatened, men will come to lead, to inspire, to articulate what must be done to preserve it or to establish a new order. Every nation continues to need the nationalists, people who are willing to submit to the greater good of the collectivity in order to maintain the nation-building process.

No entity that calls itself a nation-state is ever removed from the process of nation-building. There are always threats to the order, to the meaningful, systematized relationships within, and to the independent, distinctive existence without. Most states of Africa are at earlier stages of the process than are most states of Europe; none of them has yet reached the stage at which outside observers can be completely sure they are going to continue to exist within present frontiers. In spite of some future economic and possible union in Europe, one may be reasonably sure "there will always be an England." One may not be equally sure there will always be a Belgium, however. In spite of some possible union in the Middle East or in Africa, one may be reasonably sure there will always be an Egypt, but will there always be a Mauritania?

England, France, Egypt, Japan, and the United States, for example, will in the twentieth century continue to exist as the supreme loyalty groups for most people who live within their national frontiers. One need not hesitate to write about them out of fear they may disappear. In some parts of Africa what seem to be nations in different stages of the process may turn out to be parts of future nations, although fidelity to the frontiers established by colonial regimes has been expressed by African leaders.

African nations have *esprit* just as European nations do. They have their own problems of maintaining order. They have been influenced by varieties of the European experience in economic and political development, and "a man's a man for a' that," but human collectivities are different from one another. They try to be faithful to the ancestors; they have a style of doing things.

This does not mean that only Africans can write about African phenomena. An outsider may perceive the realities of social change, and he may make meaningful analyses about them without necessarily being able to speak all the languages spoken in the country and without necessarily living there for ten years. Social scientists constantly develop tools, and perceptive humans from other lands may use methods as relevant for an understanding of human behavior in Kalamazoo as in Kissidougou.

Africans may, however, be led to discourage research by a misinterpretation of the researcher's motives, a suspicion about to what use information is to be put, and a lack of concern with recording contemporary history. The behavior of some researchers, increasing awareness of the tensions of international relations, and past experience with some journalists whose goal has been to exaggerate, or even to lie, have of course been the basis for reticence. Records could still be better cared for. They are in some places destroyed by water and fire, and documents may be put in secret places to be forgotten by everyone except the termites. Future research is thereby endangered both for the European and African scholar.

Research in nation-building is not historical research. This has not been a study of the rise or fall of the Gabonese nation. It is a study of the forces that act on the country and people from without and from within. These forces push it toward national consolidation and away from national consolidation and make of a developing Gabonese nation a process in itself.

The ways of studying nation-building are not historical methods; they are the methods of the social sciences. The political scientist's techniques in dealing with these phenomena have been significantly influenced by those of the sociologist and the social anthropologist, whose experience in studying non-Western societies and group development is great. The most important thing the political scientist learns from his colleagues is the importance of studying certain phenomena outside urban areas in Africa.

As he conducts his study the social scientist may unwittingly influence the expression of the motive force and the processes of national consolidation. He goes to the country and does a study of, for example, the religions in Gabon rather than the religions of five ethnic groups who incidentally happen to live in a place called Gabon. He is encouraged to write about phenomena within a nation because the national frontiers furnish him with one definition or limitation of what he is studying. (And it may be too much trouble to get the different visas now necessary to visit different states.) He may then seek to justify his choice by looking for those factors which, if added together in the proper way, prove that the country has some unity, that its religions, for example, share characteristics that religions in neighboring states do not have. His book is then published and perhaps is sold in the country where the study was undertaken. It contributes to the distinctiveness the people feel, and it contributes to the idea that there is actually something called Senegal or Gabon in this world.

The social scientist may (almost) wittingly influence the expression of the motive force and the processes of national consolidation by his use of quantitative data. The political scientist is devoted to goals of unity and peace. The desire for realization of these goals influences his choice of subjects to study and the way in which he studies them. He emphasizes, perhaps, those forces which tend toward unification at a national or a supranational level. This does not mean there is falsification for all attempts to find the truth. But, truth is evasive, and perception of it is always influenced by points of view that cannot be completely discounted.

Nation-building is a good process and an inevitable process.

This is my point of view. In Gabon there is no way to add up the information and analysis to say what the future will bring or even to determine whether people are happier now than they were ten years ago. Gabon has the resources to be a viable independent nation-state, it appears. There are no absolute standards for being a nation-state. Can a nation-state have only 500,000 inhabitants? No one could say this is impossible. Can a nation-state have 650,000,000 inhabitants? No one could say this is impossible. It depends on the way in which a motive force and forces of consolidation are expressed.

In Gabon fear of a return to the State of Nature does not automatically lead to a faith in the nation as a source of order and modernity, but people in Africa have not had much choice. The nation is today the largest supreme loyalty group which among its other promises has promised order and modernity to the Fang and groups like the Omyènè. Leaders direct their people toward the nation, but they cannot be considered to be doing so only out of cynicism and a desire for power. They are also involved in a general desire for a new order and can only direct the motive force toward national construction.

National consolidation through increasing shared experience is the background process that makes one community out of several communities. This, too, must be given direction by the leaders. It is difficult to measure true feelings and to relate mobilization to assimilation. In Heartlands people have few dealings with "foreigners" and have a degree of security from fear that comes with ownership of land and the sense of continuity of living in one place for a long time with one's family. People in Contact Zones are forced to get along with their neighbors who may be of different ethnic groups; but the Heartland is not far away and they may return to it easily. A Shaké might shoot sheep owned by a Bakota neighbor and thereby destroy a statistically neat process. In the Nationalizing Zone a clearer idea of what the nation is and of the dangers of intertribal violence far from the Heartland may lead to a more conscious effort to get along with different people who also belong to the developing nation. Small groups deny the relevance of ethnic considerations because they realize that if violence occurs on the basis of ethnic-group conflict and if benefits are given on the basis of ethnic group, they will suffer. On the other hand, people may not always make rational calculations about their possible losses and gains, and they may destroy themselves.

The greatest task of nation-building as an expression of the desire for a new order is to prove to the Gabonese that what they are called upon to do is for their own benefit. One day they must be motivated to do what they must do to preserve and develop the nation. At present not all Gabonese are totally convinced they will get benefits from any group to which they belong. During the colonial era one built roads, one went to church, one went to the hospital across from Lambaréné on the Ogooué, but one believed it was for the ruler who happened to be white. The White said he was saving the Black's soul and that he was imposing his kind of peace for a civilizing mission, but the Black soon was convinced the colonialist had come to save his own soul, to fill his own purse, to bring prestige to his own nation, and perhaps to find someone before whom he could pretend to be superior. The structures set up by the European were considered exploitative, and many Gabonese believe this is true of those structures and methods now used by an independent Gabon.

The old groups to which the Gabonese belong, the pre-national or traditional groups, are often considered exploitative too. Women and young people increasingly reject rule by the men and the elders. Oppressed castes deny the pre-national belief systems that claim their inferiority, and they attempt to free themselves. All these people may feel the need to submit to a new order, but they are often hesitant and are caught between the discredited past and the unproved future.

A former colonial governor has estimated that it will take the Gabonese at least one thousand years to have a developed nation on the Ogooué, and President Léon Mba once said that five years should be enough. When something goes a bit wrong, some people outside Africa appear eager to draw conclusions that support their prejudices. When something goes a bit right, other people appear eager to draw conclusions which support *their* prejudices. Watching closely in the few years since independence it is difficult to take the long view, but watching closely represents a rare opportunity for the observer to learn about himself and about his own nation.

Nations exist, and they never exist. In the twentieth century they are strived for, they present themselves as the efficacious order, the system, the community which can best make all human life worthwhile. Among those engaged in this process of national construction in all lands there must be only the most profound feelings of respect and fellowship.

Bibliography

NATION-BUILDING AND NATIONALISM

Barrès, Maurice, *La Terre et les morts* (Paris, La Patrie Française, 1899).

Coleman, James S., *Nigeria: Background to Nationalism* (Berkeley and Los Angeles, University of California Press, 1958).

Coleman, James S., and Rosberg, Carl (eds.), *Political Parties and National Integration* (Berkeley and Los Angeles, University of California Press, 1964).

Deutsch, Karl W., *Nationalism and Social Communication: An Inquiry into the Foundations of Nationality* (New York, The Technology Press and John Wiley, 1953; second printing, Cambridge, Mass., The M.I T. Press, 1962). Basic in the study of nation-building.

Deutsch, Karl W., "Social Mobilization and Political Development," *American Political Science Review,* September 1961, Vol. 55, pp. 493–514.

Deutsch, Karl W., and Foltz, William J. (eds.), *Nation-Building* (London, Prentice-Hall International, 1963).

Doob, Leonard W., *Patriotism and Nationalism: Their Psychological Foundations* (New Haven, Yale University Press, 1964). Schematic, based on research in Europe and Africa.

Emerson, Rupert, *From Empire to Nation* (Cambridge, Mass., Harvard University Press, 1960). Basic in the study of nation-building.

Emerson, Rupert, "Self-Determination Revisited in the Era of Decolonization," Cambridge, Mass., Harvard University Center for International Affairs, December 1964. Ambiguities of idea of self-determination discussed.

Emerson, Rupert, and Kilson, Martin (eds.), *The Political Awakening of Africa* (Englewood Cliffs, Prentice-Hall, Spectrum Book, 1965). Important collection of African writings and introduction.

Etzioni, Amitai, *Political Unification: A Comparative Study of Leaders and Forces* (New York, Holt, Rinehart & Winston, 1965).
Theories and cases.

Foltz, William J., *From French West Africa to the Mali Federation* (New Haven, Yale University Press, 1965).

Geertz, Clifford (ed.), *Old Societies and New States: The Quest for Modernity in Asia and Africa* (New York, The Free Press of Glencoe, 1963).
Chapters on integration, political socialization, problems of nation-building.

Hodgkin, Thomas, *Nationalism in Colonial Africa* (New York, New York University Press, 1957).
Basic book about colonialism and nationalism.

Hoffmann, Stanley, "Une Théorie quantitative du nationalisme," *Revue Française de Science Politique*, April-June 1956, pp. 401–405.
Helpful criticism of statistical approaches.

Jacob, Philip E., and Toscano, James V. (eds.), *The Integration of Political Communities* (Philadelphia, Lippincott, 1964).

Niebuhr, Reinhold, *The Structure of Nations and Empires* (New York, Charles Scribner's Sons, 1959).
Inevitability of nations.

Pye, Lucian W., *Politics, Personality, and Nation Building: Burma's Search for Identity* (New Haven, Yale University Press, 1962).

Safran, Nadav, *Egypt in Search of Political Community* (Cambridge, Mass., Harvard University Press, 1961).
Importance of belief systems and weakening of Islam in Egypt.

Wallerstein, Immanuel, "Elites in French-Speaking Africa," *The Journal of Modern African Studies*, Vol. 3, No. 1, 1965, pp. 1–33.

GROUP ANALYSIS AND SOCIAL CHANGE

Biffot, Laurent, "La Jeunesse gabonaise face au monde rural et au monde urbain," Paris, ORSTOM, April 1964.

Durkheim, Emile, *Suicide* (Glencoe, Ill., The Free Press, 1958).
Anomie.

Girond, Jack, "Alcoolisme et pays sous-développés," *La Semaine Médicale*, 14 June 1958, pp. 730–732.
Family budgets and purchase of alcoholic beverages.

Grazia, Sebastian De, *The Political Community: A Study of Anomie* (Chicago, University of Chicago Press, 1948).
Importance of political communitiy to human being.

Hoyt, Elizabeth, "Integration of Culture: A Review of Concepts," *Current Anthropology*, December 1961, pp. 407–426
Review of theories of integration and system.

Leach, E. R., *Political Systems of Highland Burma* (Cambridge, Mass., Harvard University Press, 1954).
Attack on ideas of integration and equilibrium.

Leach, E. R., *Rethinking Anthropology* (London, University of London, 1961).
Another attack on integration. Attempt to build a model to study social structure.

Mannoni, O., *Prospero and Caliban: The Psychology of Colonization,* translated by Pamela Powesland (New York, Praeger, 1956).
Suggestive, study of complex of "dependency."

Memmi, Albert, *Portrait du colonisé* (Paris?, J. J. Pauvert, 1966).
The colonial situation and its ideologies.

Mercier, Paul, "L'Affaiblissement des processus d'intégration dans des sociétés en changement," *Bulletin de l'Institut Français de l'Afrique Noire,* January-April 1954, pp. 143–166.
Growth of Islam as traditional means of socialization grow weak in part of Dahomey.

Merton, Robert K., "Manifest and Latent Functions," in his book *Social Theory and Social Structure* (Glencoe, Ill., The Free Press, 1957), pp. 19–84.
Weakening and strengthening of social systems.

Merton, Robert K., "Anomie, Anomia, and Social Interaction: Contexts of Deviant Behavior," in Marshal B. Clinard (ed), *Anomie and Deviant Behavior: A Discussion and Critique* (New York, Free Press of Glencoe, 1964), pp. 213–242.
Clarification of concept anomie.

Mizruchi, Ephraim Harold, *Success and Opportunity: A Study of Anomie* (New York, The Free Press of Glencoe, 1964), pp. 3–12.
Alienation, anomie, anomia.

Nisbet, Robert A., *Community and Power* (formerly *The Quest for Community*) (New York, Oxford University Press, 1962).
Implications of political centralization, individualism, and contemporary insecurity.

Olivier, Akiremy, "Réflexions sur la puissance paternelle au Gabon," unpublished Mémoire of the Institut des Hautes Etudes d'Outre-Mer, Paris, 1962.
Call for occidentalization of African cultures.

Parsons, Talcott, *The Social System* (Glencoe, Ill., The Free Press, 1951).
Definitions, basic concepts.

Radcliffe-Brown, A. R., *The Andaman Islanders* (Cambridge, Cambridge University Press, 1933), pp. 233–234, 331–332, 377 particularly.
Elaboration of Durkheim. Discussion of consolidation and disintegration of systems.

Radcliffe-Brown, A. R., *Structure and Function in Primitive Society* (London, Cohen and West, 1959), introduction and pp. 49–89, 90–116, 117–132, 182–183, 188–204.

Redfield, Robert, *Peasant Society and Culture: An Anthropological Approach to Civilization* (Chicago, The University of Chicago Press, 1956).

Rouch, Jean, "Second Generation Migrants in Ghana and the Ivory Coast," in Aidan Southall (ed.), *Social Change in Modern Africa* (London, Oxford University Press, 1961), pp. 300–304.
New social system created by orphans.

Russet, Bruce M., Alker, Hayward R., Jr., *et al., World Handbook of Political and Social Indicators* (New Haven, Yale University Press, 1964).
Useful comparative data on many countries.

Schaar, John H., "Psychological Dimensions of Anomy," *American Sociological Review,* February 1965, pp. 14–40.
Feeling of normlessness seen as part of a general psychological state.

Seeman, Melvin, "On the Meaning of Alienation," *American Sociological Review,* December 1959, pp. 783–790.
Five meanings of alienation.

Shils, Edward, "Charisma, Order, and Status," *American Sociological Review,* April 1965, pp. 199–213.
"Charismatic propensity" as a reflection of the need for order.

Southall, Aidan, "Introductory Summary," in his book *Social Change in Modern Africa* (London, Oxford University Press, 1961), pp. 1–66.
Tribes in cities and the meaning of social change.

Van de Walle, Etienne, "Some Characteristic Features of Census Age Distributions in Illiterate Populations," *The American Journal of Sociology,* Vol. 5, March 1966, pp. 549–555.
Discussion of usual errors in census information.

Weinstein, Brian, "Social Communication Methodology in the Study of Nation-Building," *Cahiers d'Etudes Africaines,* No. 16, 1964, pp. 569–589.

AFRICA IN GENERAL

Administration et diplomatie d'Afrique noire et de Madagascar 1962 (Paris, Europe Outremer, 1962).
Who's Who.

"L'Afrique d'expression française et Madagascar," *Europe France Outremer,* No. 421, special number, 1965.

Badian, Seydou, *Les Dirigeants africains face à leur peuple* (Paris, Maspéro, 1964).
Belief in necessity of economic revolution.

Balandier, Georges, *Afrique Ambiguë* (Paris, Plon, 1957).
A personal view.

Biebuyck, Daniel, and Douglas, Mary, *Congo Tribes and Parties* (London, Royal Anthropological Institute, 1961).
Hardening of tribal lines in Congo-Kinshasa.

Blanchet, André, *L'Itinéraire des partis africains depuis Bamako* (Paris, Plon, 1958).
Rassemblement Démocratique Africain, problems of federalism.

Burke, Fred G., *Africa's Quest for Order* (Englewood Cliffs, N.J., Prentice-Hall, 1964).

Davies, Chief H. O., "The New African Profile," *Foreign Affairs,* January 1962, pp. 293–302.
One-party authoritarian governments.

Deschamps, Hubert, *L'Union française* (Paris, Berger-Levrault, 1952).
History and organization of French Empire under the Fourth Republic.

Dugué, Gil, *Vers les Etats-Unis d'Afrique* (Dakar, Editions Lettres Africaines, 1960).
Political history from loi-cadre to 1960 and Mali Federation.

Fanon, Frantz, *Les Damnés de la terre* (Paris, Maspéro, 1961).
Peasant revolution.

Fernandez, James W., "The Sound of Bells in a Christian Country — in Quest of the Historical Schweitzer," *The Massachusetts Review,* Vol. 5, No. 3, Spring 1964, pp. 537–562.
The ambiguities of altruism.

Hodgkin, Thomas L., "The Relevance of 'Western' Ideas for the New African States," in J. Roland Pennock (ed.), *Self-Government in Modernizing Nations* (Englewood Cliffs, N.J., Prentice-Hall, 1964), pp. 50–80.
Important. African revolution is like other revolutions.

Hommage à Jacques Richard-Molard (Paris, Présence Africaine, 1951).
Collection of some of the geographer's writings.

Jahoda, Gustav, *White Man: A Study of the Attitudes of Africans to Europeans in Ghana before Independence* (London, Oxford University Press, 1961).
Interview data on interracial attitudes.

Kalanda, Mabika, "Baluba et Lulua — une ethnie à la recherche d'un nouvel équilibre," *Collection Etudes Congolaises*, No. 2, Bruxelles, 1959.
Sources of enmity between two groups discussed.

Leighton, Alexander H., et al., *Psychiatric Disorder among the Yoruba* (Ithaca, Cornell University Press, 1963).
Important discussion of methodology and possibilities for further comparative study.

Lemarchand, René, "The Limits of Self-Determination: The Case of the Katanga Secession," *The American Political Science Review*, June 1962, pp. 404–416.

Malembe, Paul, "L'Afrique reformiste et le regroupement des états africains et malgache de langue française (le Groupe de Brazzaville) de 1960 à mars 1964," mimeo thesis for Université Catholique de Louvain, July 1964.
Rise and fall of Union Africaine et Malgache.

Maquet, Jacques J., *The Premise of Inequality in Ruanda* (London, Oxford University Press, 1961).
African caste system.

Maquet, Jacques J., *Afrique: les civilisations noires* (Paris?, Horizons de France, 1962).
Beautifully done with many photos.

Mercier, Paul, "Remarques sur la signification du 'tribalisme' actuel en Afrique noire," *Cahiers Internationaux de Sociologie*, July-December 1961, pp. 61–80.
Tribal solidarity influenced by economic and political change.

Morgenthau, Ruth Schachter, *Political Parties in French-Speaking West Africa* (London, Clarendon Press — Oxford, 1964).
Important. Detailed political history.

Radcliffe-Brown, A. R., and Forde, Daryll, *Systèmes familiaux et matrimoniaux en Afrique* (Paris, Presses Universitaires de France, 1953).
Introduction on social structure; particularly valuable.

Richard-Molard, Jacques, "Groupements ethniques et civilisations nègres d'Afrique," *Les Cahiers d'Outre-Mer*, January-March 1952.
Loyalty groups and egalitarian social systems.

Segal, Ronald, *Political Africa — A Who's Who of Personalities and Parties* (London, Stevens and Sons, 1961).

Vansina, Jan, Mauny, Raymond, and Thomas, L. V., *The Historian in Tropical Africa*, International African Institute (London, Oxford University Press, 1964).
Valuable discussions of use of oral history.

Woodtli, Robert, *L'Europe et l'Afrique: le potentiel minéral africain* (Lausanne, Université de Lausanne, 1961).
African resources and who is exploiting them.

WITCHCRAFT AND RELIGION

Birinda, Prince, *La Bible secretè des Noirs selon le Bouity* (Paris, Omnium Littéraire, 1952).
Non-Fang *Bwiti*.

Bloch-Hoell, Nils, *The Pentacostal Movement — Its Origin, Development, and Distinctive Character* (Oslo, Universitetsforlaget, 1964).
American and European beginnings of the movement.

Debrunner, Rev. H., *Witchcraft in Ghana: A Study on the Belief in Destructive Witches and Its Effect on the Akan Tribes* (Accra, Presbyterian Book Department, 1961).
Detailed information; accompanies M. J. Field book.

Evans-Pritchard, Edward, *Witchcraft, Oracles and Magic among the Azande* (London, Oxford University Press, 1937).
Basic study.

Faure, Félix, *Le Christ dans la grande forêt*, Paris, "Je Sers," 1934.
Missionary point of view of superstition.

Fernandez, James W., "Christian Acculturation and Fang Witchcraft," *Cahiers d'Etudes Africaines*, No. 6, 1961, pp. 244–270.

Fernandez, James W., "Redistributive Acculturation and Ritual Reintegration in Fang Culture," unpublished Ph.D. dissertation, Chicago, Northwestern University, 1963.
The above two works are excellent discussions of witchcraft and Fang society.

Fernandez, James W., "African Religious Movements — Types and Dynamics," *The Journal of Modern African Studies*, December 1964, pp. 531–549.
Movements in Equatorial Africa; a typology is suggested.

Fernandez, James W., "The Idea and Symbol of the Savior in a Gabon Syncretistic Cult," *International Review of Missions*, 1965, pp. 281–289.

Fernandez, James W., "Unbelievably Subtle Words Representation and Integration in the Sermons of an African Reformative Cult," manuscript, 1965.

Field, M. J., *Search for Security: An Ethno-Psychiatric Study of Rural Ghana* (London, Faber & Faber, 1960).
Economic change and insecurity.

Gollnhofer, Otto, and Sillans, Roger, "Recherche sur le mysticisme des Mitsogo — peuple de montagnards du Gabon central (Afrique équatoriale)," in *Réincarnation et vie mystique en Afrique Noire* (Paris, Presses Universitaires de France, Bibliothèque des Centres d'Etudes Supérieures Specialisées, 1965), pp. 143–173.
Bwiti of the Mitsogo.

Kluckhohn, Clyde, *Navaho Witchcraft* (Boston, Beacon Press, 1944).
Basic study with considerable case information and methodology.

Lavignotte, Henri, *L'Evur — croyance des Pahouins du Gabon* (Paris, Société des Missions Evangéliques, 1947).
Discussion of magic spirit in Fang society.

Mair, Lucy P., "Witchcraft as a Problem in the Study of Religion," *Cahiers d'Etudes Africaines,* No. 15, 1964, pp. 335–348.
Synthesis of various works.

Mennesson-Rigaud, O., "Le Rôle de Vaudou dans l'indépendence d'Haïti," *Présence Africaine,* February-May 1958, pp. 43–67.
Cults as a source of resistance to white authority.

Messing, Simon, "Group Therapy and Social Status in the Zar Cult of Ethiopia," *American Anthropologist,* 60, December 1958, pp. 1120–1126.
Functions of spirit taming.

Middleton, John, and Winter, E. H. (eds.), *Witchcraft and Sorcery in East Africa* (New York, Praeger, 1963).
Descriptive chapters and contributions to theory by editors.

Parrinder, E. G., "Les Sociétés religieuses en Afrique occidentale," *Présence Africaine,* February-May 1958, pp. 17–22.
Religion and politics, syncretism.

Parrinder, Geoffrey, *Witchcraft: European and African* (London, Faber & Faber, 1963).
Basic work.

Reynolds, Barrie, *Magic, Divination and Witchcraft among the Barotse of Northern Rhodesia* (London, Chatto & Windus, 1963).

Scotch, N. A., "Magic, Sorcery, and Football among the Zulu," *The Journal of Conflict Resolution,* March 1961, pp. 70–74.

Sundkler, B. G. M., *Bantu Prophets in South Africa* (London, Oxford University Press, 1961).
Syncretist religions.

Tait, David, "A Sorcery Hunt in Dagomba," *Africa,* April 1963, pp. 136–147.

Tempels, Rev. Placide, *Bantu Philosophy* (Paris, Présence Africaine, 1959).
Force vitale.

Turner, Victor, "Witchcraft and Sorcery: Taxonomy versus Dynamics," *Africa,* October 1964, pp. 314–325.
Criticism of Middleton.

Veciana Vilaldach, Antonio de, *La Secta del Bwiti en la Guinea Española* (Madrid, Instituto de Estudios Africanes, 1958).
Traditional ethnography.

Vernaud, G. *Etablissement d'une mission du plein Evangile au Gabon* (Peseux/NE, Editions Evangéliques, 1957).

Vernaud, G., *Réveil au Gabon* (Les Andelys (Euro), Editions Viens et Vois, n.d.).
The Revival by the man who preached it.

Walker, Abbé A. R., "Le Bouiti," *Bulletin de la Société des Recherches Congolaises,* No. 4, 1924, pp. 3–7.

Walker, Abbé A. R., and Sillans, Roger, *Rites et croyances des peuples du Gabon* (Paris, Présence Africaine, 1962).
Traditional Gabonese religions.

Wilson, Monica Hunter, "Witch Beliefs and Social Structure," *The American Journal of Sociology,* January 1951, pp. 307–313.
Two peoples are compared.

Youlou, Abbé Fulbert, "Le Rêve, le sorcier, le devin, et le féticheur en Afrique Centrale," *Communauté France-Eurafrique,* No. 133, July-August 1962, pp. 32–35.
Witchcraft beliefs considered as functional.

Equatorial Africa

Ansprenger, Franz, *Politik im schwarzen Afrika: die modernen politischen Bewegungen im Afrika französischer Prägung* (Köln und Opladen, Westdeutscher Verlag, 1961).
    More information on Afrique Occidentale Française but still useful.

Augagneur, Victor, "L'Afrique Equatoriale Française," 23 January 1922, Extracts from Numbers 30 and 31 of *Lyon Colonial, 1922.*
    Point of view of governor general who favored economic development of A.E.F.

Balandier, Georges, *Sociologie actuelle de l'Afrique noire: dynamique des changements sociaux en Afrique Centrale* (Paris, Presses Universitaires de France, 1955).
    Important book about Fang and Bakongo. Methodology.

Bruel, Georges, *Bibliographie de l'Afrique Equatoriale Française* (Paris, Larose, 1914).

Bruel, Georges, *La France Equatoriale Africaine* (Paris, Larose, 1935).
    Indispensable source book for comparisons with present. Bibliography indicates rare references.

Charbonnier, F., "Les Espoirs de l'A.E.F.: Barrage de Kouilou, fer de Mékambo, pétroles du Gabon," *La Vie Française,* 23 August 1957.

Eboué, Félix, "La Nouvelle Politique indigène (pour l'Afrique Equatoriale Française)," Office Français d'Edition, 1941, or Brazzaville, Afrique Française Libre, 1941.
    Changes proposed by governor general.

Jayle, Christian, "L'U.R.A.C. est née à Fort-Lamy," *Démocratie,* 60, 26 May 1960.
    Descriptive, citations by Youlou.

Joseph, Gaston, "L'AEF d'Hier," *France Outremer,* July 1953, pp. 20–21.

LaPierre, René, "Les Investissements publics et privés dans l'ancienne Afrique Equatoriale Française et au Cameroun anciennement sous tutelle française," unpublished Mémoire of the Institut d'Etudes Politiques de Paris, Paris, 1960.

Lasserre, Guy, *Libreville — la ville et sa région,* Paris, Colin, 1958.
    A model for the study of African cities.

Maran, René, *Afrique Equatoriale Française — Terres et Races d'Avenir* (Paris, Ghalandre?, 1937).

Poquin, Jean-Jacques, "Les Relations économiques extérieures des pays d'Afrique noire de l'Union Française 1925–1955" (Centre d'Etudes Economiques, Paris, Colin, 1957).
    Data on nature and value of imports and exports.

"Production et consommation en Afrique Equatoriale," *Europe France Outremer,* No. 413, pp. 31–33.

Gouverneur-Général Reste, *Action politique, économique et sociale en Afrique Equatoriale Française 1936–1938* (Brazzaville, Gouvernement Général?, 1938).
    Report to Governors and administrators on future of A.E.F.

de la Roche, Jean, *Le Gouverneur Général Félix Eboué 1884–1944* (Paris, Hachette, 1957).
    Details about Afrique Equatoriale Française history.

R. S., Colon du Congo, *Victor Augagneur et l'A.E.F.* (Bordeaux, Imprimerie Coopérative, 1923).
Conflict between administration and business.

Thompson, V., and Adloff, R., *The Emerging States of French Equatorial Africa* (Stanford, Stanford University Press, 1960).
General Survey.

Zieglé, H., *Afrique Equatoriale Française* (Paris, Berger-Levrault, 1952).
General and short.

GABONESE AND AFRICAN HISTORY

Annuaire de l'Archidiocèse de Libreville et du Diocèse de Mouila (Libreville, Gabon, 1964).
History of Roman Catholic Church in Gabon.

Antonelli, Etienne, *Manuel de legislation coloniale* (Paris, Presses Universitaires de France, 1927?), pp. 57–149.
Descriptive.

Bessieux, Mgr., "Missions catholiques françaises" (letters of Bishop Bessieux), *Revue Coloniale*, August 1847, pp. 443–451.
Description of establishment of first Roman Catholic mission in Gabon.

Borella, François, *L'Evolution politique et juridique de l'Union Française depuis 1946* (Paris, Librairie Générale de Droit, 1958).

Bouët-Willaumez, Comte, "Les Colonies françaises en 1852," *Revue des Deux Mondes*, 1 June 1852, extract in Bibliothèque Nationale.
Importance of colonies for the navy.

Bowdich, Thomas E., *Mission from Cape Coast Castle to Ashantee* (London, John Murray, 1819), pp. 422–452.
Sketch of Gaboon.

Brown, Arthur Judson, *One Hundred Years* (New York, Revell, 1936).
History of the beginning of American Missionary work in Gabon.

Brunschwig, Henri, *Mythes et réalités de l'impérialisme colonial français 1871–1914* (Paris, Colin, 1960).
Important. Intellectual History.

Brunschwig, Henri, "Expéditions punitives au Gabon (1875–1877)," *Cahiers d'Etudes Africaines*, No. 7, 1962, pp. 347–361.
Expeditions against the Fang.

Brunschwig, Henri, *L'Avènement de l'Afrique noire du XIX siècle à nos jours* (Paris, Colin, 1963).
Important, new information on Savorgnan de Brazza.

Brunschwig, Henri, "La Négociation du traité Makoko," *Cahiers d'Etudes Africaines*, No. 17, 1965, pp. 5–56.
Publication of an important text by Savorgnan de Brazza.

Brunschwig, Henri, *Brazza Explorateur: L'Ogooué 1875–1879* (Paris, Mouton, 1966).
Report by de Brazza published.

Buell, Raymond Leslie, *The Native Problem in Africa*, two volumes (New York, Macmillan, 1928).

Charbonnier, François, *Gabon — terre d'avenir* (Paris, Encyclopédie d'Outre-Mer, 1957).

Chavannes, Ch. de, *Avec Brazza: Souvenirs de la Mission de l'Ouest Africain (Mars 1883–Janvier 1886)* (Paris, Plon, 1935).
Three de Brazza missions are described.

Compiègne, le Marquis de, *L'Afrique Equatoriale: Gabonais, Pahouins, Gallois,* third edition (Paris, Plon, 1878).

Compiègne, le Marquis de, *L'Afrique Equatoriale: Okanda, Bangouens, Osyeba,* third edition (Paris, Plon, 1885).
Voyage along the Ogooué.

Coquery-Vidrovitch, Catherine, "Les Idées économiques de Brazza et les premières tentatives de compagnie de colonisation au Congo Français 1885–1898," *Cahiers d'Etudes Africaines,* No. 17, 1965, pp. 57–82.
Part of a general project on de Brazza under direction of Professor Brunschwig.

Cottes, A., "La Guinée espagnole," *Annales de Géographie,* Paris, 1909, pp. 433–450.
Connections between Woleu-Ntem and Rio Muni.

Deschamps, Hubert, *Traditions orales et archives au Gabon* (Paris, Berger-Levrault, 1962).
Ethnohistory; the first part of a general history of Gabon.

Deschamps, Hubert, "Quinze ans de Gabon — les débuts de l'établissement français," Paris, Société Française d'Histoire d'Outre-mer, 1965; extract from *La Revue Française d'Histoire d'Outre-Mer,* 1963 and 1965.
Important details.

La Documentation Française, "Les territoires espagnols d'Afrique," Notes et études documentaires, Paris, 3 January 1963, pp. 20–39.
General information on Rio Muni and Fernando Poo.

La Documentation Française, "Les territoires portugais d'Afrique," Notes et études documentaires, Paris, 26 January 1962, pp. 44–47.
Saint Thomas and Prince islands.

Du Chaillu, Paul B., *Explorations and Adventures in Equatorial Africa* (London, John Murray, 1961).

Farine, B., *Sites préhistoriques gabonais* (Libreville, Ministère de l'Information, 1963).
Description of artifacts discovered in Libreville area mainly.

Fernandez, James W., "The Fall of the Noble Cannibal: The Fang Perceived 1840–1910," manuscript, Hanover, N.H., 1965.
Attitudes of explorers and colonialists toward Fang.

Gide, André, *Voyage au Congo* (Paris, Gallimard, 1927).
Criticism of concessions.

His Majesty's Stationery Office, *Spanish Guinea* (London, 1920).
General description and early history.

Ireland, William, "Historical Sketch of Gabon Mission," *Sketches of the ABCFM,* 1863; extract in Library of United Church Board for World Ministries, Boston.
Excellent account of the arrival of American Protestants.

Kingsley, M. H., *Travels in West Africa — Congo Français, Corisco and Cameroons* (London, Macmillan, 1897).
Famous lady traveler met the Fang and others in Gabon.

Lestrille, M., "Note sur le comptoir du Gabon," *Revue Coloniale,* October 1856, pp. 424–449.

Luchaire, François, *Manuel de droit d'Outre-mer* (Paris, Sirey, 1949).

Mannix, Daniel, and Cowley, Malcolm, *Black Cargoes* (New York, Viking Press, 1962).
Transatlantic slave trade.

Maran, René, *Batouala* (Paris, Albin Michel, 1921), pp. 9–18.
Early criticism of colonial regime in A.E.F.

Maran, René, *Brazza et la fondation de l'A.E.F.* (Paris, Gallimard, 1941).

Mariol, Henri, *La Chronologie coloniale* (Paris, Larose, 1921), pp. 68–85.
Useful tables, succinct history.

Ménier, Marie-Antoinette, "Conceptions politiques et administratives de Brazza — 1885–1898," *Cahiers d'Etudes Africaines*, No. 17, 1965, pp. 83–95.

Mveng, Engelbert, *Histoire du Cameroun* (Paris, Présence Africaine, 1963).
Massive work but little about Gabon and Neu-Kamerun.

Nassau, Robert Hill, *My Ogowe* (New York, Neale, 1914).
Adventures of an American missionary remembered particularly by the Omyènè.

Neuhoff, Hans-Otto, "German-Gabonese Relations from the mid-19th Century to the Present Day," *Afrika*, August 1964, pp. 122–127.

Ney, Napoléon (ed.), *Conférences et lettres de P. Savorgnan de Brazza sur ses trois explorations dans l'Ouest Africain* (Paris, Maurice Dreyfous, 1887).

Parsons, Ellen C. (ed.), *A Life for Africa: Rev. Adolphus Clemens Good* (New York, Revell, 1900).
Biography and letters of one of the last American missionaries in Gabon. He went to Cameroun to found a Presbyterian mission there.

Pélissier, René, "La Guinée espagnole," *Revue Française de Science Politique*, September 1963, pp. 624–644.
Point of view of Spain.

Pélissier, René, "Political Movements in Spanish Guinea," *Africa Report*, May 1964, pp. 3–7.

Pélissier, René, "Spain's Discreet Decolonization," *Foreign Affairs*, April 1965, pp. 519–527.
Point of view of Spain.

Pélissier, René, "Le Mouvement nationaliste en Afrique espagnole," *Le Mois en Afrique*, July 1966, No. 7, pp. 72–96.

Raponda-Walker, Abbé André, "Notes d'histoire du Gabon," *Brazzaville*, Mémoire de l'Institut d'Etudes Centrafricaines, No. 9, 1960.
Omyènè history in detail with some information on other people and France.

Raponda-Walker, Abbé André, "Toponymie de l'estuaire du Gabon et de ses environs," *Bulletin de l'Institut de Recherches Scientifiques au Congo*, Tome 2, 1962, pp. 87–122.
Origin of some Gabonese names explained.

Raponda-Walker, Abbé André, "Longevité des missionaires du Gabon," Libreville, 1964.
Short biographies of Roman Catholic missionaries.

Ritter, Karl, *Neu-Kamerun*, Veröffentlichungen des Reichskolonialamts, Nummer 4 (Jena, Gustav Fischer, 1912), particularly pp. 21–26, 91–92, 118–119, 179–180.
Important economic information; German view of Fang, Franco-German agreements reprinted.

Roberts, Stephen H., *History of French Colonial Policy (1870–1925)* (London, King, 1929).

Rouchon, André, "Le Ministère de la France d'Outre-Mer," *Penant,* July-August 1950, pp. 159–171.

Rouget, Fernand, *L'Expansion coloniale au Congo Français* (Paris, Larose, 1906).
Almost an official history.

Runner, Jean, *Les Droits politiques des indigènes des colonies* (Paris, Larose, 1927).
Description of powerless councils set up in colonies.

Savorgnan de Brazza, Pierre, "Expéditions sur les cours supérieurs de l'Ogooué," speeches by P. S. de Brazza and N. Baillay to the Société de Géographie, Sorbonne, 24 January 1879; extract of *Bulletin de la Société de Géographie,* February 1879.

Savorgnan de Brazza, Pierre, *Exposé présenté par M. P. Savorgnan de Brazza, Lt. de vaisseau, dans la séance générale extraordinaire, 21 Janvier 1886* (Paris, Société de Géographie, 1886).

Schnapper, Bernard, *La Politique et le commerce français dans le Golfe de Guinée de 1838 à 1871* (Paris, Mouton, 1961).
Best book on colonialism in that area at that time.

Sicé, A., *L'Afrique Equatoriale Française et le Cameroun au service de la France* (Paris, Presses Universitaires de France, 1946).
Rally of A.E.F. to de Gaulle. Eboué is barely mentioned, however.

Sousatte, René-Paul, *L'A.E.F. — berceau de l'Union Française* (Paris, Collection — La Voix de l'A.E.F., 1952).
Loyalty of A.E.F. to France and the importance of Gabon, by a political leader.

Suret-Canale, Jean, *Afrique noire: L'ère coloniale 1900–1945* (Paris, Editions Sociales, 1964).
Second volume of colonial history. Marxist-Leninist interpretation but many facts not revealed elsewhere. Most useful.

Vansina, J. "Long-Distance Trade Routes in Central Africa," *Journal of African History,* No. 2, 1962, pp. 375–390.
Trade routes linking Gabon to Congo in the sixteenth to nineteenth centuries.

Wilson, J. Leighton, *Western Africa: Its History, Condition, and Prospects* (New York, Harper and Brothers, 1856).
First American missionary.

Zimmermann, Emil, *Neu-Kamerun* (Berlin, Mittler, 1913).
Description of advantages to Germany of addition of parts of Gabon and Congo to Kamerun.

THE FANG

Alexandre, Pierre, "Le Mouvement fang ou regroupement pahouin," unpublished Mémoire, Centre des Hautes Etudes d'Administration Musulmane, tome 190, No. 2518, pp. 7–13.

Alexandre, Pierre and Binet, J., *Le Groupe dit Pahouin (Fang-Boulou-Beti)* (Paris, Presses Universitaires de France, 1958).
Excellent succinct study, based mainly on work in southern Cameroun. Long bibliography.

Alexandre, Pierre, *Manuel élémentaire de langue Bulu (Sud Cameroun)* (Paris, Centre des Hautes Etudes d'Administration Musulmane, 1956).

Alexandre, Pierre, "Proto-histoire du groupe beti-bulu-fang: essai de synthèse provisoire," Cahiers d'études africaines, No. 20, Autumn 1965, pp. 503–560.
Important additions.

Aranzadi, Inigi de, *La Adivinanza en la zona de los Ntumu: tradiciones orales del bosque fang* (Madrid, Instituto de Estudios Africanos, 1962).

Balandier, Georges, "Le Fan du Gabon: des conquérants en disponibilité," *Tropiques*, No. 316, December 1949, pp. 23–26.
One of the dynamic aspects of the Fang personality.

Balandier, Georges, "Problèmes économiques et problèmes politiques au niveau du village fang," *Bulletin de l'Institut d'Etudes Centrafricaines*, No. 1, 1950.

Balandier, Georges, "Phénomènes sociaux totaux et dynamique sociale," *Cahiers Internationaux de Sociologie*, Vol. XXX, January-June 1961, pp. 23–34.
Discussion of a type of potlatch among the Fang and Bakongo.

Balandier, Georges and Pauvert, J.-Cl., "Les Villages gabonais," Mémoire (Brazzaville, Institut des Recherches Congolaises, 1952).
Village depopulation and attempts to regroup them.

Biffot, Laurent, *Contribution à la connaissance et compréhension des populations rurales du nord-est du Gabon* (Paris, ORSTROM, 1965).
Fang peasants and their neighbors.

Bôt ba Njock, Henri-Marcel, "Prééminences sociales et systèmes politico-religieux dans la société traditionnelle Bulu et Fang," *Journal de la Société des Africanistes*, tome XXX, fasc. II, 1960, pp. 150–171.
Important study of Fang egalitarianism.

Brunhès, J., "Exploitations de primitifs: type complexe de dévastation végétale et animale dans la forêt équatoriale: les Fang," *La Géographie Humaine*, 1947, pp. 199–204.

Chauvet, Stephane, *L'Art Funéraire au Gabon* (Paris, Maloine, 1933).
Bieri.

Curault, Capitaine, "Etudes congolaises — monographie du secteur de N'Djolé au Gabon," *Revue des Troupes Coloniales*, No. 68, February 1908, pp. 186–209.

Ekogha Mengue, Edouard, "Un Gros Problème: populations gabonaises en voie d'anéantissement," unpublished manuscript, Bitam, 8 June 1962.

Eno-Belinga, M. S., *Littérature et musique populaires en Afrique Noire*, (Paris?, Cujas, Collection Culture et Coopération, 1965).
Author comes from Southern Cameroun; therefore, much on Fang and Bulu.

Faure, Félix, *Obam et son fétiche* (Paris, Société des Missions Evangéliques, 1949).
Missionary view.

Fernandez, James W., "Folklore as an Agent of Nationalism," *African Studies Bulletin*, May 1962, pp. 3–8.
Fang history as a source of Fang unity.

Fernandez Cabezas, Jesus, *La Persona pamue desde el punto de vista bioti-pologico* (Madrid, Instituto de Estudios Africanos, 1951).

Galley, Samuel, *Dictionnaire français-fang, fang-français* (Neuchâtel, Editions Henri Messeiller, 1964).

Grébert, F., "La Famille pahouine en 1931," *Africa*, April 1932, pp. 192–201.

Horner, George R., "The Allocation of Power and Responsibility in Bulu Society," *Cahiers d'Etudes Africaines*, June 1964, pp. 400–434.
Methodology of Marion Levy applied to Bulu.

Largeau, V., *Encyclopédie pahouine* (Paris, Leroux, 1901).
An important early French study of Fang.

Lenz, Oskar, "Reise auf dem Okande in Westafrika," *Zeitschrift der Gesellschaft für Erdkunde zu Berlin*, Vol. X, Berlin, 1875.

Leroux, L.-C., "Etude sur le Ngil," *Bulletin de la Société des Recherches Congolaises*, No. 6, 1925, pp. 3–10.
Pre-national society for social control.

Martrou, L., "Les Ekis des Mfang," *Anthropos*, Vol. I, 1906, extract.
Dietary laws and interdictions.

Martrou, L., "Le Nomadisme des 'Fang,'" *Revue de Géographie*, No. III, 1909, pp. 497–524.

Mayila, Augustin, "Une Séance de Bouiti," *Réalités Gabonaises*, November-December 1961, pp. 17–20.
Not only about the Fang.

Mba, Léon, "Essai de droit coutumier pahouin," *Bulletin de la Société des Recherches Congolaises*, 25 June 1938, pp. 5–51.
Many Fang customs discussed by the man who became first President of Gabon.

Mbah, Jules, "Coutume gabonaises et civilisation française," unpublished Mémoire, Institut des Hautes Etudes d'Outre-Mer, 1958–1959.
Fang culture and conflicts with French culture.

M'Beng, Simon, "Elar-Ayong chez les Fangs au Gabon," *Liaison*, September 1951, pp. 15–16.
Account of regroupment movement.

Montaignac, J. de, "L'Ogooué: ses populations et son avenir commercial," *Revue des Deux Mondes*, 1 November 1884, pp. 187–198.
Fang penetration of new territory.

Mvone-Obiang, Thomas, "Les Fang — des origines à nos jours," unpublished Mémoire, Ecole Nationale de la France d'Outre-Mer, 1944-1945.
Story of Afrikara.

Nang-Ondo, J., "Le Mariage," unpublished Mémoire, Institut des Hautes Etudes d'Outre-Mer, 1963.
Role of women.

Nkogho-Mvé, M-O, "Abrégé des coutumes fang," unpublished manuscript, Mitzic, 4 April 1962.

Nkogho-Mvé, M-O, L'Histoire de Mitzic 1910–1962," unpublished manuscript, Mitzic, 4 April 1962.

Ondoua, Engute, "Dulu Bon Be Afri Kara" (The Migration of the Children of Afrikara) (Elat, Ebolowa, Cameroun, Mission Presbytérienne, 1948, 1954, and 1956).
Origin of the Fang.

Oschwald, P., "La Danse 'de Gaulle' à Lambaréné," *Journal des Missions Evangéliques*, 1950, pp. 7–13.

Panyella, Augusto, *Esquema de Etnologia de los Fang Ntumu de la Guinea Española* (Madrid, Instituto de Estudios Africanos, 1959).
Traditional ethnography.

Perrault, G., "Les Fang du pays Yaoundé," *Les Cahiers d'Outre-Mer,* October-December 1949, pp. 313–333.
Similarities between Fang of Cameroun and those of Gabon.

Pervès, Maurice, "Parmi les Fang de la forêt équatoriale: le jeu de l'Abbia," *La Revue de Géographie Humaine et d'Ethnologie,* July-September, 1948, pp. 26–41.

Rolland, M. "Le Mouvement fang au Moyen-Congo," unpublished mémoire, Centre des Hautes Etudes d'Administration Musulmane, Paris, Vol. 24, March 1955.

Sautter, Gilles, "Le Cacao dans l'économie rurale du Woleu N'Tem," *Bulletin de l'Institut d'Etudes Centrafricaines,* No. 1, 1950, pp. 7–24.

Sautter, Gilles, "Les Paysans noirs du Gabon septentrional: essai sur le peuplement et l'habitat du Woleu N'Tem," 14, *Les Cahiers d'Outre-Mer,* April-June 1951, pp. 119–159.
Changes in Fang society since the introduction of cocoa and coffee cultivation.

Tardy, Mgr. Louis, "Contribution à l'étude du folklore bantou," *Anthropos,* Vol. XXVIII, 1933, pp. 277–303.
Fang stories as seen by a missionary.

Tessmann, Günter, *Die Pangwe: Völkerkundliche Monographie eines westafrikanisches Negerstammes* (Berlin, Ernst Masmuth, 1913, 2 Vols.).
Classic German study of the Fang.

Trezenem, E. "Notes ethnographiques sur les tribus fan du Moyen-Ogooué," *Journal de la Société des Africanistes,* tome VI, 1936, pp. 65–93.
An administrator who worked for many years among the Fang.

Trilles, H., *Chez les Fang, ou quinze années de séjour au Congo Français* (Lille, Brouwer, 1912).

Trilles, H., "Proverbes, légendes et contes fans," *Bulletin de la Société Neuchâteloise de Géographie,* 1905, extract.

Trilles, H., "Les Légendes des Bena Kanioka et le folk-lore bantou," *Anthropos,* Vols. IV, V, 1909, 1910, pp. 945–971, 163–180.

Trilles, H., *Le Totémisme chez les Fans* (Münster, Bibliothèque-Anthropos, 1912), pp. 97–143, 549–558, 593–600.
Valuable material about the Fang, with some exaggeration.

Other Tribes

Adam, Mgr. J., "Dialectes du Gaban — la famille des langues téké," *Bulletin de l'Institut d'Etudes Centrafricaines,* Nouvelle Série, Nos. 7–8, 1954, pp. 33–107.

Avaro, J. Ambourouré, "Le Bas-Ogowe au XIX siècle," unpublished thesis, Faculté des Lettres et Sciences Humaines de l'Université de Paris, May 1964.

Avelot, R., "Recherches sur l'histoire des migrations dans le bassin de l'Ogooué et la région littorale adjacente," *Bulletin Géographique Historique et Descriptive,* No. XX, 1905, extract.

Buléon, R. P., *Voyage d'exploration au pays des Eshiras* (Lyon, Aux Bureaux des Missions Catholiques, 1895).

Carret, J. M., "Le Problème métis au Cameroun," *Le Courier d'Afrique,* 5–6 December 1943.
Favoritism proposed.

Duriez, Jean, "Les Mpongwe, intermédiaires commerciaux en A.E.F.," unpublished Mémoire, Ecole Coloniale, Paris, No. 16, 1933–1934.
Early trade routes and commerce between tribes.

Gautier, R. P., Etude historique sur les Mpongouès et tribus avoisinantes, Mémoire (Brazzaville, Institut d'Etudes Centrafricaines), No. 3, 1950.
The ideas of Père Gautier about the origin of Mpongouè differ from those of Msgr. Raponda-Walker.

Grébert, F., "'La Famille galoase et son évolution désirée par la jeunesse," *Africa,* Vol. X, No. 3, pp. 329–334.

Hauser, André, "Notes sur les Omyènè du Bas Gabon," *Bulletin de l'Institut Français d'Afrique Noire,* 3–4 Series B, July-October 1954, pp. 402–415.
Excellent short article on Omyènè.

Hubert, Jacques, "Esquisse de la coutume bapounou et généralités sur la dégradation des coutumes au Gabon," Mémoire, Paris, Centre des Hautes Etudes d'Administration Musulmane, n.d.
Some inaccuracies.

Jean, S., "Organisation sociale et familiale et problèmes fonciers des populations banjabi et bapunu de la N'Gounié-Nyanga," Paris, Bureau pour le Développement de la Production Agricole, 1960.
Material on Bapounou and Bandjabi history.

Jean, S., "Deuxième Mission: Moyen-Ogooué-Estuaire," preliminary report, Paris, Bureau pour le Développement de la Production Agricole, 1963.
Movement of populations near the coast.

Jean, S., "Région économique de la Ngounié-Nyanga: étude sociologique," Paris, Bureau pour le Développement de la Production Agricole, 1964.
Land ownership.

Le Garrec, Eugène (ed.), *Au Fernan-Vaz: la rencontre de deux civilisations* (Abbeville, C. Paillart, 1896).
Missionaries' views and comments on role of missionaries in colonization.

Le Testu, Georges, *Notes sur les coutumes bapounou dans la circonscription de la Nyanga* (Caen, J. Hauland, 1918?).

Lotte, A. J., "Situation démographique du district de Franceville (Gabon)," *Bulletin de l'Institut d'Etudes Centrafricaines,* Nouvelle Série, No. 6, 1953, pp. 161–180.

Miletto, Dr., "Notes sur les ethnies du Haut-Ogooué," *Bulletin de l'Institut d'Etudes Centrafricaines,* Nouvelle Série, No. 2, 1951, pp. 19–48.

Millot, Jacques, "De Pointe-Noire au pays tsogo," *Objets et Mondes,* Autumn-Winter, 1961, pp. 65–80.
Author views Mitsogo as a closed society.

Ogoula-M'Beye, Pasteur, "Galoa ou Edongo d'antan," unpublished, translated from the Galoa and annotated by Paul-Vincent Pounah, Port-Gentil, 1957.
Written to prove Galoa are Omyènè and not Eshira.

Papy, Louis, "Les Populations Batéké," *Les Cahiers d'Outre-Mer,* January-March, 1949, pp. 112–134.
Decrease in Batéké power and prestige.

Sautter, Gilles, "Le Plateau congolais de Mbe," *Cahiers d'Etudes Africaines,*
No. 2, 1960, pp. 5–48.
Batéké.

Soret, M., "Carte ethno-démographique de l'Afrique Equatoriale Française:
note préliminaire," *Bulletin de l'Institut d'Etudes Centrafricaines,*
Nouvelle Série, No. 11, 1956, pp. 27–52.

Tonjokoue, Marc-Aurelien, "La Famille — son aspect juridique chez les
Bakèlè," unpublished Mémoire, Institut des Hautes Etudes d'Outre-Mer,
1963.
Disappearance of Bakèlè.

Walker, Abbé A. R., "Voyage au pays des Ishogos," unpublished manuscript
in Library of Chambre de Commerce, Libreville, 1907.
Amusing missionary account.

GABONESE POLITICS AND ECONOMY

Anguilè, André G., and David, Jacques E., *L'Afrique sans frontières* (Monaco,
Paul Bory, 1965).
Regionalism and planning in Equatorial Africa.

Aubame, Jean-Hilaire, *Renaissance gabonaise: programme de regroupement
des villages* (Brazzaville, Imprimerie Officielle, 1947).
Plans of deputy Aubame for village regroupment.

Balandier, G., "Les Problèmes du travailleur africain au Gabon et au Congo,"
Bulletin International des Sciences Sociales, No. 3, 1954, pp. 504–513.

Ballard, John A., "The Development of Political Parties in French Equatorial
Africa," unpublished thesis, Fletcher School of Law and Diplomacy,
December 1963.
Important study. Very detailed political history.

Ballard, John, "Four Equatorial States," in Gwendolen Carter, *National
Unity and Regionalism in Eight African States* (Ithaca, Cornell University
Press, 1966), pp. 321–335.
Succinct political history of Gabon, Congo, Chad, Central African
Republic.

Biarnes, Pierre, "U.D.E.A.C. — Espoirs et inquiétudes," *Le Mois en Afrique,*
July 1966, No. 7, pp. 19–22.

Bichon, M., *Etude sur la palmeraie de Moabi* (Paris, Compagnie Générale
des Oléagineux Tropicaux, July 1959).
Difficulties faced by small industry.

Bidault, F., "Résultats provisoires de l'enquête agricole par sondage 1960,"
for Ministère de l'Agriculture, République Gabonaise, 1961?.
Study made to help planners. Gabonese peasants.

Biffot, Laurent, "Facteurs d'intégration et de désintégration du travailleur
gabonais à son entreprise" Paris, Office de la Recherche Scientifique et
Technique Outre-Mer, 1960–1961.
Important study of Gabonese workers.

Birinda, Prince, "Manifeste," Grand Village, Port-Gentil (Gabon), October
1959.
"Monstrueux complot des missionnaires et colonialistes en Afrique
noire."

"Le Bois dans l'économie de l'Afrique noire," *Europe France Outremer,* No.
422, 1965, pp. 26–29.

Bounguendza, Jean-Arsème, "La Voirie au Gabon en région forestière," unpublished Mémoire, Institut des Hautes Etudes d'Outre-Mer, 1962.
Roadbuilding.

Bureau pour le Développement de la Production Agricole Outre-Mer, "Etude de la région économique de Ngounié-Nyanga," Paris, 1962.
Data on agricultural production.

Courbot, Roger, "Le Mouvement commercial du Gabon de 1928 à 1939," unpublished Mémoire, Ecole Nationale de la France d'Outre-Mer, No. 12, 1944–1945.

Cruiziat, Gaudefroy-Demombynes, Magnen, "Les Problèmes du développement rural au Gabon," République Française, Secrétariat d'Etat aux Relations avec les Etats de la Communauté, 1959?.
Data on income.

Decraene, Philippe, "Le Gabon est soumis aux sollicitations de l'Est et de l'Ouest," Le Monde, 22 August 1961.

Dermigny, L., and Serre, G., "Au Gabon: le district du beut du monde," Les Cahiers d'Outre-Mer, July-September 1954, pp. 213–214.

"Discours prononcés par Monsieur Léon Mba à l'Assemblée Territoriale du Gabon," Libreville, 21 April 1958.

"Discours prononcés par M. Léon Mba et M. Paul Gondjout," Ouverture de la session budgétaire de l'Assemblée Territoriale du Gabon, Libreville, 18 November 1957.

Dumas, M., "L'Economie cacaoyère du Gabon," unpublished Mémoire, Paris, Ecole Nationale de la France d'Outre-Mer, No. 59, 1958–1959.

Ekogha, Julien, "Neuvième Session de formation de cadres de la coopération pour l'Afrique noire et Madagascar," unpublished Mémoire, Paris, Institut des Hautes Etudes d'Outre-Mer, 1960.
Problems facing peasantry.

Essonghe, Jean-Baptiste, "Les Partis politiques au Gabon," unpublished report from Cycle des auditeurs, Paris, Ecole Nationale de la France d'Outre-Mer, No. 63, 1958–1959.

"Gabon — Putsch or Coup d'Etat?," Africa Report, March 1964, pp. 12–15.

Guilbot, J., Absentéisme et mobilité des travailleurs en Afrique Equatoriale (Paris, Ministère de la Coopération, December 1962).
Data on movement of workers.

Hermary, Michel, "Les Paysannats de l'Ogooué-Ivindo," unpublished Mémoire, Paris, Institut des Hautes Etudes d'Outre-Mer, No. 77, 1958–1959.
History of the idea of a type of regrouped village and its economic basis.

Institut de Science Economique Appliquée, "La Planification de l'encadrement — problèmes et méthodes," series on planning sponsored by the Ministère de la Coopération, Paris, pp. 95–104, 153–176.
Theory of Africanization of cadres applied to Gabon.

Labat, René, Le Gabon devant le Gaullisme (Bordeaux, Delams, 1941).
Written by a leader of Vichyist group in Gabon.

Marcus, Edward, "Large-Scale Investment and Development — The Dilemma of the Gabon Republic," Economic Development and Cutural Change, October 1960, pp. 64–74.

Mauric, Alain, "Le Gabon de la loi-cadre au referendum," unpublished Mémoire, Paris, Ecole Nationale de la France d'Outre-Mer, 28 May 1959.
Detailed study of Gabonese party politics 1957–1958.

De Montigny, Suzanne, "Une réalisation gabonaise: le chemin de fer du nord," *Afrique contemporaine,* Vol. 23, January-February 1966, pp. 17–21.
History of attempts to build a railroad.

Neuhoff, Hans-Otto, *Die Rohstoffwirtschaft Gabuns — Geschichte, Struktur und Probleme,* thesis, Ludwig-Maximilians-Universität, Munich, 1966.
Important economic study. Much on early Germans.

Ondo-Bonjean, François, "Les Problèmes actuels de la jeunesse au Gabon," unpublished Mémoire, Paris, Ecole Nationale de la France d'Outre-Mer, No. 123, 1958–1959.

"Le Président Léon Mba vous parle," Direction de l'Information de la République Gabonaise, Libreville, 1960.
Collection of Mba's speeches.

Oschwald, Pierre, "Cent ans d'efforts scolaires au Gabon," in *Encyclopédie Mensuelle d'Outre-Mer,* Vol. 1, No. 22, 1952, pp. 175–178.
Little history but advocates expansion of education. Protestant point of view.

Oschwald, Pierre, *Randonnée au Gabon* (Paris, Société des Missions Evangéliques, 1956).
Impressions of Protestant missions.

Proust, Jacques, "Essai d'analyse des mouvements d'effectifs dans l'enseignement du premier degré au Gabon," *Tiers-monde* (études), 1964, pp. 107–162.
Problems of failures and movement of students.

Sautter, Gilles, *De l'Atlantique au fleuve Congo: une Géographie du sous-peuplement* (Paris, Mouton, 1966).
Important geographic and economic study.

Société Française de Développement, "La Population active: la politique de l'emploi et de la formation dans le cadre du plan," Paris, 1960–1961.
Workers and wages and needs.

Société Française de Développement, "Gabonisation de la première zone," Paris, January 1962.
Gabonese participation in forestry exploitation.

Société Française de Développement, "Problèmes d'infrastructure posés au Gabon par le passage en second zone," Paris, June 1962.
Lumbering industry moves further into interior.

Soppo Priso, Paul, "Face à l'harmonisation de lAfrique: le Cameroun et la Guinée espagnole," *Communauté France-Eurafrique,* September 1962, pp. 6–8.

Wadlow, René, "Aprés un coup d'état à rebours," *La Tribune de Genève,* 1–2 March 1964.
An account of the political situation in 1964, the coup, the intervention.

Wagret, Jean-Michel, *Histoire et sociologie politiques de la République du Congo (Brazzaville)* (Paris, Librairie Générale de Droit et de Jurisprudence, 1963).
Pro-Youlou.

DOCUMENTS

Archives Nationales Coloniales (Arch. Nat. Col.), Gabon-Congo IV-9, IV-10, IV-11, XI-10, XIII-12, XVI-1, XVI-12, XVI-13bis, Missions carton 24, Affaires Politiques 116/1, Affaires Politiques 1919-338/4, and others.

Many documents from Brazzaville have been shipped to France but are not available.

Assemblée Nationale de la République Gabonaise, *Journal des Débats,* 1960–1962.

Assemblée Territoriale, *Débats,* Libreville, 1953–1957.

Bureau de Statistiques, Ministère de l'Economie Nationale, "Recensement 1960–1961," unpublished village reports, Libreville.

Chambre de Commerce, "Statistique générale du commerce extérieur, exportations et importations de la République de Gabon," Libreville, December 1961, December 1963.

Conseil Représentatif du Gabon, Libreville, *Procès Verbaux,* 1947, 1948.

Direction de l'Information de la République Gabonaise, "Assemblée Nationale 1961," Libreville, 1962.

La Documentation Française, "La République Gabonaise," series "Notes et Etudes Documentaires," 10 July 1961, No. 2.795.

La Documentation Française, "Le Problème des chefferies en Afrique noire française," series "Notes et Etudes Documentaires," 10 February 1959, No. 2.508.

Dubly, A., and Fiemeyer, M., "Etude pour orienter une politique de développement du Gabon," Paris, Fondation d'Assistance Mutuelle pour l'Afrique au sud du Sahara, March-June 1961.

Eap, Ty Long, "Essai de systématisation d'utilisation du calendrier historique dans les enquêtes N-Gounié-Gabon 1963," mimeo *Rapport de stage,* Institut National de la Statistique et des Etudes Economiques, 1965?

Eap, Ty Long, "Migrations des hommes de 14 ans et plus — N'Gounié-Gabon 1963," mimeo rapport de stage, Institut National de la Statistique et des Etudes Economiques, 1965?

Gouvernement Général de l'Afrique Equatoriale Française, "Histoire et organisation générale de l'enseignement en A.E.F.," Paris, 1931.

Gouvernement Général de l'Afrique Equatoriale Française, "Congrès pahouin de Mitzic (26–28 Février 1947): Voeux."

Gouvernement Général de l'Afrique Equatoriale Française, "Doctrines et bilans de la modernisation rurale en A.E.F.," July 1956.

Grand Conseil de l'Afrique Equatoriale Française, *Débats du Grand Conseil,* Brazzaville, 1953–1958.

La Guinea Ecuatorial y su Régimen de Autonomía, Madrid, Instituto de Estudios Africanos, 1964.

Journal Officiel, Afrique Equatoriale Française, Paris, 1930, 1935, 1940, 1945, 1950, 1955, 1957.

Journal Officiel de la République Gabonaise, Libreville, 1959–1965.

Ministère de l'Agriculture, République Gabonaise, "Rapport Annuel — 1962," Libreville, 1964.

Ministère de la Coopération, République Française, "Economie et plan de développement: République Gabonaise," Paris, May 1963.

Ministère de l'Economie Nationale de la République Gabonaise, "Rapport annuel sur la situation économique, financière et sociale de la République Gabonaise — Fin 1961," Libreville, March 1962.

Ministère de l'Economie Nationale de la République Gabonaise, "Rapport annuel sur la situation économique, financière et sociale de la République Gabonaise — Fin 1963," Libreville, July 1964.

Ministère de l'Economie Nationale du Plan et des Mines, "Situation économique et sociale de la République Gabonaise en 1964," Libreville, June 1965.

Ministère de l'Economie Nationale, "Note sur l'enquête 'Conditions de vie en milieu africain' effectuée à Libreville en 1961 et 1962," Libreville, n.d.

Ministère de l'Education Nationale de la République Gabonaise, "Notions d'instruction civique," special number of *Réalités Gabonaises*, July-August 1962.

Ministère d'Etat chargé de l'Economie Nationale, "Situation économique, financière et sociale de la République Gabonaise — Fin 1962," Libreville, May 1963.

Ministère de l'Information et du Tourisme, "Gabon: ma patrie," Libreville, n.d.

Ministère de l'Information et du Tourisme, "Gabon: mon pays," Libreville, n.d.

"Le Prince Birinda vous parle — Lettre ouverte," *Journal des Débats*, Assemblèe Nationale, 28 October 1960.

Rapport Annuel, Banque Centrale des Etats de l'Afrique Equatoriale et du Cameroun, Paris, 1960–1963.

"Rapport de P. Savorgnan de Brazza sur son expédition dans l'Afrique Equatoriale," August 1875-November 1878, in Archives Nationales Coloniales, séries BB4, Vol. 1448, 30 August 1879.

Service de Statistique, République Gabonaise, "Le Commerce extérieur du Gabon 1959," Libreville, n.d.

Service de Statistique, République Gabonaise, "Recensement et enquête démographiques 1960–1961: Résultats pour Libreville," Paris, 1962.

Service de Statistique, République Gabonaise, "Recensement et enquête démographiques 1960–1961: Résultats définitifs ensemble du Gabon," Paris, 1965.

Service de Statistique, République Gabonaise, "Recensement et enquête démographiques 1960–1961: Résultats provisoires ensemble du Gabon," Paris, May 1963.
The census was taken in collaboration with the Service de Coopération of the French Institut National de la Statistique et des Etudes économiques and the Ministère de la Coopération.

Service de Statistique, République Gabonaise, "Dix Ans d'économie gabonaise," August 1963.

Service de Statistique, République Gabonaise, "La Parc automobile du Gabon au 1er Janvier 1962," Libreville, August 1963.

Vincent, Disaine, Feron, "Essai de systématisation d'utilisation du calendrier historique dans les enquêtes Woleu N'Tem, Gabon 1963" (Paris, Institut National de la Statistique et des Etudes Economiques, Direction des Travaux Régionaux et de la Coopération, 9 August 1966), mimeo.
One of several papers done by students at INSEE based on census data.

NEWSPAPERS AND JOURNALS

Actualités Culturelles du Woleu-Ntem (Mitzic), 1962.

Bulletin Général de la Congrégation du St. Esprit et du St. Coeur de Marie (Paris), 1863–1933.

A.E.F. Nouvelle (Brazzaville), 1948–1949.
  Rassemblement Démocratique Africain (RDA) newspaper.
Afrique Nouvelle (Dakar).
  Roman Catholic.
Bulletin de l'Institut d'Etudes Centrafricaines (Brazzaville).
  Social Sciences.
Bulletin Mensuel (Paris), Banque Centrale des Etats de l'Afrique Equatoriale et du Cameroun.
Bulletin Mensuel de Statisique (Libreville).
  Published by Service National de Statistique.
Bulletin Quotidien, Agence Gabonaise d'Information (Libreville).
Cahiers d'Etudes Africaines (Paris).
L'Echo Gabonais: Organe d'union et de défense des interêts généraux de l'A.E.F. (Dakar), 1922–1932.
  Founded by Laurent Anchouey, concerned with affairs all over Africa and in Antilles.
L'Educateur (Libreville), 1964–1966.
  Pedagogical review.
L'Effort Gabonais (Libreville), 1962–1964.
  Government weekly, succeeded by *Gabon d'Aujourd'hui*.
L'Etudiant d'Afrique Noire (Paris).
  Fédération des Étudiants d'Afrique Noire en France.
L'Etudiant du Gabon (Paris).
  Association Générale des Etudiants du Gabon.
L'Etincelle de L'A.E.F. (Brazzaville).
  Gaullist.
Femmes Gabonaises (Libreville).
  Paper of Organisation Nationale des Femmes Gabonaises.
Gabon d'Aujourd'hui (Libreville), 1964–1966.
  Government weekly.
Jeunesse Gabonaise (Paris), 1953–1954.
  First Gabonese students in France.
Liaison (Brazzaville).
  "Organe des cercles culturels en A.E.F."
Le Moniteur Africain (Paris).
  Economic review.
Missionary Herald (Boston), 1848–1951.
  American Board of Commissioners for Foreign Missions.
Nkegeni Kiki-Ndoa (Talagouga, Gabon).
  Paper of Protestant mission, founded about 1903.
Patrie Gabonaise (Paris).
  Monthly, pro-government.
Le Patriote (Libreville), 1964–1965.
  Pro-government, published by French.
Le Pilote (Paris), 1949–?
  Aubame's paper.
Réalités Gabonaises (Libreville).
  Cultural and pedogogical review.
Revue Mensuelle (Libreville).
  Published by Chamber of Commerce.

Union Gabonaise (Libreville).
  Bloc Démocratique Gabonais (B.D.G.) newspaper.
La Voix Coloniale (Nice), 1923.
  Took over from *L'Echo Gabonais*.
La Voix du Coges (Paris), 1948.
  René-Paul Sousatte's newspaper; transformed into *Réalités Africaines* in 1949 and then into *La Voix de l'A.E.F. et de l'Union Française* in 1952.

Index

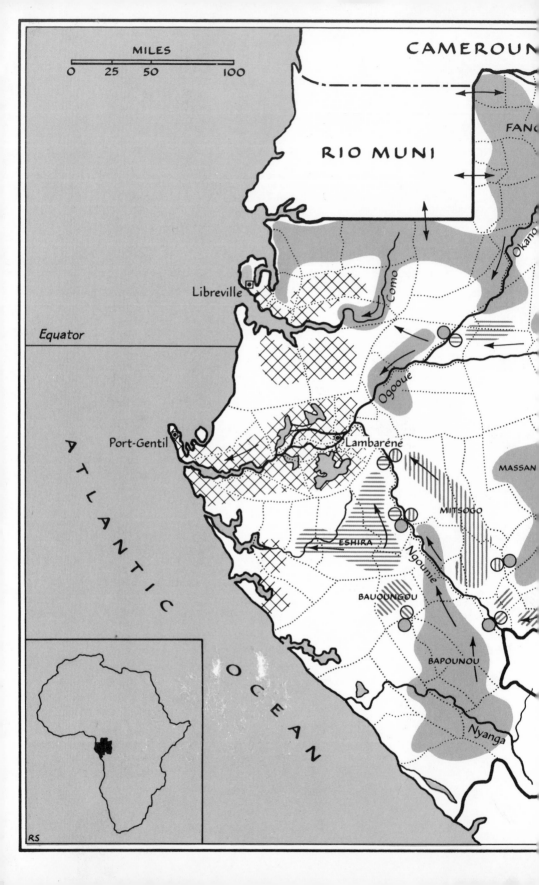